Mastering Python: A Comprehensive Crash Course for Beginners

Kameron Hussain and Frahaan Hussain

Published by Sonar Publishing, 2024.

MASTERING PYTHON: A COMPREHENSIVE CRASH COURSE FOR BEGINNERS

First edition. October 31, 2024.

ISBN: 979-8227289209

Written by Kameron Hussain and Frahaan Hussain.

Mastering Python

A Comprehensive Crash Course for Beginners

FIRST EDITION

Table of Contents

1. Argument

2. Assignment

3. Boolean

4. Class

5. Data Types

6. Dictionary

7. Exception

8. Function

9. Immutable

10. List

11. Loop

12. Method

13. Mutable

14. Object-Oriented Programming (OOP)

15. Parameter

16. Slice

17. Tuple

18. Variable

19. Virtual Environment

20. Whitespace

Preface

This book is designed to guide both novice and intermediate programmers through the journey of mastering Python, one of the most versatile and powerful programming languages available today. Whether you're new to coding or looking to expand your knowledge, this text will provide a comprehensive overview of Python's core concepts, practical applications, and advanced features.

We begin with the basics, covering everything from installing Python to writing your first program. We'll move through fundamental topics such as variables, data types, control flow, and functions, ensuring a solid foundation before diving into more advanced areas like object-oriented programming (OOP), file handling, and error handling.

Along the way, we'll explore how to leverage Python's extensive libraries and modules for web scraping, data analysis, and more. Special attention is given to real-world applications, equipping you to use Python for everything from automating tasks to analyzing large datasets. Additionally, this book introduces key data structures and algorithms, preparing you for more complex projects that require efficient solutions.

The final chapters focus on advanced Python programming techniques, touching on exciting fields such as machine learning and artificial intelligence. You will also learn how to contribute to open-source projects and connect with the vibrant Python community to continue your learning journey.

Each chapter is crafted with practical examples and exercises that reinforce the concepts discussed. As you progress through this book, you'll not only gain a deep understanding of Python, but you'll also build the confidence needed to tackle larger projects, both personal and professional.

Welcome to the world of Python programming!

Chapter 1: Introduction to Python Programming

Understanding Python: A High-Level Overview

PYTHON IS AN INTERPRETED, high-level, general-purpose programming language. Created by Guido van Rossum and first released in 1991, Python has grown to become one of the most popular programming languages in the world, thanks to its simplicity, readability, and flexibility. Python allows developers to write code that is clear and easy to understand, making it ideal for both beginners and experienced programmers alike.

One of Python's greatest strengths lies in its versatility. It can be used for a wide range of tasks, from web development and automation to data analysis, machine learning, and scientific computing. Additionally, Python is supported by a vast ecosystem of libraries and frameworks, which extend its functionality and make it suitable for almost any project.

Python's design philosophy emphasizes code readability and simplicity. Its syntax allows programmers to express concepts in fewer lines of code than in languages such as C++ or Java, while still maintaining the clarity and functionality of the code. Python code is often said to be "executable pseudocode" because it mirrors how humans think, making it a fantastic language for learning programming concepts.

Some of the core features of Python include:

- **Interpreted language**: Python code is executed line by line, which allows for rapid prototyping and testing.

- **High-level language**: Python abstracts away many of the details that other languages require, such as memory management.

- **Dynamically typed**: You don't need to declare variable types in Python; the interpreter infers the type automatically.

- **Cross-platform compatibility**: Python runs on Windows, macOS, Linux, and other platforms, making it a truly cross-platform language.

Python's versatility and ease of use have made it the go-to language for professionals in a variety of fields, from web developers to data scientists and software engineers.

The Python Philosophy

PYTHON'S DEVELOPMENT is guided by a set of principles that are codified in the "Zen of Python," a collection of aphorisms that reflect the language's design philosophy. You can access the Zen of Python by typing the following into a Python interpreter:

import this

Some key tenets of the Zen of Python include:

- **Readability counts**: Code should be easy to read and understand, even to someone unfamiliar with the codebase.

- **There should be one—and preferably only one—obvious way to do it**: Python encourages a single, clear solution to a problem, as opposed to multiple ways of achieving the same result.

- **Simple is better than complex**: The language favors simple and straightforward solutions over convoluted or overly abstract ones.

- **Explicit is better than implicit**: Code should clearly show its intent and purpose.

These principles are designed to make Python a language that is enjoyable to use, promotes clean code, and fosters collaboration within development teams.

Why Learn Python?

PYTHON'S WIDESPREAD adoption in both industry and academia is a testament to its power and usability. Here are just a few reasons why learning Python is a smart investment of your time:

1. **Ease of Learning**: Python's simple syntax makes it one of the easiest languages for beginners to learn. The code is not cluttered with unnecessary punctuation, and the language's structure is intuitive, which allows learners to focus on mastering programming concepts rather than grappling with the language itself.
2. **Versatility**: Python can be used in a wide range of domains, from web development (Django, Flask) and automation (scripts) to scientific computing (NumPy, SciPy) and data analysis (Pandas). It's also a popular choice for machine learning and artificial intelligence (TensorFlow, PyTorch).
3. **Strong Community Support**: Python has one of the largest and most active programming communities in the world. This means there are endless resources—such as

tutorials, libraries, and forums—available to help you solve problems and continue learning.

4. **Career Opportunities**: Python developers are in high demand across a variety of industries, including tech, finance, healthcare, and more. Learning Python can open doors to a wide range of job opportunities, including roles as software developers, data scientists, machine learning engineers, and more.

Python's Growing Popularity

PYTHON'S POPULARITY has grown rapidly over the past decade. According to the TIOBE Index, a measure of programming language popularity, Python consistently ranks among the top programming languages in the world. This growth can be attributed to several factors:

- **Data Science and Machine Learning**: Python has become the language of choice for data scientists and machine learning engineers due to its powerful libraries such as Pandas, NumPy, and TensorFlow. Python's simple syntax allows data scientists to focus on solving problems without getting bogged down in complex code.

- **Automation and Scripting**: Many professionals, particularly in IT and systems administration, use Python to automate routine tasks. From writing small scripts to automate file management to developing complex automation pipelines, Python is invaluable for increasing productivity.

- **Web Development**: Python's web frameworks, such as Django and Flask, have made it a popular choice for building websites and web applications. These frameworks simplify the development process and allow developers to focus on building features rather than worrying about low-level details.

Python vs. Other Programming Languages

WHEN COMPARING PYTHON to other programming languages, such as Java, C++, or JavaScript, there are several key differences that set Python apart:

- **Simplicity**: Python's syntax is much simpler than many other programming languages, which makes it easier to write and maintain code. For example, Python uses indentation to define blocks of code, eliminating the need for braces or semicolons. This results in cleaner and more readable code.

- **Dynamic Typing**: Python is dynamically typed, meaning that variables do not need to be explicitly declared with a type. This makes the language more flexible and reduces boilerplate code. However, it also means that Python is slightly slower than statically typed languages such as C++ or Java, as type checks are performed at runtime.

- **Interpreted Language**: Unlike compiled languages like C or C++, Python code is executed line by line by the Python interpreter. This makes Python slower for certain performance-critical applications, but it also allows for quicker development and testing since there's no need to recompile code after making changes.

- **Extensive Libraries**: Python has an extensive standard library that covers many common programming tasks, such as file I/O, regular expressions, and networking. Additionally, Python's ecosystem of third-party libraries is vast, allowing you to quickly add functionality to your programs without reinventing the wheel.

The Future of Python

PYTHON'S FUTURE LOOKS bright. As more industries recognize the value of data and the importance of automation, Python is well-positioned to remain one of the top programming languages. Its applications in emerging fields such as artificial intelligence, machine learning, and data science are particularly promising.

Moreover, the Python community is continuously improving the language, ensuring that it remains relevant in a rapidly changing technology landscape. With regular updates and new libraries being developed all the time, Python will continue to be a vital tool for developers for years to come.

In conclusion, Python is more than just a programming language—it's a tool that empowers you to build anything from small scripts to large, complex applications. Whether you're a beginner just starting out or an experienced programmer looking to expand your skill set, Python offers endless opportunities for growth and development.

Installing Python: Step-by-Step Guide

BEFORE YOU CAN START programming in Python, you need to have Python installed on your computer. Python is available on a wide range of platforms, including Windows, macOS, and Linux. The installation process is relatively straightforward, but there are a few different methods depending on your operating system and the environment you plan to use. This section will guide you through the process of installing Python, setting up your environment, and ensuring everything is configured properly.

Installing Python on Windows

TO INSTALL PYTHON ON Windows, follow these steps:

1. **Download the Python Installer**: Go to the official Python website atpython.org[1] and navigate to the "Downloads" section. The Python website should automatically detect that you're using Windows and suggest the latest version of Python for your system. Click the "Download Python" button to download the installer.
2. **Run the Installer**: Once the installer has been downloaded, open it to start the installation process. The installer gives you two options: install Python with the default settings or customize the installation. Before proceeding, ensure that the option **"Add Python to PATH"** is checked. This is important as it allows you to use Python from the command line without additional configuration.
3. **Customize Installation (Optional)**: If you choose to customize the installation, you'll be able to select optional

1. https://www.python.org

features like installing pip (Python's package manager) or setting the installation path. It's generally recommended to leave the default options selected unless you have specific requirements.

4. **Complete the Installation**: Click "Install" to begin the installation process. After a few moments, Python will be installed on your system, and you should see a message confirming the successful installation.

Verify the Installation: To ensure that Python is installed correctly, open a command prompt by typing cmd in the Windows search bar and hitting Enter. In the command prompt, type:

bash

python—version

This should return the version number of the installed Python interpreter. For example:

Python 3.9.1

1. If you see the version number, Python is successfully installed. You can now use Python from the command line.

Installing Python on macOS

MACOS COMES WITH PYTHON pre-installed, but it is often an older version (Python 2.x), which is no longer supported. Therefore, it's a good idea to install the latest version of Python (Python 3.x) on your system.

There are two main ways to install Python on macOS: using the official Python installer or using the Homebrew package manager. Below are instructions for both methods.

Method 1: Installing Python Using the Official Installer

1. **Download the Python Installer**: Go topython.org[2] and navigate to the "Downloads" section. The website should detect your operating system and provide a download link for the latest version of Python compatible with macOS. Download the installer.
2. **Run the Installer**: Open the downloaded .pkg file to start the installation process. Follow the on-screen instructions to install Python. This process is similar to installing any other macOS application.

VERIFY THE INSTALLATION: After the installation is complete, open the terminal by searching for "Terminal" in Spotlight (Command + Space). In the terminal, type:

bash

python3—version

This command should return the installed Python version, such as:

Python 3.9.1

1. By typing python3, you ensure that you are using the latest version of Python, rather than the older, pre-installed version.

2. https://www.python.org

Method 2: Installing Python Using Homebrew

HOMEBREW IS A POPULAR package manager for macOS that makes it easy to install and manage software, including Python. If you don't have Homebrew installed, you can install it by running the following command in the terminal:

/bin/bash -c "$(curl -fsSL https://raw.githubusercontent.com/Homebrew/install/HEAD/install.sh)"

Once Homebrew is installed, you can install Python by running:

brew install python

After the installation completes, verify it by typing:

python3—version

This will confirm that the latest version of Python has been installed.

Installing Python on Linux

MOST LINUX DISTRIBUTIONS come with Python pre-installed, but like macOS, it is often an older version. To install or upgrade to the latest version of Python, you can use your system's package manager. Here's how you can install Python on popular Linux distributions.

Ubuntu/Debian

UPDATE THE PACKAGE List: Open a terminal and run the following command to update the list of available packages:

bash

sudo apt update

1.

Install Python: To install Python 3.x, run the following command:

bash

sudo apt install python3

1.

Verify the Installation: Once the installation is complete, verify it by typing:

bash

python3—version

1.

Fedora

UPDATE THE SYSTEM: Open a terminal and run the following command:

bash

sudo dnf update

1.

Install Python: To install Python 3.x, use the following command:

bash

sudo dnf install python3

1.

Verify the Installation: After the installation completes, verify it by typing:

bash

python3—version

1.

Setting Up a Python Virtual Environment

ONCE PYTHON IS INSTALLED, it's a good idea to use virtual environments to manage your Python projects. A virtual environment is a self-contained directory that includes its own Python installation and package dependencies. This is useful because it prevents conflicts between different projects that may require different versions of Python libraries.

To create a virtual environment, follow these steps:

Install the venv module: The venv module is included in Python 3.x, so no additional installation is required. However, if you're using an older version of Python or your system does not have venv installed, you can install it using:

bash

sudo apt install python3-venv

1.

Create a Virtual Environment: To create a virtual environment, open a terminal or command prompt, navigate to the directory where you want your project to be, and run:

bash

python3 -m venv myenv

2. This creates a new directory called myenv, which contains the virtual environment. You can name your environment anything you like.

3. **Activate the Virtual Environment**: Once the virtual environment is created, you need to activate it. The process for activating the environment varies depending on your operating system:

On Windows:

bash

myenv\Scripts\activate

o

On macOS and Linux:

bash

source myenv/bin/activate

o

4. After activating the environment, you will notice that the command prompt or terminal now shows the name of the environment in parentheses. This indicates that you are now working inside the virtual environment.

Install Packages in the Virtual Environment: While inside the virtual environment, you can install packages using pip, Python's package manager. For example, to install the requests library, run:

bash

```
pip install requests
```

5.

Deactivate the Virtual Environment: When you are done working in the virtual environment, you can deactivate it by running the following command:

bash

```
deactivate
```

6.

Using an Integrated Development Environment (IDE)

WHILE PYTHON CAN BE run from the command line, using an Integrated Development Environment (IDE) can greatly enhance your programming experience by providing features like syntax highlighting, debugging tools, and code suggestions. Some popular Python IDEs include:

- **PyCharm**: A feature-rich IDE specifically designed for Python. PyCharm offers powerful tools for debugging, testing, and project management. It's available in both a free community edition and a paid professional edition.

- **Visual Studio Code**: A lightweight and highly customizable code editor with excellent Python support through extensions. Visual Studio Code is free and open-source.

- **Jupyter Notebooks**: Jupyter is popular in data science and research. It allows you to create and share documents that contain live code, visualizations, and narrative text.

Once you've installed Python and set up your development environment, you're ready to start coding. Whether you choose to work in an IDE or directly from the terminal, having Python installed and configured correctly ensures that you're prepared for the exciting journey ahead.

Python IDEs: Choosing the Right Environment

CHOOSING THE RIGHT Integrated Development Environment (IDE) is crucial for enhancing your productivity and streamlining your Python development process. An IDE provides a comprehensive environment that offers syntax highlighting, debugging tools, project management capabilities, code suggestions, and more. There are several popular IDEs available for Python, each with its strengths and weaknesses, and the choice often depends on your specific needs and preferences.

This section will walk you through the most popular Python IDEs, how to install them, and some key features that can help you decide which one is right for you. Additionally, we'll discuss the advantages and disadvantages of using an IDE versus writing Python code directly in a text editor or from the command line.

Why Use an IDE?

AN IDE IS MORE THAN just a text editor. It integrates all the tools you need for software development into a single application. Using an IDE can significantly speed up your development process, help you catch errors early, and provide a more structured way to manage your projects. Here are some key benefits of using an IDE:

- **Code Completion**: IDEs often provide suggestions as you type, making it easier to recall Python syntax and library functions.

- **Debugging Tools**: IDEs include built-in debuggers, allowing you to set breakpoints, step through code, and inspect variables, which makes debugging much more efficient.

- **Version Control Integration**: Many IDEs integrate with version control systems like Git, making it easier to manage your codebase, track changes, and collaborate with other developers.

- **Project Management**: IDEs help you organize files, libraries, and dependencies in large projects, ensuring everything is easily accessible.

While you can write Python code in a simple text editor like Notepad or Vim, IDEs provide additional features that enhance the overall programming experience, especially for larger or more complex projects.

Popular Python IDEs

1. PyCharm

PYCHARM, DEVELOPED by JetBrains, is one of the most popular IDEs specifically designed for Python. It is a powerful, feature-rich environment that offers everything from code completion to advanced debugging tools, making it suitable for both beginners and experienced developers.

Features:

- **Intelligent Code Editor**: PyCharm's editor provides smart code completion, on-the-fly error checking, and powerful refactoring tools.

- **Debugging and Testing**: PyCharm offers an integrated debugger that supports breakpoints, step execution, and variable inspection. It also supports unit testing frameworks like unittest, pytest, and nose.

- **Version Control Integration**: PyCharm seamlessly integrates with Git, Mercurial, and other version control systems, allowing you to manage your code directly from the IDE.

- **Support for Web Development**: PyCharm supports web frameworks like Django, Flask, and Pyramid, making it an excellent choice for web development projects.

Installation: You can download PyCharm from the official JetBrains website. There are two editions: the free Community Edition, which is suitable for most Python development needs, and the paid Professional Edition, which includes additional features for web development and database management.

To install PyCharm on Windows:

1. Go to theJetBrains website[3] and download the installer.

---

3. https://www.jetbrains.com/pycharm/

2. Run the installer and follow the on-screen instructions.
3. Once installed, you can create a new Python project, set up a virtual environment, and start coding.

For macOS and Linux, installation instructions are similar. You can download the appropriate installer and follow the setup process.

2. Visual Studio Code (VS Code)

VISUAL STUDIO CODE is a free, open-source code editor developed by Microsoft. Although it is not specifically designed for Python, it is highly customizable and supports Python through extensions. VS Code is lightweight, fast, and packed with features that can make Python development more efficient.

Features:

- **Python Extension**: The Python extension for VS Code provides support for IntelliSense (smart code completion), linting, debugging, and testing.

- **Integrated Terminal**: VS Code has a built-in terminal, allowing you to run Python scripts, manage virtual environments, and execute shell commands without leaving the IDE.

- **Customization**: You can customize the look and feel of VS Code, as well as install various extensions for Python, Git integration, Docker, and more.

- **Support for Multiple Languages**: If you're working with multiple programming languages (e.g., JavaScript, HTML, CSS), VS Code supports them all, making it a versatile choice for full-stack developers.

Installation: You can download VS Code from theofficial website[4]. After installation, you'll need to install the Python extension:

1. Open VS Code.
2. Go to the Extensions view by clicking the Extensions icon on the Activity Bar on the side of the window or using the keyboard shortcut Ctrl+Shift+X.
3. Search for "Python" and install the extension provided by Microsoft.

Once the Python extension is installed, VS Code will provide code suggestions, error checking, and debugging capabilities.

3. Spyder

SPYDER IS AN OPEN-SOURCE IDE that is specifically designed for scientific computing and data analysis. It comes pre-installed with the Anaconda distribution of Python, which is popular among data scientists and researchers. Spyder is lightweight and includes several features that make it an excellent choice for working with scientific libraries like NumPy, SciPy, Pandas, and Matplotlib.

Features:

- **Variable Explorer**: Spyder provides a variable explorer that allows you to inspect variables and data structures in real-time, which is particularly useful for data analysis and debugging.

---

4. https://code.visualstudio.com/

- **Integrated IPython Console**: The IPython console in Spyder offers enhanced interactive capabilities, including inline plotting and command history.

- **Editor and Debugging Tools**: Spyder includes a multi-language editor with code completion, syntax highlighting, and a debugger that supports breakpoints and step execution.

Installation: You can install Spyder by installing the Anaconda distribution of Python, which includes Spyder and a host of scientific libraries.

To install Anaconda on Windows:

1. Go to the Anaconda website and download the installer.
2. Run the installer and follow the on-screen instructions.
3. After installation, open Anaconda Navigator, where you will see Spyder as one of the available IDEs.

For macOS and Linux, the installation process is similar. You can download the Anaconda installer and set it up by following the instructions.

4. Jupyter Notebook

JUPYTER NOTEBOOK IS not an IDE in the traditional sense, but it is one of the most popular environments for data science and research projects. Jupyter allows you to create notebooks that contain both code and text, making it ideal for data visualization, interactive coding, and educational purposes.

Features:

- **Interactive Coding**: Jupyter allows you to run code in small chunks called "cells," making it easy to test and iterate on your code.
- **Visualizations**: Jupyter supports inline plotting with libraries like Matplotlib and Seaborn, making it ideal for data visualization.
- **Rich Text and Markdown**: In addition to code, Jupyter supports rich text formatting using Markdown, making it easy to document your work and create reports.

Installation: If you have installed the Anaconda distribution, Jupyter Notebook comes pre-installed. If you prefer to install it separately, you can do so using pip:

```
pip install notebook
```

After installation, you can start Jupyter Notebook by running the following command in your terminal:

```
jupyter notebook
```

This will open a new browser window where you can create and manage notebooks.

IDE vs. Text Editor

WHILE IDES OFFER A comprehensive environment for development, some developers prefer the simplicity of using a text editor, especially for smaller projects. Text editors like Sublime Text, Atom, and Vim are popular choices for Python development because they are lightweight and can be easily extended with plugins. However, they may lack some of the advanced features of a full-fledged IDE, such as debugging tools, project management, and version control integration.

Here are some advantages of using a text editor over an IDE:

- **Lightweight**: Text editors tend to be faster and use fewer resources than IDEs, making them a good choice for developers working on older or less powerful machines.

- **Flexibility**: Text editors can be customized to suit your needs with plugins and extensions, but they do not force you into a particular workflow.

- **Focus**: Some developers prefer the minimalism of text editors, which allows them to focus on writing code without distractions.

On the other hand, the main disadvantage of using a text editor is that you may need to manually configure additional tools like linters, debuggers, and version control integration, which can be time-consuming.

Conclusion: Choosing the Right Tool

WHEN CHOOSING THE RIGHT environment for Python development, consider the size and complexity of your projects, your workflow preferences, and the type of development you'll be doing. Here are some recommendations based on different use cases:

- **For Web Development**: PyCharm is an excellent choice, especially if you're working with frameworks like Django or Flask. Its built-in tools for database management and debugging make it ideal for web projects.

- **For Data Science**: Spyder or Jupyter Notebook are the best options. Spyder's real-time variable explorer and Jupyter's interactive coding environment are both designed for data analysis and scientific computing.

- **For General Python Development**: Visual Studio Code offers a great balance between simplicity and functionality. With the right extensions, it can handle almost any Python project, from web development to automation scripts.

- **For Lightweight Development**: If you prefer a fast and minimal environment, consider using a text editor like Sublime Text or Atom. These editors can be extended with plugins to suit your needs, but they won't overwhelm you with features you may not need for small projects.

Choosing the right IDE or editor can make a big difference in your productivity and enjoyment as a developer. Take the time to explore different environments and find the one that best suits your needs. Whether you're building a complex web application or writing simple scripts, there's an IDE or editor out there that will help you write better Python code more efficiently.

Running Your First Python Program

RUNNING YOUR FIRST Python program is an exciting step in your programming journey. Whether you're entirely new to programming or transitioning from another language, Python's simplicity and readability make it easy to get started. This section will guide you through the different methods of running Python programs, from writing simple scripts in the command line to developing larger projects using an Integrated Development Environment (IDE). We'll also explore the process of debugging and interpreting error messages, key aspects of working with Python programs.

Writing Your First Python Script

TO BEGIN, LET'S START by writing a simple Python script that prints a message to the screen. One of the most common introductory programs in any language is the "Hello, World!" program. This program does nothing more than output the text "Hello, World!" to the console, but it is a great first step in understanding how Python works.

Here's what the "Hello, World!" program looks like in Python:

```
print("Hello, World!")
```

That's it! Just a single line of code to display a message. Now, let's go over the different ways you can run this program.

Running Python from the Command Line

THE COMMAND LINE (ALSO known as the terminal or shell) is a powerful tool that allows you to interact with your operating system directly through text commands. Python can be run from the command line in several ways, depending on how you've set up your environment. Let's walk through the steps to run Python from the command line.

Step 1: Open the Command Line

- **On Windows**: Open the Command Prompt by typing cmd in the search bar and pressing Enter.
- **On macOS**: Open the Terminal by searching for it using Spotlight (Command + Space) or from the Applications folder.
- **On Linux**: Open the terminal using your preferred method, such as searching for "Terminal" in the application menu.

Step 2: Check Python Installation

BEFORE RUNNING ANY Python code, it's a good idea to verify that Python is installed correctly. In the command line, type the following command to check the version of Python installed on your system:

python—version

On some systems, particularly macOS and Linux, you may need to type python3 instead of python to access Python 3.x:

python3—version

PYTHON 3.9.1

Step 3: Write a Python Script

NEXT, CREATE A PYTHON script file. You can use any text editor to do this, such as Notepad, Visual Studio Code, or a built-in editor like Nano on Linux. Save the file with a .py extension, which is the standard file extension for Python scripts. For example, create a file named hello.py and add the following code:

```
print("Hello, World!")
```

Step 4: Run the Python Script

NAVIGATE TO THE DIRECTORY where you saved your Python script using the cd (change directory) command. For example, if your script is saved on the desktop, you would type:

```
cd Desktop
```

Once you're in the correct directory, run your Python script by typing:

```
python hello.py
```

Or, if you're using Python 3.x and python3 is required, type:

```
python3 hello.py
```

HELLO, WORLD!

Congratulations! You've just run your first Python program.

Running Python Interactively

PYTHON ALSO HAS AN interactive mode that allows you to type Python commands and execute them immediately. This is especially useful for testing small snippets of code or experimenting with Python syntax without the need to create a full script.

To start Python in interactive mode, simply type python (or python3 for Python 3.x) in the command line:

python

You should see something like this:

Python 3.9.1 (default, Dec 8 2020, 07:51:42)

[GCC 7.3.0] on linux

Type "help", "copyright", "credits" or "license" for more information.

>>>

This >>> prompt indicates that you're in Python's interactive shell. You can now enter Python code directly, and the results will be displayed immediately. For example, type:

print("Hello, World!")

HELLO, WORLD!

To exit the interactive mode, you can type exit() or press Ctrl+D (on macOS/Linux) or Ctrl+Z followed by Enter (on Windows).

Running Python in an IDE

WHILE RUNNING PYTHON from the command line or interactively is useful for small scripts or testing, most developers prefer using an Integrated Development Environment (IDE) for larger projects. IDEs provide advanced features such as debugging tools, code completion, and project management, which make them more suitable for developing complex applications.

Example: Running Python in PyCharm

PYCHARM IS A POPULAR Python IDE that streamlines the process of writing, running, and debugging Python code. Here's how to run a Python script in PyCharm:

1. **Create a New Project**:

○ Open PyCharm and select "Create New Project."

○ Choose a location for your project and set up a Python interpreter if needed.

2. **Create a New Python File**:

○ Right-click the project folder in the left-hand sidebar and select "New > Python File."

○ Name the file hello.py and write the following code:

```python
print("Hello, World!")
```

3.

4. **Run the Script**:

○ Click the green "Run" button at the top right of the PyCharm window, or right-click the file and select "Run."

```
Hello, World!
```

5.

Most IDEs follow a similar process: create a file, write code, and run the script with a single click. IDEs like Visual Studio Code, Spyder, and Jupyter Notebook also provide similar workflows.

Debugging Your Python Code

WRITING CODE IS ONLY part of the programming process—debugging is equally important. Debugging is the process of identifying and fixing errors (bugs) in your code. Python provides several tools and techniques to help you debug your programs effectively.

Syntax Errors

THE FIRST TYPE OF ERROR you're likely to encounter is a syntax error. Syntax errors occur when Python encounters code that does not conform to the language's grammar rules. For example, if you forget to close a parenthesis, Python will raise a SyntaxError. Here's an example:

```
print("Hello, World!"
```

Running this code will result in the following error:

```
SyntaxError: unexpected EOF while parsing
```

Python is telling you that it expected to find a closing parenthesis but reached the end of the file instead. To fix this error, simply add the missing parenthesis:

```
print("Hello, World!")
```

Runtime Errors

A RUNTIME ERROR OCCURS while the program is running. For example, attempting to divide by zero will raise a ZeroDivisionError. Consider the following code:

```
x = 10 / 0
```

When you run this code, Python will raise an error:

```
ZeroDivisionError: division by zero
```

Python provides detailed error messages that tell you the type of error and where it occurred, which makes it easier to fix the issue.

Using a Debugger

MOST MODERN IDES, INCLUDING PyCharm and Visual Studio Code, come with built-in debuggers that allow you to pause the execution of your program and inspect its state. You can set breakpoints (places where the debugger will pause the program), step through code line by line, and inspect the values of variables.

To use the debugger in PyCharm:

1. Set a breakpoint by clicking in the gutter next to the line of code where you want the program to pause.
2. Run the program in debug mode by clicking the "Debug" button (it looks like a bug).
3. The program will run until it reaches the breakpoint, at which point the debugger will pause the execution. You can now inspect the variables and step through the code to identify any issues.

The debugger is an essential tool for finding and fixing more complex bugs that are difficult to catch with basic error messages.

Handling Errors with try/except

PYTHON PROVIDES A WAY to handle errors gracefully using the try and except blocks. These blocks allow you to catch exceptions (runtime errors) and execute alternative code instead of crashing the program. Here's an example of how to use try and except to handle a division by zero error:

```
try:

x = 10 / 0

except ZeroDivisionError:

print("Error: Cannot divide by zero!")
```

In this case, Python will catch the ZeroDivisionError and print the error message instead of terminating the program:

```
Error: Cannot divide by zero!
```

You can also catch multiple types of errors or handle them in different ways. For example:

```
try:

x = 10 / 0

except ZeroDivisionError:

print("Error: Cannot divide by zero!")

except Exception as e:

print(f"An unexpected error occurred: {e}")
```

This example will catch any unexpected errors and display a message without crashing the program.

Conclusion: Understanding How to Run Python Programs

RUNNING PYTHON PROGRAMS is a straightforward process, but the methods you choose depend on your specific use case and environment. Whether you're writing quick scripts, working on interactive projects, or developing large applications, Python provides a range of tools to suit your needs. From the command line to sophisticated IDEs, Python's flexibility allows you to adapt your workflow to your personal preferences.

By understanding the basics of running Python programs, handling errors, and using debugging tools, you're well on your way to becoming a proficient Python developer.

Basic Syntax and Structure

UNDERSTANDING THE BASIC syntax and structure of Python is crucial for writing clear and efficient code. Python's simplicity and readability make it an excellent choice for beginners and experienced developers alike. However, even though Python's syntax is relatively straightforward, there are key rules and conventions that you must follow to write proper Python code.

This section will cover Python's essential syntactical features, including indentation, comments, variables, data types, operators, and control structures. By the end of this section, you should have a firm grasp of Python's core syntax and be able to write basic programs that adhere to Python's best practices.

Indentation

ONE OF THE MOST UNIQUE and recognizable features of Python is its reliance on indentation to define the structure of the code. Unlike many other programming languages, which use braces {} or other markers to denote blocks of code, Python uses indentation to determine the grouping of statements. This makes the code cleaner and more readable but requires strict attention to indentation.

Consider the following example:

```
if 5 > 2:

print("Five is greater than two")
```

In this case, the indented print statement belongs to the if block. If you don't properly indent your code, Python will raise an IndentationError:

```
if 5 > 2:

print("Five is greater than two") # This will raise an IndentationError
```

By convention, Python uses four spaces for each level of indentation. Most modern text editors and IDEs will automatically handle indentation for you, but it's important to ensure consistency throughout your code.

Comments

COMMENTS ARE AN ESSENTIAL part of writing readable code. They allow you to annotate your code with explanations or reminders, which can be especially useful when revisiting a project later or when collaborating with others.

In Python, comments are created using the # symbol. Any text following the # on the same line is ignored by the Python interpreter:

```
# This is a comment

print("Hello, World!") # This comment is next to a line of code
```

Comments do not affect the execution of your program, but they are critical for maintaining clarity, especially in larger projects.

Python also supports multi-line comments, although there is no specific syntax for them. The most common way to write multi-line comments is by using consecutive # symbols or triple-quoted strings """, though the latter is more commonly used for docstrings:

```
"""

This is a multi-line comment.

It can span multiple lines.

"""
```

Variables and Assignments

VARIABLES IN PYTHON are used to store values that can be referenced and manipulated throughout your program. Python is dynamically typed, which means you don't need to explicitly declare the type of a variable; the interpreter infers it based on the value assigned.

Here's an example of variable assignment:

```
x = 5

name = "John"
```

is_active = True

In this example, x is an integer, name is a string, and is_active is a boolean. Python allows you to change the type of a variable by assigning a new value to it:

x = "Now I'm a string"

Variable Naming Rules

PYTHON VARIABLE NAMES must follow these rules:

- A variable name must start with a letter or an underscore _.
- A variable name cannot start with a number.
- Variable names can contain letters, numbers, and underscores, but no other characters (such as spaces or punctuation marks).
- Variable names are case-sensitive (age and Age are different variables).

It's important to choose descriptive names for your variables to make your code more readable:

Less descriptive

x = 10

y = 20

z = x + y

More descriptive

num_apples = 10

num_oranges = 20

total_fruits = num_apples + num_oranges

Data Types

PYTHON SUPPORTS SEVERAL built-in data types, each designed for specific types of data. Here are some of the most commonly used types:

- **Integers**: Whole numbers, such as 1, 100, or -3.
- **Floats**: Numbers with decimal points, such as 3.14 or -0.001.
- **Strings**: Text values, such as "hello" or "Python". Strings are enclosed in either single or double quotes.
- **Booleans**: True/False values, represented by True and False.
- **Lists**: Ordered collections of values, such as [1, 2, 3] or ["apple", "banana", "cherry"].
- **Tuples**: Immutable ordered collections, such as (1, 2, 3) or ("apple", "banana", "cherry").
- **Dictionaries**: Key-value pairs, such as {"name": "John", "age": 30}.

Python is dynamically typed, meaning that variables can change types during execution. Here's an example that demonstrates different data types:

```
age = 30 # Integer

height = 5.9 # Float

name = "Alice" # String

is_student = False # Boolean

fruits = ["apple", "banana", "cherry"] # List

person = {"name": "Alice", "age": 30} # Dictionary
```

You can check the type of a variable using the type() function:

```
print(type(age)) # Output: <class 'int'>

print(type(height)) # Output: <class 'float'>

print(type(name)) # Output: <class 'str'>
```

Operators

PYTHON PROVIDES VARIOUS operators to perform operations on variables and values. The most common operators are arithmetic operators, comparison operators, and logical operators.

Arithmetic Operators

ARITHMETIC OPERATORS are used to perform basic mathematical operations:

- +: Addition
- -: Subtraction
- *: Multiplication

- /: Division
- //: Floor division (division without the remainder)
- %: Modulus (remainder of a division)
- **: Exponentiation (raise to the power)

Here's an example of using arithmetic operators:

x = 10

y = 3

print(x + y) # Output: 13

print(x - y) # Output: 7

print(x * y) # Output: 30

print(x / y) # Output: 3.3333333333333335

print(x // y) # Output: 3

print(x % y) # Output: 1

print(x ** y) # Output: 1000

Comparison Operators

COMPARISON OPERATORS are used to compare two values, returning True or False:

- ==: Equal to
- !=: Not equal to
- >: Greater than

- <: Less than
- >=: Greater than or equal to
- <=: Less than or equal to

Here's an example of comparison operators in action:

```
x = 10
y = 5
print(x == y) # Output: False
print(x != y) # Output: True
print(x > y) # Output: True
print(x < y) # Output: False
```

Logical Operators

LOGICAL OPERATORS ARE used to combine conditional statements:

- and: Returns True if both statements are true
- or: Returns True if at least one statement is true
- not: Returns the opposite of the statement

Here's an example of logical operators:

```
x = 10
y = 5
print(x > 5 and y < 10) # Output: True
```

print(x > 5 or y > 10) # Output: True

print(not(x == y)) # Output: True

Control Flow

CONTROL FLOW STATEMENTS allow you to control the execution of your program based on certain conditions. Python's primary control flow mechanisms include if statements, loops, and function calls.

If Statements

THE IF STATEMENT ALLOWS you to execute a block of code only if a certain condition is true. Here's an example of an if statement in Python:

age = 20

if age >= 18:

print("You are an adult.")

else:

print("You are a minor.")

In this example, the print statement inside the if block will only be executed if the condition (age >= 18) is true.

For Loops

A FOR LOOP IS USED to iterate over a sequence, such as a list, tuple, or string. Here's an example:

fruits = ["apple", "banana", "cherry"]

```
for fruit in fruits:

print(fruit)
```

The for loop iterates over the fruits list and prints each element.

While Loops

A WHILE LOOP REPEATS as long as a condition is true. Here's an example of a while loop:

```
count = 0

while count < 5:

print(count)

count += 1
```

This loop will print the numbers from 0 to 4 because the condition (count < 5) is true.

Functions

FUNCTIONS ALLOW YOU to encapsulate reusable blocks of code. You can define a function using the def keyword, followed by the function name and parentheses. Here's an example:

```
def greet(name):

print(f"Hello, {name}!")

greet("Alice") # Output: Hello, Alice!
```

In this example, the function greet() takes a parameter name and prints a greeting.

Conclusion

UNDERSTANDING PYTHON'S basic syntax and structure is essential for writing clear and efficient code. By mastering indentation, variables, data types, operators, control flow, and functions, you'll be well-equipped to build more complex Python programs. Following Python's clean and simple syntax will not only make your code easier to write but also easier to read and maintain.

Chapter 2: Variables and Data Types

What Are Variables?

IN PYTHON, A **variable** is a symbolic name that is a reference or pointer to an object. Once an object is assigned to a variable, you can refer to that object by that name. But what does this mean, and why are variables important? Let's break this down.

Understanding Variables

A VARIABLE IN PYTHON acts as a storage container where data is kept temporarily. The data stored in this container can be of various types, such as numbers, strings, or more complex objects. The idea is that you can use a variable to hold a value and then use that value throughout your program without retyping it multiple times.

For example, let's define a variable x and assign it a number:

```
x = 10
```

In this case, x is a variable, and it holds the value 10. You can then use x wherever you need the number 10 in your code. For instance, you can print the value of x:

```
print(x)
```

10

Rules for Naming Variables

THERE ARE SOME RULES you need to follow when naming variables in Python:

1. **Variable names must start with a letter or an underscore** (_). They cannot start with a number. For example, my_var, _my_var, and var1 are valid, but 1var is not.
2. **Variable names can only contain letters, numbers, and underscores**. No special characters like @, #, or $ are allowed.
3. **Variable names are case-sensitive**. This means my_var and My_Var are two different variables.
4. **Avoid using Python keywords as variable names.** Keywords like class, if, and for have special meanings in Python and cannot be used as variable names.

Good Practices for Naming Variables

ALTHOUGH PYTHON ALLOWS various ways to name variables, adhering to best practices ensures that your code is easy to read and maintain. Here are some good practices:

Use meaningful names: Always name your variables based on what they represent. For example, instead of x, use age if you are storing someone's age.

python

age = 25

•

- **Use snake_case**: When your variable name contains multiple words, separate them with underscores (_), like user_name or total_price.

- **Avoid single-letter names**: Single-letter variables like x, y, or z should only be used for simple cases, like loops or mathematical operations. For more complex scenarios, use descriptive names.

total_price = 100

user_name = "Alice"

Variable Assignment

IN PYTHON, ASSIGNING a value to a variable is simple. You use the = operator. The syntax looks like this:

variable_name = value

Here are some examples of variable assignments:

age = 30 # Assigning an integer

name = "John" # Assigning a string

is_active = True # Assigning a boolean

In each of these examples, the variable is assigned a value of a specific data type (more on that later). Python doesn't require you to declare the type of variable beforehand, making it a dynamically typed language.

Reassigning Variables

ONCE A VARIABLE HAS been assigned a value, you can change its value by reassigning it. For example:

```
x = 10

x = 20

print(x)
```

```
20
```

The value of x was initially 10, but it was overwritten with 20.

Multiple Assignments

PYTHON ALSO ALLOWS you to assign multiple variables in a single line:

```
a, b, c = 5, 10, 15
```

In this case, a is assigned the value 5, b the value 10, and c the value 15. This is a handy way to initialize multiple variables simultaneously.

You can also assign the same value to multiple variables:

```
x = y = z = 100
```

In this example, all three variables x, y, and z are assigned the value 100.

Variable Types

PYTHON VARIABLES CAN hold different types of values. The most common types include:

Integers: Whole numbers, such as 10, 25, or -100.

python

number = 10

•

Floats: Decimal numbers, such as 3.14, 0.001, or -2.5.

python

pi = 3.14

•

Strings: Text, such as "Hello, World!" or 'Python'.

python

message = "Hello, World!"

•

Booleans: True or False values.

python

is_valid = True

•

NoneType: A special type that represents the absence of a value. The keyword None is used to denote this.

python

```
value = None
```

•

Dynamic Typing

PYTHON IS A **dynamically typed language**, which means that you don't need to explicitly declare the type of a variable when you create it. The type of the variable is determined based on the value you assign to it.

For example:

```
x = 10 # x is an integer

x = "hello" # x is now a string
```

In the above code, x is first assigned the integer value 10, and later reassigned the string "hello". Python handles the type changes automatically. However, this can lead to confusion if you're not careful, so it's essential to keep track of variable types in your code.

Type Checking

IF YOU WANT TO CHECK the type of a variable, you can use the type() function:

```
x = 10

print(type(x)) # Output: <class 'int'>

y = "Hello"
```

print(type(y)) # Output: <class 'str'>

This is helpful when debugging or when you're unsure what type a particular variable holds.

Constants in Python

ALTHOUGH PYTHON DOES not have built-in constant types, you can use a naming convention to indicate that a variable should be treated as a constant. Typically, constants are written in all uppercase letters with underscores between words:

PI = 3.14159

MAX_CONNECTIONS = 100

In Python, there's no enforcement of immutability for constants. You could technically reassign a constant, but it's considered bad practice to do so.

Memory Management and Variable Lifetimes

PYTHON MANAGES MEMORY automatically, and variables are stored in memory locations. Python uses an internal mechanism known as **reference counting** to keep track of how many references (or links) a particular object has. When an object's reference count drops to zero (i.e., no variables or references point to it), Python's garbage collector automatically frees up the memory associated with the object.

Here's a basic example to understand how this works:

a = 10

b = a # Now both 'a' and 'b' refer to the same object (10)

print(id(a)) # Output: memory address of 'a'

print(id(b)) # Output: same memory address as 'a'

a = 15 # Now 'a' points to a different object (15)

print(id(a)) # Output: different memory address

print(id(b)) # Output: still the memory address of 'b'

In the above example, you can see how a and b initially point to the same memory location (the number 10), but when a is reassigned, it points to a new memory location.

Global vs Local Variables

VARIABLES IN PYTHON can have **global** or **local** scope. A global variable is one that is defined outside of any function and can be accessed anywhere in the program. A local variable is one that is defined inside a function and can only be accessed within that function.

Here's an example of both global and local variables:

x = 50 # Global variable

def my_function():

y = 10 # Local variable

print(y)

my_function() # Output: 10

print(x) # Output: 50

Attempting to access the local variable y outside of my_function() would result in an error, because y is not defined globally.

Working with Numbers and Arithmetic Operations

NUMBERS ARE ONE OF the most fundamental data types in Python, allowing you to perform a wide variety of calculations and manipulations. Python supports several types of numbers, including integers, floating-point numbers, and complex numbers. In this section, we will explore how to work with different kinds of numbers and perform arithmetic operations in Python.

Types of Numbers in Python

PYTHON PROVIDES THREE main numeric types:

Integers: These are whole numbers without a decimal point. They can be positive, negative, or zero. For example: 10, -5, 0.

Example of assigning an integer to a variable:

python

```
a = 10

b = -5
```
1.

Floating-point numbers: These are numbers with a decimal point, also known as floats. For example: 3.14, -0.001, 100.0.

Example of assigning a float:

python

```
pi = 3.14159
```
1.

Complex numbers: These consist of a real and an imaginary part. The imaginary part is denoted by the letter j in Python. For example: 2 + 3j, -1j.

Example of assigning a complex number:

python

```
z = 2 + 3j
```

1.

Most day-to-day calculations are done using integers and floats, but Python supports complex numbers for more specialized applications, such as in certain fields of mathematics or engineering.

Basic Arithmetic Operations

PYTHON SUPPORTS A RANGE of basic arithmetic operations, such as addition, subtraction, multiplication, and division. Here's how to perform each of them:

Addition (+): Adds two numbers together.

python

```
x = 10

y = 5

result = x + y

print(result) # Output: 15
```

1.

Subtraction (-): Subtracts one number from another.

python

result = x - y

print(result) # Output: 5

1.

Multiplication (*): Multiplies two numbers.

python

result = x * y

print(result) # Output: 50

1.

Division (/): Divides one number by another, returning a float.

python

result = x / y

print(result) # Output: 2.0

1.

Note that in Python, division always results in a floating-point number, even if both operands are integers.

Floor Division (//): This operator performs integer (or floor) division. It divides two numbers and discards the fractional part, returning the largest integer less than or equal to the result.

python

result = x // y

print(result) # Output: 2

1.

Modulus (%): The modulus operator returns the remainder of a division operation.

python

```
result = x % y

print(result) # Output: 0
```

1. The modulus operation is useful when you want to determine if one number is divisible by another.

Exponentiation (**): Raises one number to the power of another.

python

```
result = x ** 2

print(result) # Output: 100
```

1.

Order of Operations

PYTHON FOLLOWS THE standard order of operations, also known as **PEMDAS**:

- **P**: Parentheses first
- **E**: Exponents (i.e., powers and square roots, etc.)
- **MD**: Multiplication and Division (left to right)
- **AS**: Addition and Subtraction (left to right)

For example:

```
result = 2 + 3 * 4
```

print(result) # Output: 14

Here, multiplication takes precedence over addition, so 3 * 4 is calculated first, resulting in 12, and then 2 is added.

If you want to change the order, you can use parentheses:

result = (2 + 3) * 4

print(result) # Output: 20

Now, addition is done first, followed by multiplication.

Working with Negative Numbers

PYTHON ALLOWS FOR EASY manipulation of negative numbers. You can add, subtract, multiply, and divide negative numbers just like positive ones:

a = -5

b = 10

Addition

print(a + b) # Output: 5

Subtraction

print(b - a) # Output: 15

Multiplication

print(a * b) # Output: -50

Division

print(b / a) # Output: -2.0

Negative numbers behave predictably when combined with positive numbers in arithmetic operations.

Working with Floats

FLOATING-POINT NUMBERS (floats) are useful when working with decimals or when precision is needed. Python handles floats with a high degree of accuracy, but there are some limitations due to how computers represent floating-point numbers internally.

For example, you might see a slight difference in the result due to precision limitations:

```
x = 0.1 + 0.2

print(x) # Output: 0.30000000000000004
```

This is a common issue in many programming languages and is not specific to Python.

You can also use arithmetic operations with floats in the same way as with integers:

```
a = 5.5

b = 2.0

# Addition

print(a + b) # Output: 7.5

# Subtraction

print(a - b) # Output: 3.5

# Multiplication
```

```
print(a * b) # Output: 11.0

# Division

print(a / b) # Output: 2.75
```

Integer and Float Conversion

IN PYTHON, INTEGERS and floats are two distinct types, but you can convert between them as needed. Python allows you to convert an integer to a float and vice versa using the int() and float() functions:

```
x = 5

y = 10.5

# Convert integer to float

x_float = float(x)

print(x_float) # Output: 5.0

# Convert float to integer

y_int = int(y)

print(y_int) # Output: 10
```

Note that when you convert a float to an integer, the decimal part is truncated, not rounded. If you need rounding, you can use the round() function.

Rounding Numbers

THE ROUND() FUNCTION is used to round a number to the nearest integer or to a specified number of decimal places.

For example, to round a float to the nearest whole number:

x = 3.14159

rounded_value = round(x)

print(rounded_value) # Output: 3

To round to a specific number of decimal places, pass a second argument to round():

rounded_value = round(x, 2)

print(rounded_value) # Output: 3.14

Augmented Assignment Operators

PYTHON ALSO PROVIDES shorthand operators for performing arithmetic operations and updating the value of a variable in one step. These are known as **augmented assignment operators.**

Here are some examples:

Addition assignment (+=):

python

x = 10

x += 5 # Equivalent to x = x + 5

print(x) # Output: 15

1.

Subtraction assignment (-=):

python

x -= 3 # Equivalent to x = x - 3

print(x) # Output: 12

1.

Multiplication assignment (*=):

python

x *= 2 # Equivalent to x = x * 2

print(x) # Output: 24

1.

Division assignment (/=):

python

x /= 4 # Equivalent to x = x / 4

print(x) # Output: 6.0

1.

These operators are convenient for updating a variable's value based on its current value.

Mathematical Functions with the math Module

FOR MORE ADVANCED MATHEMATICAL operations, Python provides a built-in math module. This module includes functions for performing complex mathematical calculations such as trigonometry, logarithms, and powers.

Here are some common functions in the math module:

Square root (math.sqrt()):

python

```
import math
result = math.sqrt(16)
print(result) # Output: 4.0
```

1.

Power (math.pow()):

python

```
result = math.pow(2, 3) # 2 raised to the power of 3
print(result) # Output: 8.0
```

1.

Logarithm (math.log()):

python

```
result = math.log(100) # Natural logarithm
print(result) # Output: 4.605170185988092
```

You can also specify the base for logarithms:

python

```
result = math.log(100, 10) # Logarithm base 10
print(result) # Output: 2.0
```

1.

Trigonometric Functions:

The math module includes functions like math.sin(), math.cos(), and math.tan() for trigonometric calculations:

python

```
angle = math.radians(90) # Convert degrees to radians

result = math.sin(angle)

print(result) # Output: 1.0
```

1.

Handling Large Numbers

PYTHON NATIVELY SUPPORTS arbitrarily large integers. Unlike some other programming languages, you don't have to worry about integer overflow in Python. You can work with extremely large numbers without any issues:

```
big_number = 10 ** 100 # 10 raised to the power of 100

print(big_number)
```

Conclusion

NUMBERS ARE A FOUNDATIONAL aspect of Python programming, enabling you to perform calculations and operations with ease. From basic arithmetic to advanced mathematical functions using the math module, Python provides all the tools you need to manipulate numbers. Understanding how to work with integers, floats, and even complex numbers is essential for writing efficient and effective code.

Strings: Manipulating Text in Python

IN PYTHON, STRINGS are one of the most common and versatile data types, used to represent text. A string in Python is a sequence of characters enclosed in either single (' ') or double (" ") quotes. Python provides powerful tools and methods to manipulate strings, making text processing both easy and efficient. In this section, we will explore string creation, manipulation, and advanced operations that you can perform with strings in Python.

Creating Strings

YOU CAN CREATE A STRING by assigning text to a variable. The text must be enclosed in either single or double quotes. Here are some examples:

greeting = "Hello, World!"

name = 'Alice'

Python treats single and double quotes the same, so you can use either. However, it is important to be consistent with your choice to avoid errors.

You can also create multi-line strings using triple quotes (''' ''' or """ """). This is particularly useful when working with long blocks of text.

message = """This is a multi-line string.

It spans multiple lines, and can be very useful

for storing long text content."""

String Indexing and Slicing

STRINGS IN PYTHON ARE **indexed** starting from zero. Each character in a string has an index, and you can access individual characters using square brackets ([]).

For example, to access the first character of a string:

```
word = "Python"

first_letter = word[0]

print(first_letter) # Output: P
```

Similarly, you can access characters from the end of the string using negative indexing:

```
last_letter = word[-1]

print(last_letter) # Output: n
```

String slicing allows you to extract a portion of a string. The syntax for slicing is string[start:end], where start is the index to begin slicing, and end is the index to stop (exclusive). For example:

```
substring = word[0:4]

print(substring) # Output: Pyth
```

You can also omit the start or end index to slice from the beginning or until the end of the string:

```
print(word[:4]) # Output: Pyth (from start to index 4)

print(word[2:]) # Output: thon (from index 2 to the end)
```

You can specify a step value in slicing by adding a third argument, which determines how many characters to skip:

step_slice = word[::2]

print(step_slice) # Output: Pto (characters at even indices)

String Immutability

STRINGS IN PYTHON ARE **immutable**, which means once a string is created, its characters cannot be changed. If you need to modify a string, you must create a new string. For example:

word = "Hello"

word[0] = "h" # This would raise an error since strings are immutable

To change the first letter, you would need to create a new string

new_word = "h" + word[1:]

print(new_word) # Output: hello

String Concatenation

YOU CAN CONCATENATE (combine) two or more strings using the + operator:

greeting = "Hello, " + "World!"

print(greeting) # Output: Hello, World!

String concatenation is a powerful feature, but it can become inefficient when working with large amounts of text. In those cases, it's better to use other methods like **join** (discussed later).

Repeating Strings

YOU CAN REPEAT A STRING multiple times using the * operator:

```
repeat_string = "Python! " * 3

print(repeat_string) # Output: Python! Python! Python!
```

This can be useful for generating repeated patterns or structures in your output.

String Methods

PYTHON PROVIDES A RICH set of built-in methods for manipulating strings. These methods can be used to perform various operations like formatting, searching, replacing, and more.

Changing Case

YOU CAN CONVERT THE case of a string using methods like lower(), upper(), capitalize(), and title():

```
word = "python programming"

print(word.upper()) # Output: PYTHON PROGRAMMING

print(word.lower()) # Output: python programming

print(word.capitalize()) # Output: Python programming

print(word.title()) # Output: Python Programming
```

- upper() converts all characters to uppercase.
- lower() converts all characters to lowercase.

- capitalize() converts only the first character to uppercase and the rest to lowercase.
- title() converts the first character of each word to uppercase.

Stripping Whitespace

THE STRIP() METHOD removes leading and trailing whitespace (spaces, tabs, or newline characters) from a string:

```
text = " Hello, World! "

print(text.strip()) # Output: Hello, World!
```

If you want to remove only leading or trailing whitespace, you can use lstrip() (left strip) or rstrip() (right strip):

```
print(text.lstrip()) # Output: Hello, World!

print(text.rstrip()) # Output: Hello, World!
```

Replacing Substrings

THE REPLACE() METHOD allows you to replace occurrences of a substring within a string with another substring:

```
message = "Hello, World!"

new_message = message.replace("World", "Python")

print(new_message) # Output: Hello, Python!
```

You can replace multiple occurrences by specifying a substring that appears more than once in the string.

Splitting and Joining Strings

THE SPLIT() METHOD splits a string into a list of substrings based on a delimiter. By default, it splits on whitespace, but you can specify any delimiter:

sentence = "This is a sample sentence."

words = sentence.split()

print(words) # Output: ['This', 'is', 'a', 'sample', 'sentence.']

You can split on other characters, like commas or periods:

data = "apple,orange,banana"

fruits = data.split(',')

print(fruits) # Output: ['apple', 'orange', 'banana']

The join() method does the opposite of split(). It joins a list of strings into a single string, with a specified delimiter:

word_list = ['This', 'is', 'a', 'sentence']

sentence = " ".join(word_list)

print(sentence) # Output: This is a sentence

Finding Substrings

YOU CAN SEARCH FOR substrings using the find() and index() methods. Both return the index of the first occurrence of the substring, but they handle cases where the substring is not found differently.

- find() returns -1 if the substring is not found:

```
text = "Python is fun"

print(text.find("fun")) # Output: 10

print(text.find("boring")) # Output: -1
```

- index() raises an error if the substring is not found:

```
print(text.index("fun")) # Output: 10

# print(text.index("boring")) # Raises ValueError
```

Checking for Substrings

YOU CAN CHECK WHETHER a string contains a specific substring using the in operator:

```
text = "Python programming"

print("Python" in text) # Output: True

print("Java" in text) # Output: False
```

This is a simple and efficient way to check for the existence of substrings.

Formatting Strings

PYTHON PROVIDES SEVERAL ways to format strings, allowing you to insert variables or values into a string in a clean and readable way.

Using the format() Method

THE FORMAT() METHOD allows you to insert variables into a string by placing placeholders {} in the string. The values are passed as arguments to format():

name = "Alice"

age = 30

message = "My name is {} and I am {} years old.".format(name, age)

print(message) # Output: My name is Alice and I am 30 years old.

You can also use positional or keyword arguments in format():

message = "My name is {0} and I am {1} years old.".format(name, age)

print(message) # Output: My name is Alice and I am 30 years old.

message = "My name is {name} and I am {age} years old.".format(name="Bob", age=25)

print(message) # Output: My name is Bob and I am 25 years old.

Using f-strings

INTRODUCED IN PYTHON 3.6, **f-strings** (formatted string literals) are a more concise way to format strings. You prefix the string with an f, and use curly braces {} to insert variables directly:

name = "Alice"

age = 30

message = f"My name is {name} and I am {age} years old."

print(message) # Output: My name is Alice and I am 30 years old.

f-strings are not only shorter but also more readable than the format() method.

String Encoding and Decoding

IN PYTHON, STRINGS are stored as sequences of Unicode characters. However, when dealing with data from external sources, such as files or the internet, you may encounter different encodings.

The most common encoding is **UTF-8**, which can represent any Unicode character. You can encode a string into bytes using the encode() method, and decode bytes back into a string using decode():

text = "Hello, World!"

encoded_text = text.encode("utf-8")

print(encoded_text) # Output: b'Hello, World!'

decoded_text = encoded_text.decode("utf-8")

print(decoded_text) # Output: Hello, World!

Conclusion

STRINGS ARE AN ESSENTIAL part of Python programming, providing a wide range of functionalities for text manipulation. Whether you're concatenating strings, searching for substrings, formatting text, or splitting and joining strings, Python's built-in methods make working with text efficient and easy. Understanding string manipulation is crucial for tasks like parsing user input, generating dynamic content, or handling data from files and APIs.

By mastering string operations, you unlock powerful tools to make your Python programs more versatile and effective.

Booleans and Logical Expressions

BOOLEANS ARE ONE OF the simplest yet most powerful data types in Python. They represent truth values and are the foundation of logical operations in programming. A Boolean can only have two possible values: True or False. Booleans are commonly used in decision-making structures, control flow, and conditions in Python, making them essential for writing robust and dynamic code.

Understanding Booleans in Python

A **Boolean** is a data type that can hold one of two values: True or False. These values are not strings or numbers but rather distinct values with special significance in Python. They are often the result of comparison operations or logical expressions.

For example, assigning Boolean values:

is_sunny = True

is_raining = False

Here, is_sunny holds the Boolean value True, indicating that the condition "it is sunny" is true. is_raining, on the other hand, holds False, meaning the condition "it is raining" is false.

Boolean Expressions

A **Boolean expression** is any expression that evaluates to either True or False. This often happens as a result of comparison operations or logical tests. Let's examine some common Boolean expressions in Python.

Comparison Operators

PYTHON PROVIDES SEVERAL comparison operators that are used to compare values. The result of these comparisons is always a Boolean value (True or False).

Equal to (==): This operator checks whether two values are equal.

python

result = 5 == 5 # True

result = 5 == 6 # False

1.

Not equal to (!=): This operator checks whether two values are not equal.

python

result = 5 != 6 # True

result = 5 != 5 # False

1.

Greater than (>): This operator checks if the value on the left is greater than the value on the right.

python

result = 10 > 5 # True

result = 3 > 5 # False

1.

Less than (<): This operator checks if the value on the left is less than the value on the right.

python

```
result = 3 < 5 # True

result = 5 < 5 # False
```

1.

Greater than or equal to (>=): This operator checks if the value on the left is greater than or equal to the value on the right.

python

```
result = 5 >= 5 # True

result = 4 >= 5 # False
```

1.

Less than or equal to (<=): This operator checks if the value on the left is less than or equal to the value on the right.

python

```
result = 3 <= 5 # True

result = 6 <= 5 # False
```

1.

Logical Operators

PYTHON ALSO PROVIDES **logical operators** that allow you to combine multiple Boolean expressions. These operators are used to build more complex conditions.

and: This operator returns True if both operands (the expressions on its left and right) are True. If either operand is False, it returns False.

python

```
result = (5 > 3) and (7 > 6) # True

result = (5 > 3) and (7 < 6) # False
```

1. In the first example, both conditions are True, so the overall expression is True. In the second example, since one condition is False, the result is False.

or: This operator returns True if at least one of its operands is True. If both operands are False, it returns False.

python

```
result = (5 > 3) or (7 < 6) # True

result = (5 < 3) or (7 < 6) # False
```

1. In the first example, since one condition is True, the overall expression is True. The second example evaluates to False because both conditions are False.

not: This operator negates the Boolean value of its operand. If the operand is True, not returns False; if the operand is False, not returns True.

python

```
result = not (5 > 3) # False

result = not (5 < 3) # True
```

1.

Combining Logical and Comparison Operators

OFTEN, YOU WILL NEED to combine both logical and comparison operators to create more complex Boolean expressions. These expressions can be used to control the flow of your program by making decisions based on multiple conditions.

For example:

```
age = 20

is_student = True

# A person is eligible for a student discount if they are under 25 and are a student

eligible_for_discount = (age < 25) and is_student

print(eligible_for_discount) # True
```

Here, we use both the and operator and a comparison (<) to determine whether someone is eligible for a student discount.

Boolean Values in Python Control Flow

BOOLEAN EXPRESSIONS are at the heart of Python's control flow. Python evaluates conditions in control flow statements such as if, elif, and while. Based on the result (either True or False), the program will decide whether to execute certain blocks of code.

The if Statement

THE **if statement** is one of the most common ways to control the flow of a program. It allows you to execute a block of code only if a certain condition is True.

```
x = 10

if x > 5:

print("x is greater than 5")
```

In this example, the program checks whether x is greater than 5. Since the condition is True, the program executes the print statement. If the condition were False, the code inside the if block would be skipped.

The else Statement

YOU CAN USE THE **else statement** to specify a block of code to run if the condition in the if statement is False.

```
x = 3

if x > 5:

print("x is greater than 5")

else:

print("x is not greater than 5")
```

Here, since x is not greater than 5, the code inside the else block is executed, and the output will be:

```
x is not greater than 5
```

The elif Statement

THE **elif statement** (short for "else if") allows you to check multiple conditions. It is used after an if statement, and before an else statement, to test additional conditions if the first condition is False.

```
x = 7

if x > 10:

print("x is greater than 10")

elif x > 5:

print("x is greater than 5 but less than or equal to 10")

else:

print("x is 5 or less")
```

In this case, the first condition (x > 10) is False, so the program checks the next condition (x > 5), which is True, and executes the corresponding block of code.

The output will be:

```
x is greater than 5 but less than or equal to 10
```

The while Loop

THE **while loop** executes a block of code as long as a given condition is True. It is often used when you need to repeat a task until a certain condition is met.

```
count = 0

while count < 5:

print(count)

count += 1
```

In this example, the loop continues to run as long as count is less than 5. Each time the loop runs, count is incremented by 1. Once count reaches 5, the condition becomes False, and the loop exits.

0

1

2

3

4

Truthy and Falsy Values

IN PYTHON, CERTAIN values are considered **truthy** or **falsy**, meaning they are treated as True or False when evaluated in a Boolean context.

Truthy values are values that evaluate to True in a Boolean context. In general, any non-zero number, non-empty string, non-empty list, or non-empty object is truthy.

For example:

python

if 1:

print("This is truthy!") # Output: This is truthy!

if "hello":

print("This string is truthy!") # Output: This string is truthy!

-

Falsy values are values that evaluate to False. These include 0, None, False, an empty string (""), an empty list ([]), and other empty data structures.

For example:

python

if not 0:

print("0 is falsy!") # Output: 0 is falsy!

if not []:

print("An empty list is falsy!") # Output: An empty list is falsy!

-

Understanding truthy and falsy values is crucial for writing concise and efficient code, especially when working with conditions and loops.

Short-Circuit Evaluation

PYTHON USES **short-circuit evaluation** for logical operators. This means that Python stops evaluating an expression as soon as it knows the result.

For the and operator, if the first operand is False, the overall expression will be False, so Python will not evaluate the second operand:

result = (5 < 3) and (2 > 1) # The second expression is not evaluated because the first is False

print(result) # Output: False

For the or operator, if the first operand is True, the overall expression will be True, and Python will not evaluate the second operand:

result = (5 > 3) or (2 < 1) # The second expression is not evaluated because the first is True

print(result) # Output: True

Short-circuit evaluation can help optimize your code by avoiding unnecessary computations.

Boolean Functions

SEVERAL BUILT-IN PYTHON functions return Boolean values, including all(), any(), and bool().

all()

THE **all() function** returns True if all the elements in an iterable (e.g., a list or a tuple) are truthy. If any element is falsy, it returns False.

numbers = [1, 2, 3, 4]

result = all(numbers) # True, because all elements are truthy

print(result)

If the list contains a falsy value, all() will return False:

numbers = [1, 0, 3, 4]

result = all(numbers) # False, because 0 is falsy

print(result)

any()

THE **any() function** returns True if at least one element in an iterable is truthy. If all elements are falsy, it returns False.

numbers = [0, 0, 0, 1]

result = any(numbers) # True, because 1 is truthy

print(result)

If all elements are falsy, any() will return False:

numbers = [0, 0, 0, 0]

result = any(numbers) # False, because all elements are falsy

print(result)

bool()

THE **bool() function** is used to convert a value into its Boolean equivalent. It returns True for truthy values and False for falsy values.

print(bool(1)) # Output: True

print(bool(0)) # Output: False

print(bool("hi")) # Output: True

print(bool("")) # Output: False

Conclusion

BOOLEANS AND LOGICAL expressions are fundamental concepts in Python that enable decision-making and control flow in your programs. By mastering Boolean logic, comparison operators, and logical operators, you can write more dynamic and flexible code. Understanding how to combine conditions, use truthy and falsy values, and take advantage of short-circuit evaluation will make your Python code more efficient and readable.

Lists, Tuples, and Dictionaries: Working with Data Collections

PYTHON PROVIDES SEVERAL built-in data structures that allow you to store and manage collections of data. Three of the most commonly used data structures are **lists**, **tuples**, and **dictionaries**. Each of these structures serves a different purpose and provides different capabilities for managing data collections in Python.

Lists: Mutable Ordered Sequences

A **list** in Python is an ordered collection of items (or elements) that can contain any type of data: integers, floats, strings, or even other lists. Lists are **mutable**, meaning their contents can be changed after they are created. This flexibility makes lists one of the most commonly used data structures in Python.

Creating Lists

YOU CAN CREATE A LIST by placing a comma-separated sequence of items inside square brackets ([]):

```
fruits = ["apple", "banana", "cherry"]

numbers = [1, 2, 3, 4, 5]

mixed_list = [1, "apple", 3.14, True]
```

A list can hold elements of different types, as shown in the mixed_list example above. Lists can also be empty:

empty_list = []

Accessing List Elements

YOU CAN ACCESS INDIVIDUAL elements in a list using **indexing**. Python lists are zero-indexed, meaning the first element has an index of 0:

fruits = ["apple", "banana", "cherry"]

print(fruits[0]) # Output: apple

print(fruits[2]) # Output: cherry

You can also use negative indexing to access elements from the end of the list:

print(fruits[-1]) # Output: cherry (last element)

print(fruits[-2]) # Output: banana

Modifying Lists

ONE OF THE KEY FEATURES of lists is that they are mutable, meaning you can modify the contents of a list after it has been created.

Changing Elements

YOU CAN CHANGE THE value of an element at a specific index:

fruits[1] = "orange"

print(fruits) # Output: ['apple', 'orange', 'cherry']

Adding Elements

THERE ARE SEVERAL WAYS to add elements to a list. You can use the append() method to add a single element to the end of the list:

fruits.append("grape")

print(fruits) # Output: ['apple', 'orange', 'cherry', 'grape']

To add multiple elements at once, you can use the extend() method, which takes an iterable (like another list) and adds each element to the end of the list:

fruits.extend(["mango", "pineapple"])

print(fruits) # Output: ['apple', 'orange', 'cherry', 'grape', 'mango', 'pineapple']

Alternatively, you can insert an element at a specific index using the insert() method:

fruits.insert(1, "strawberry")

print(fruits) # Output: ['apple', 'strawberry', 'orange', 'cherry', 'grape', 'mango', 'pineapple']

Removing Elements

TO REMOVE ELEMENTS from a list, Python provides several methods:

remove(): Removes the first occurrence of a specified element.

python

fruits.remove("orange")

print(fruits) # Output: ['apple', 'strawberry', 'cherry', 'grape', 'mango', 'pineapple']

•

pop(): Removes and returns the element at a specified index. If no index is provided, pop() removes and returns the last element.

python

last_fruit = fruits.pop()

print(last_fruit) # Output: pineapple

print(fruits) # Output: ['apple', 'strawberry', 'cherry', 'grape', 'mango']

first_fruit = fruits.pop(0)

print(first_fruit) # Output: apple

•

clear(): Removes all elements from the list, leaving it empty.

python

fruits.clear()

print(fruits) # Output: []

•

Slicing Lists

YOU CAN USE **slicing** to access a portion of a list. The syntax for slicing is list[start:end], where start is the index to begin the slice and end is the index to stop (the element at the end index is not included in the result):

```
fruits = ["apple", "banana", "cherry", "date", "elderberry"]

slice_fruits = fruits[1:4]

print(slice_fruits) # Output: ['banana', 'cherry', 'date']
```

You can also omit the start or end index to slice from the beginning or to the end of the list:

```
print(fruits[:3]) # Output: ['apple', 'banana', 'cherry']

print(fruits[2:]) # Output: ['cherry', 'date', 'elderberry']
```

List Comprehensions

A **list comprehension** is a concise way to create lists based on existing lists. It allows you to generate a new list by applying an expression to each element of an iterable.

```
squares = [x**2 for x in range(1, 6)]

print(squares) # Output: [1, 4, 9, 16, 25]
```

List comprehensions can also include conditions:

```
even_squares = [x**2 for x in range(1, 11) if x % 2 == 0]

print(even_squares) # Output: [4, 16, 36, 64, 100]
```

Tuples: Immutable Ordered Sequences

A **tuple** is similar to a list, but it is **immutable**, meaning that once a tuple is created, its elements cannot be changed. Tuples are useful when you want to create a collection of items that should not be modified.

Creating Tuples

TUPLES ARE CREATED by placing a comma-separated sequence of items inside parentheses (()):

coordinates = (10, 20)

colors = ("red", "green", "blue")

Tuples can also be created without parentheses, simply by separating items with commas:

dimensions = 1920, 1080

If you want to create a tuple with only one element, you need to include a trailing comma:

single_item_tuple = (5,)

Accessing Tuple Elements

YOU CAN ACCESS ELEMENTS in a tuple using indexing, just like with lists:

colors = ("red", "green", "blue")

print(colors[0]) # Output: red

print(colors[-1]) # Output: blue

Tuple Unpacking

A COMMON USE OF TUPLES is **tuple unpacking**, where you assign the elements of a tuple to multiple variables at once:

```
coordinates = (10, 20)

x, y = coordinates

print(x) # Output: 10

print(y) # Output: 20
```

This is particularly useful when functions return multiple values as tuples.

Immutability of Tuples

SINCE TUPLES ARE IMMUTABLE, you cannot modify their elements. Attempting to change an element of a tuple will result in an error:

```
colors = ("red", "green", "blue")

# colors[0] = "yellow" # This would raise a TypeError
```

If you need to modify a tuple, you would need to convert it to a list, make the changes, and then convert it back to a tuple:

```
colors_list = list(colors)

colors_list[0] = "yellow"

colors = tuple(colors_list)

print(colors) # Output: ('yellow', 'green', 'blue')
```

Dictionaries: Key-Value Pairs

A **dictionary** in Python is a collection of key-value pairs. Each key is associated with a specific value, and the key is used to access the corresponding value. Unlike lists and tuples, dictionaries are **unordered** collections, and they are **mutable**.

Creating Dictionaries

YOU CAN CREATE A DICTIONARY by placing a comma-separated sequence of key-value pairs inside curly braces ({}). Each key-value pair is separated by a colon (:):

person = {"name": "Alice", "age": 30, "city": "New York"}

Dictionaries can also be created using the dict() constructor:

person = dict(name="Alice", age=30, city="New York")

Keys in a dictionary must be unique and immutable (e.g., strings, numbers, or tuples). Values can be of any data type.

Accessing Dictionary Values

YOU CAN ACCESS A VALUE in a dictionary by using its key inside square brackets:

print(person["name"]) # Output: Alice

print(person["age"]) # Output: 30

You can also use the get() method to access a value. This method allows you to specify a default value to return if the key is not found:

print(person.get("name")) # Output: Alice

print(person.get("address", "Unknown")) # Output: Unknown

Modifying Dictionaries

DICTIONARIES ARE MUTABLE, so you can add, modify, or remove key-value pairs.

Adding or Updating Key-Value Pairs

TO ADD A NEW KEY-VALUE pair or update an existing one, use the assignment operator:

person["job"] = "Engineer"

print(person) # Output: {'name': 'Alice', 'age': 30, 'city': 'New York', 'job': 'Engineer'}

Removing Key-Value Pairs

YOU CAN REMOVE A KEY-value pair using the del statement or the pop() method:

del person["age"]

print(person) # Output: {'name': 'Alice', 'city': 'New York', 'job': 'Engineer'}

job = person.pop("job")

print(job) # Output: Engineer

print(person) # Output: {'name': 'Alice', 'city': 'New York'}

Dictionary Methods

PYTHON PROVIDES SEVERAL useful methods for working with dictionaries:

keys(): Returns a view of the dictionary's keys.

python

```
print(person.keys()) # Output: dict_keys(['name', 'city'])
```

-

values(): Returns a view of the dictionary's values.

python

```
print(person.values()) # Output: dict_values(['Alice', 'New York'])
```

-

items(): Returns a view of the dictionary's key-value pairs.

python

```
print(person.items()) # Output: dict_items([('name', 'Alice'), ('city', 'New York')])
```

-

Nested Data Structures

PYTHON ALLOWS YOU TO create **nested** lists, tuples, and dictionaries, meaning that these data structures can contain other data structures as elements.

Nested Lists

A LIST CAN CONTAIN other lists as elements:

```
matrix = [[1, 2, 3], [4, 5, 6], [7, 8, 9]]

print(matrix[0]) # Output: [1, 2, 3]

print(matrix[0][1]) # Output: 2
```

Nested Dictionaries

A DICTIONARY CAN CONTAIN other dictionaries as values:

```
people = {

"Alice": {"age": 30, "job": "Engineer"},

"Bob": {"age": 25, "job": "Artist"}

}

print(people["Alice"]["job"]) # Output: Engineer
```

Conclusion

LISTS, TUPLES, AND dictionaries are versatile data structures that allow you to organize and manage collections of data in Python. Each structure has its strengths: lists are mutable and ordered, tuples are immutable and ordered, and dictionaries provide fast lookups with key-value pairs. By mastering these data structures, you can handle complex data sets and design efficient, readable code in Python.

Chapter 3: Control Flow in Python

Conditional Statements: if, else, elif

CONTROL FLOW IS ONE of the most important concepts in any programming language, as it allows developers to dictate how the program should behave in different situations. In Python, control flow is primarily achieved using conditional statements (if, else, and elif) and loops. In this section, we'll focus on conditional statements and how they can be used to add logic to your Python programs.

What Are Conditional Statements?

A CONDITIONAL STATEMENT is a way to execute certain pieces of code only when a particular condition or set of conditions is true. Python provides a simple syntax for defining conditions using the if, else, and elif keywords.

Here's the basic structure of an if statement:

if condition:

Code to execute if condition is true

When Python encounters an if statement, it evaluates the condition. If the condition is true (i.e., evaluates to True), Python will execute the block of code inside the if statement. If the condition is false, Python will skip the block of code.

For example:

x = 10

if x > 5:

```
print("x is greater than 5")
```

In this case, the condition x > 5 is true, so the program prints "x is greater than 5". If x were less than or equal to 5, the code inside the if block would not be executed.

Adding else and elif

WHILE AN IF STATEMENT can stand alone, it is often useful to add alternative actions for when the condition is not true. This is where the else and elif statements come in.

The else statement provides an alternative block of code that will execute if the if condition is false:

```
x = 2

if x > 5:

print("x is greater than 5")

else:

print("x is less than or equal to 5")
```

Here, because x is less than 5, the else block is executed, and the program prints "x is less than or equal to 5".

If you have multiple conditions to check, you can use the elif (short for "else if") statement. This allows you to check additional conditions if the first one is false:

```
x = 3

if x > 5:

print("x is greater than 5")
```

elif x == 3:

print("x is equal to 3")

else:

print("x is less than 3")

In this example, since x is equal to 3, the program prints "x is equal to 3". If x were greater than 5, the first condition would trigger, and if x were less than 3, the else block would execute.

Complex Conditions with Logical Operators

IN MANY CASES, YOU'LL want to check multiple conditions at once. Python supports logical operators like and, or, and not to help you combine multiple conditions in a single statement.

Using and

THE AND OPERATOR ALLOWS you to combine two or more conditions that must all be true for the entire condition to evaluate to true:

x = 7

if x > 5 and x < 10:

print("x is between 5 and 10")

In this case, both conditions (x > 5 and x < 10) are true, so the block of code is executed, and the program prints "x is between 5 and 10". If either condition were false, the block would not be executed.

Using or

THE OR OPERATOR ALLOWS you to combine conditions where only one needs to be true for the entire condition to evaluate to true:

```
x = 4

if x < 5 or x > 10:

print("x is either less than 5 or greater than 10")
```

Here, because x is less than 5, the program prints "x is either less than 5 or greater than 10". Even though x is not greater than 10, the condition still evaluates to true because the or operator only requires one of the conditions to be true.

Using not

THE NOT OPERATOR NEGATES a condition, meaning that it returns true if the condition is false, and false if the condition is true:

```
x = 7

if not x == 5:

print("x is not equal to 5")
```

Since x is not equal to 5, the not operator causes the condition to evaluate to true, and the program prints "x is not equal to 5".

Nested Conditions

SOMETIMES YOU'LL NEED to check conditions inside other conditions. This is known as nesting, and it allows for more complex logic in your programs.

```
x = 10

y = 20

if x > 5:

if y > 15:

print("x is greater than 5 and y is greater than 15")
```

In this example, the first condition (x > 5) is true, so Python evaluates the second if statement inside it. Since y > 15 is also true, the program prints "x is greater than 5 and y is greater than 15".

You can also combine if, else, and elif statements inside each other to handle even more complex scenarios.

```
x = 7

y = 3

if x > 5:

if y > 5:

print("Both x and y are greater than 5")

else:

print("x is greater than 5, but y is not")

else:
```

print("x is not greater than 5")

In this case, the program first checks if x is greater than 5. Since that's true, it then checks if y is greater than 5. Because y is not, the program prints "x is greater than 5, but y is not".

Ternary Conditional Operator

PYTHON ALSO PROVIDES a more concise way to write simple if-else statements using the ternary operator. This operator allows you to write a condition in a single line of code:

x = 10

result = "x is greater than 5" if x > 5 else "x is less than or equal to 5"

print(result)

In this case, the program prints "x is greater than 5" because the condition x > 5 is true. If the condition were false, the program would print the alternative message.

Indentation in Python Conditionals

PYTHON USES INDENTATION to define the blocks of code associated with each condition. It's important to be consistent with your indentation; otherwise, you'll encounter syntax errors. By default, most Python code uses four spaces for indentation, although tabs are also allowed as long as you are consistent throughout the program.

Here's an example of incorrect indentation that will raise an error:

x = 5

if x > 3:

print("This will cause an error")

In this case, Python expects the code block inside the if statement to be indented, and since it's not, the interpreter will raise an IndentationError.

Practical Applications of Conditional Statements

CONDITIONAL STATEMENTS are fundamental to any Python program, and they can be used in a wide variety of scenarios, such as:

Making decisions based on user input:

python

```
age = int(input("Enter your age: "))

if age >= 18:

print("You are eligible to vote.")

else:

print("You are not eligible to vote.")
```

-

Checking the validity of data:

python

```
password = input("Enter password: ")

if len(password) < 8:

print("Password too short")
```

else:

print("Password accepted")

-

Controlling program flow in games or applications:

python

health = 50

if health <= 0:

print("Game Over")

elif health <= 20:

print("Low Health! Find a health pack.")

else:

print("Keep going!")

-

These examples illustrate how if, else, and elif statements can be used to create more interactive and dynamic Python programs.

Conclusion

MASTERING CONDITIONAL statements is crucial for building more sophisticated Python programs. By understanding how to use if, else, and elif, you can control the flow of your program and make it respond intelligently to different inputs and conditions. Combine this knowledge with logical operators and nested conditions, and you'll be well on your way to writing complex, efficient Python code that can handle a wide range of scenarios.

Loops: for and while

LOOPS ARE FUNDAMENTAL programming structures that allow you to repeat a block of code multiple times, either a set number of times or until a certain condition is met. In Python, there are two primary loop types: for loops and while loops. Each serves a specific purpose and is used in different scenarios depending on the problem you're trying to solve.

The for Loop

THE FOR LOOP IN PYTHON is used to iterate over a sequence (like a list, tuple, dictionary, or string) or any other iterable object. It allows you to repeat a block of code for each element in the sequence.

Here is the basic structure of a for loop:

```
for variable in sequence:

# Code to execute for each item in sequence
```

For example, if you want to iterate over a list of numbers and print each number, you can use the following code:

```
numbers = [1, 2, 3, 4, 5]

for number in numbers:

print(number)
```

1

2

3

4

5

Iterating Over Strings

A FOR LOOP CAN ALSO be used to iterate over strings, where each character in the string is treated as an individual item in the sequence.

```
word = "Python"

for letter in word:

print(letter)
```

This will print each character of the word "Python" on a new line:

```
P

y

t

h

o

n
```

Using the range() Function

OFTEN, YOU'LL WANT to iterate over a sequence of numbers, and the range() function is a convenient way to generate those numbers. The range() function can take one, two, or three arguments depending on how you want to define the sequence.

Single argument: Generates a sequence from 0 to the argument minus one.

python

for i in range(5):

print(i)

Output:

0

1

2

3

4

1.

Two arguments: The first argument is the starting point, and the second argument is the endpoint (exclusive).

python

for i in range(2, 6):

print(i)

Output:

2

3

4

5

1.

Three arguments: The third argument specifies the step value (i.e., how much to increment the counter after each iteration).

python

for i in range(0, 10, 2):

print(i)

Output:

0

2

4

6

8

1.

The while Loop

A WHILE LOOP IS USED when you want to repeat a block of code as long as a condition remains true. Unlike the for loop, which iterates over a sequence of items, the while loop continues until the specified condition becomes false.

Here's the basic structure of a while loop:

```
while condition:

# Code to execute while condition is true
```

For example, you can create a loop that keeps printing numbers as long as a certain condition holds:

```
i = 0

while i < 5:

print(i)

i += 1
```

```
0

1

2

3

4
```

Infinite Loops

A WHILE LOOP WILL CONTINUE to run as long as the condition remains true. If the condition never becomes false, the loop will run indefinitely, which is known as an infinite loop. This can happen if you forget to update the loop variable within the loop body.

```
i = 1

while i > 0:

print("This is an infinite loop")
```

To avoid infinite loops, always ensure that the loop's condition eventually becomes false by updating the loop variable or changing the condition appropriately.

Breaking Out of Loops with break

SOMETIMES, YOU'LL WANT to exit a loop before it has completed all its iterations. You can use the break statement to exit a loop early when a specific condition is met.

```
for i in range(10):

if i == 5:

break

print(i)
```

In this example, the loop will print numbers from 0 to 4. Once the value of i becomes 5, the break statement will terminate the loop, and the remaining iterations will not be executed.

```
0

1

2

3
```

4

Skipping Iterations with continue

THE CONTINUE STATEMENT allows you to skip the current iteration of the loop and move to the next iteration. This is useful when you want to ignore certain values or conditions but continue the loop.

```
for i in range(5):

if i == 3:

continue

print(i)
```

Here, the loop will print numbers from 0 to 4, but when i equals 3, the continue statement will skip that iteration, and 3 will not be printed.

0

1

2

4

Using else with Loops

IN PYTHON, LOOPS CAN have an else clause that executes once the loop finishes all its iterations, provided the loop wasn't terminated prematurely by a break statement. This is a feature not commonly seen in other programming languages.

```
for i in range(5):
```

print(i)

else:

print("Loop finished")

In this case, after the loop prints all the numbers from 0 to 4, the else block will be executed, and "Loop finished" will be printed.

Output:

0

1

2

3

4

Loop finished

However, if the loop is terminated early using break, the else block will not be executed:

for i in range(5):

if i == 3:

break

print(i)

else:

print("Loop finished")

0

1

2

In this example, the else block is not executed because the loop is terminated when i equals 3.

Nested Loops

PYTHON ALLOWS YOU TO nest loops inside one another. This means you can place one loop inside another loop, and the inner loop will be executed for each iteration of the outer loop.

For example, you can use nested loops to print a multiplication table:

```
for i in range(1, 6):

for j in range(1, 6):

print(i * j, end=' ')

print()
```

---

1 2 3 4 5

2 4 6 8 10

3 6 9 12 15

4 8 12 16 20

5 10 15 20 25

Nested loops can also be used for more complex tasks, such as iterating over a matrix (a two-dimensional list) or performing operations on multi-level data structures.

Practical Applications of Loops

LOOPS ARE INCREDIBLY versatile and can be used in various real-world programming scenarios:

Processing user input:

python

while True:

name = input("Enter your name (or 'exit' to quit): ")

if name == 'exit':

break

print(f"Hello, {name}!")

1. This loop continues to ask for the user's name until they enter 'exit', at which point the loop terminates.

Calculating factorials:

python

number = 5

factorial = 1

for i in range(1, number + 1):

factorial *= i

print(f"Factorial of {number} is {factorial}")

1. This for loop calculates the factorial of a given number.

Summing values in a list:

python

numbers = [1, 2, 3, 4, 5]

total = 0

for number in numbers:

total += number

print(f"Sum of the list is {total}")

1. This loop sums all the values in a list.

Finding prime numbers:

python

for num in range(2, 20):

for i in range(2, num):

if num % i == 0:

break

else:

print(f"{num} is a prime number")

1. This nested loop finds and prints all prime numbers between 2 and 20.

Conclusion

LOOPS ARE AN ESSENTIAL part of any programming language, and mastering them will help you build more efficient and flexible Python programs. Whether you're iterating over a sequence with a for loop or repeating actions until a condition is met with a while loop, understanding how to use loops effectively is key to writing robust and maintainable code.

Nested Loops and Complex Conditions

IN PYTHON, LOOPS ARE not limited to single, straightforward structures. You can nest loops inside one another, creating more complex and powerful patterns for processing data or solving problems. Nested loops allow you to repeat actions on multiple levels, making them ideal for tasks that involve multi-dimensional data structures or multiple layers of iteration. Additionally, combining loops with complex conditions gives you precise control over your code's flow, allowing for intricate logic in your programs.

Understanding Nested Loops

A NESTED LOOP IS A loop inside another loop. The inner loop will run entirely for each iteration of the outer loop. Here's a simple example to illustrate the concept:

```
for i in range(1, 4):

for j in range(1, 4):

print(f"Outer loop iteration {i}, inner loop iteration {j}")
```

In this example, the outer loop runs three times, and for each iteration of the outer loop, the inner loop also runs three times. The output will be:

Outer loop iteration 1, inner loop iteration 1

Outer loop iteration 1, inner loop iteration 2

Outer loop iteration 1, inner loop iteration 3

Outer loop iteration 2, inner loop iteration 1

Outer loop iteration 2, inner loop iteration 2

Outer loop iteration 2, inner loop iteration 3

Outer loop iteration 3, inner loop iteration 1

Outer loop iteration 3, inner loop iteration 2

Outer loop iteration 3, inner loop iteration 3

As you can see, the inner loop completes its full cycle before the outer loop moves to the next iteration.

Practical Example: Creating a Multiplication Table

NESTED LOOPS ARE COMMONLY used to work with multi-dimensional data structures like grids or tables. Let's use a nested loop to generate a multiplication table:

```
for i in range(1, 11):

for j in range(1, 11):

print(f"{i * j:3}", end=" ")

print()
```

1 2 3 4 5 6 7 8 9 10

2 4 6 8 10 12 14 16 18 20

3 6 9 12 15 18 21 24 27 30

4 8 12 16 20 24 28 32 36 40

5 10 15 20 25 30 35 40 45 50

6 12 18 24 30 36 42 48 54 60

7 14 21 28 35 42 49 56 63 70

8 16 24 32 40 48 56 64 72 80

9 18 27 36 45 54 63 72 81 90

10 20 30 40 50 60 70 80 90 100

This demonstrates how nested loops can be used to perform repeated actions within a structured, multi-layered format.

Nested Loops with Lists of Lists

ANOTHER COMMON USE of nested loops is to iterate over lists of lists (2D lists or matrices). Suppose you have a list that contains other lists, representing a grid of numbers:

```
matrix = [
[1, 2, 3],
[4, 5, 6],
[7, 8, 9]
```

]

You can use nested loops to iterate over both the outer list (rows) and the inner lists (columns):

```
for row in matrix:

for item in row:

print(item, end=" ")

print()
```

```
1 2 3

4 5 6

7 8 9
```

In this case, the outer loop iterates through each sublist (or row), and the inner loop iterates through each item in those sublists.

Combining Nested Loops with Conditional Statements

BY COMBINING NESTED loops with conditional statements, you can introduce complex logic to your loops. For example, let's say you want to print only the even numbers from the multiplication table:

```
for i in range(1, 11):

for j in range(1, 11):

product = i * j
```

```
if product % 2 == 0:
print(f"{product:3}", end=" ")
else:
print(" ", end=" ")
print()
```

```
2 4 6 8 10
4 8 12 16 20
6 12 18 24 30
8 16 24 32 40
10 20 30 40 50
12 24 36 48 60
14 28 42 56 70
16 32 48 64 80
18 36 54 72 90
20 40 60 80 100
```

This demonstrates how conditional logic within nested loops can add layers of complexity to your code.

Nested Loops with break and continue

THE BREAK AND CONTINUE statements work in nested loops just as they do in regular loops, but with some added complexity. When you use break or continue inside a nested loop, they only affect the innermost loop.

For example, let's say you want to stop both loops when a specific condition is met:

```
for i in range(1, 6):

for j in range(1, 6):

if i == 3 and j == 3:

break

print(f"i = {i}, j = {j}")

if i == 3:

break
```

The output will be:

```
i = 1, j = 1

i = 1, j = 2

i = 1, j = 3

i = 1, j = 4

i = 1, j = 5

i = 2, j = 1

i = 2, j = 2

i = 2, j = 3

i = 2, j = 4
```

i = 2, j = 5

Once both i and j equal 3, the inner break statement is triggered, exiting the inner loop. The outer loop then checks if i == 3, and since it's true, the outer break is triggered, exiting both loops.

Similarly, you can use continue to skip over certain iterations of the inner loop:

for i in range(1, 6):

for j in range(1, 6):

if i == 3 and j == 3:

continue

print(f"i = {i}, j = {j}")

In this case, when both i and j equal 3, the continue statement skips that iteration of the inner loop, but both loops continue running. The output will be:

i = 1, j = 1

i = 1, j = 2

i = 1, j = 3

i = 1, j = 4

i = 1, j = 5

i = 2, j = 1

i = 2, j = 2

i = 2, j = 3

i = 2, j = 4

i = 2, j = 5

i = 3, j = 1

i = 3, j = 2

i = 3, j = 4

i = 3, j = 5

i = 4, j = 1

i = 4, j = 2

i = 4, j = 3

i = 4, j = 4

i = 4, j = 5

i = 5, j = 1

i = 5, j = 2

i = 5, j = 3

i = 5, j = 4

i = 5, j = 5

Notice that the pair (3, 3) is skipped, but the loops continue for all other values of i and j.

Complex Conditions with Logical Operators in Nested Loops

WHEN WORKING WITH NESTED loops, you often need to apply more complex conditions. Python's logical operators (and, or, and not) allow you to combine multiple conditions inside your loops for greater control.

For instance, let's modify the previous multiplication table example to only print products that are both even and greater than 20:

```
for i in range(1, 11):

for j in range(1, 11):

product = i * j

if product % 2 == 0 and product > 20:

print(f"{product:3}", end=" ")

else:

print(" ", end=" ")

print()
```

In this case, the if statement checks two conditions: whether the product is even and whether it's greater than 20. If both conditions are met, the product is printed; otherwise, an empty space is printed.

The output will be:

```
24 30

28 36
```

32 40

36 48

42 54

48 60

56 72

64 80

72 90

84 100

This example illustrates how combining logical operators with nested loops can create highly specific conditions for controlling the behavior of your code.

Conclusion

NESTED LOOPS AND COMPLEX conditions offer a way to extend the functionality of basic loops, allowing you to solve more advanced problems and handle multi-dimensional data. By nesting loops and using conditional statements within them, you can introduce intricate logic into your Python programs, enabling you to tackle tasks that involve multiple layers of iteration, such as processing grids, matrices, or multi-layered data sets. As you become more familiar with these techniques, you'll be able to build more efficient and sophisticated programs.

Break, Continue, and Pass: Controlling Loop Execution

IN PYTHON, LOOP CONTROL mechanisms allow you to manage the flow of your loops more efficiently and with greater flexibility. Three key statements that help in this regard are break, continue, and pass. These statements allow you to either stop a loop prematurely, skip iterations, or simply pass over certain pieces of code without executing them. Each has a specific use case that helps to structure your loops more elegantly, improving the readability and functionality of your code.

The break Statement

THE BREAK STATEMENT is used to exit a loop before it has completed all of its iterations. When Python encounters a break, it immediately stops the loop and moves on to the next section of the code. This is particularly useful when you are searching for a specific condition and no longer need to continue the loop once that condition is met.

Example: Exiting a Loop When a Condition is Met

CONSIDER THE FOLLOWING example where we want to find the first even number in a list:

```
numbers = [1, 3, 7, 9, 10, 13, 15]

for number in numbers:

if number % 2 == 0:

print(f"Found an even number: {number}")

break
```

```
print(f"Checked number: {number}")
```

Output:

```
Checked number: 1

Checked number: 3

Checked number: 7

Checked number: 9

Found an even number: 10
```

Here, the loop checks each number in the list to see if it's even. As soon as it finds the first even number (10), the break statement is triggered, and the loop exits. This avoids unnecessary iterations after the desired condition is met.

Using break in Nested Loops

WHEN BREAK IS USED in nested loops, it only terminates the innermost loop where it is placed. The outer loops continue to run unless explicitly broken. Let's look at an example of how this works in practice:

```
for i in range(1, 4):

for j in range(1, 4):

if j == 2:

break

print(f"i = {i}, j = {j}")
```

Output:

i = 1, j = 1

i = 2, j = 1

i = 3, j = 1

In this case, the break statement stops the inner loop whenever j equals 2. However, the outer loop continues to execute, resulting in the printed output only for j = 1 in each iteration of the outer loop.

The continue Statement

THE CONTINUE STATEMENT allows you to skip the current iteration of a loop and proceed directly to the next iteration. This is useful when you want to skip certain values or conditions without completely exiting the loop.

Example: Skipping Odd Numbers

HERE'S A SIMPLE EXAMPLE where the loop skips over odd numbers and only prints even numbers:

for number in range(1, 10):

if number % 2 != 0:

continue

print(f"Even number: {number}")

Output:

Even number: 2

Even number: 4

Even number: 6

Even number: 8

The continue statement skips the current iteration when the number is odd (number % 2 != 0). As a result, only even numbers are printed, and the loop continues running until it has iterated through all the numbers in the range.

Using continue in Nested Loops

SIMILAR TO BREAK, THE continue statement only affects the innermost loop in the case of nested loops. It skips the current iteration of the inner loop but does not affect the outer loop. Here's an example:

for i in range(1, 4):

for j in range(1, 4):

if j == 2:

continue

print(f"i = {i}, j = {j}")

Output:

i = 1, j = 1

i = 1, j = 3

i = 2, j = 1

i = 2, j = 3

i = 3, j = 1

i = 3, j = 3

In this case, whenever j equals 2, the continue statement skips the rest of the inner loop for that iteration. The outer loop continues to execute normally, allowing the other values of j to be processed.

The pass Statement

THE PASS STATEMENT is used when a statement is required syntactically but you don't want any code to be executed. It can be thought of as a placeholder in your code. While break and continue actively change the flow of the loop, pass does nothing and allows the loop to continue running as usual.

Example: Using pass as a Placeholder

YOU MIGHT ENCOUNTER situations where you need to define a loop, function, or class, but you haven't written the code yet. In such cases, pass can be used to avoid errors and allow your program to run:

```
for i in range(1, 6):

if i == 3:

pass # Placeholder for future code

else:

print(i)
```

1

2

4

5

Here, when i equals 3, the pass statement is encountered, and no action is taken. The loop continues with the next iteration without interruption.

Practical Uses of pass

WHILE PASS IS OFTEN used as a placeholder, it can also be useful in loops where you want to maintain the loop structure but don't want to execute any code under specific conditions. For example, you may have a scenario where certain conditions need to be checked but no action is required at that point in the loop:

```
for char in "Python":

if char == "h":

pass

else:

print(f"Processing character: {char}")
```

Output:

Processing character: P

Processing character: y

Processing character: t

Processing character: o

Processing character: n

In this case, when the loop encounters the character 'h', it simply passes over it without doing anything, continuing to process the remaining characters.

Combining break, continue, and pass

IT'S COMMON TO COMBINE break, continue, and pass within the same loop to handle various conditions dynamically. For example, consider a scenario where you're processing a list of numbers and want to stop processing if a certain condition is met, skip over certain numbers, and just pass on others:

```
numbers = [1, 2, 3, 4, 5, 6, 7, 8, 9]

for number in numbers:

if number == 5:

break # Stop processing entirely

elif number % 2 == 0:

continue # Skip even numbers

elif number == 3:

pass # Placeholder for future logic

print(f"Processing number: {number}")
```

Output:

```
Processing number: 1

Processing number: 3
```

In this example:

- The loop stops completely when it encounters 5 because of the break statement.

- The loop skips over even numbers because of the continue statement.

- The loop passes over 3 due to the pass statement, but since pass does nothing, the number is still processed in this case.

Real-World Example: Searching Through a File

LET'S NOW CONSIDER a more complex example of using break, continue, and pass in a real-world scenario, such as searching through a text file for specific information.

Suppose you have a log file that contains error messages, and you want to find the first critical error, skip over warnings, and just pass through info logs.

```
logs = [

"INFO: Starting process",

"WARNING: Low memory",

"ERROR: Unable to connect to server",

"CRITICAL: System failure",

"INFO: Process completed"

]

for log in logs:

if "CRITICAL" in log:
```

```
print(f"Critical log found: {log}")
break # Exit the loop after finding the critical error
elif "WARNING" in log:
continue # Skip warnings
elif "INFO" in log:
pass # Do nothing for info logs
else:
print(f"Log entry: {log}")
```

Output:

```
Critical log found: CRITICAL: System failure
```

In this example, the loop processes each log entry, skipping over warnings and ignoring info logs. Once a critical error is found, the break statement stops further processing, and the program terminates the loop.

Conclusion

UNDERSTANDING HOW TO use break, continue, and pass is essential for controlling the flow of loops in Python. These statements allow you to stop loops, skip iterations, and use placeholders, respectively. By combining these statements with conditional logic, you can handle a wide range of scenarios and improve the flexibility of your programs. Whether you're processing user input, searching through data, or building complex iterative algorithms, mastering loop control will help you write more efficient, readable, and maintainable code.

Practical Examples of Control Flow

CONTROL FLOW IS AN essential aspect of programming that allows you to dictate the order in which statements are executed. With tools like conditional statements (if, else, elif), loops (for, while), and control mechanisms (break, continue, pass), you can create dynamic programs that respond to various conditions and inputs. In this section, we'll explore practical examples that demonstrate how to apply control flow effectively in real-world programming scenarios.

Example 1: User Input Validation

ONE COMMON USE OF CONTROL flow is in validating user input. Let's consider a program that asks a user to enter their age. The program should validate the input to ensure it's a positive integer. If the user enters an invalid value, the program will prompt them to try again until they provide a valid input.

```
while True:

age = input("Please enter your age: ")

if age.isdigit() and int(age) > 0:

print(f"Thank you! You entered a valid age: {age}")

break

else:

print("Invalid input. Please enter a positive integer.")
```

In this example, the while True loop ensures that the program will keep running until a valid age is entered. The if statement checks whether the input is a digit and greater than zero. If the input is valid, the program prints a confirmation message and breaks out of the loop. Otherwise, it prompts the user to try again.

Why This Approach Works

- The while True loop provides a continuous loop that allows repeated user input attempts.
- The isdigit() method ensures the user input consists only of digits.
- The int(age) > 0 condition ensures that the number is positive.

THIS KIND OF INPUT validation is crucial for preventing errors and ensuring that your program behaves as expected when interacting with users.

Example 2: Calculating Factorials Using a Loop

ANOTHER PRACTICAL APPLICATION of control flow is calculating mathematical functions, such as the factorial of a number. The factorial of a number n is the product of all positive integers less than or equal to n. For example, the factorial of 5 (5!) is 5 * 4 * 3 * 2 * 1 = 120.

Here's how you can calculate the factorial of a number using a for loop:

```
number = int(input("Enter a number to calculate its factorial: "))

factorial = 1

if number < 0:
```

```
print("Factorial is not defined for negative numbers.")

elif number == 0:

print("The factorial of 0 is 1.")

else:

for i in range(1, number + 1):

factorial *= i

print(f"The factorial of {number} is {factorial}")
```

In this example:

- The program first checks if the number is negative, in which case it prints an error message.
- If the number is zero, the factorial is defined as 1.
- For any positive integer, the for loop multiplies the numbers from 1 to the input number to calculate the factorial.

Why This Approach Works

- The range(1, number + 1) function ensures that the loop iterates through all numbers from 1 to the input number.
- The multiplication factorial *= i builds the product step by step.

THIS SIMPLE BUT POWERFUL approach demonstrates how loops can be used to perform repetitive calculations.

Example 3: Finding Prime Numbers

CONTROL FLOW CAN ALSO be used to solve more complex problems, such as finding prime numbers. A prime number is a number greater than 1 that is divisible only by 1 and itself. Let's write a program that finds all prime numbers up to a given limit.

```
limit = int(input("Enter a limit to find all prime numbers up to that number: "))

for num in range(2, limit + 1):

is_prime = True

for i in range(2, int(num ** 0.5) + 1):

if num % i == 0:

is_prime = False

break

if is_prime:

print(f"{num} is a prime number")
```

Here's how the program works:

- The outer loop iterates over each number from 2 to the given limit.
- For each number, a flag is_prime is set to True.
- The inner loop checks if the current number is divisible by any number up to the square root of that number. If it is divisible, the number is not prime, and the inner loop breaks.

- If no divisors are found, the number is printed as prime.

Why This Approach Works

- Checking divisibility up to the square root of the number (int(num ** 0.5) + 1) optimizes the program by reducing unnecessary checks.

- The break statement efficiently exits the inner loop once a divisor is found, avoiding further unnecessary computations.

THIS EXAMPLE ILLUSTRATES how nested loops, combined with break and conditional statements, can solve a classic computational problem.

Example 4: Simulating a Simple ATM System

LET'S APPLY CONTROL flow to a more interactive and practical scenario: simulating a simple ATM system. The program will prompt the user to choose an action (check balance, deposit, withdraw, or exit) and perform the appropriate task.

```
balance = 1000.0 # Initial balance

while True:

print("\nATM Menu:")

print("1. Check Balance")

print("2. Deposit")

print("3. Withdraw")
```

```
print("4. Exit")

choice = input("Enter your choice: ")

if choice == "1":

print(f"Your balance is: ${balance:.2f}")

elif choice == "2":

deposit = float(input("Enter amount to deposit: "))

if deposit > 0:

balance += deposit

print(f"${deposit:.2f} deposited successfully.")

else:

print("Invalid deposit amount.")

elif choice == "3":

withdraw = float(input("Enter amount to withdraw: "))

if 0 < withdraw <= balance:

balance -= withdraw

print(f"${withdraw:.2f} withdrawn successfully.")

else:

print("Insufficient balance or invalid amount.")

elif choice == "4":

print("Thank you for using our ATM. Goodbye!")
```

break

else:

print("Invalid choice. Please try again.")

In this example:

- The while True loop ensures that the ATM menu keeps displaying until the user chooses to exit.
- The if-elif structure handles the user's choice of actions:
  - Checking the balance
  - Depositing money (with a validation check)
  - Withdrawing money (with a validation check for sufficient balance)
  - Exiting the system using break.

Why This Approach Works

- The loop structure and conditional statements provide an intuitive way to model user interaction.
- Input validation ensures that invalid actions (e.g., withdrawing more than the available balance) are handled gracefully.

THIS EXAMPLE DEMONSTRATES how loops and control flow mechanisms can be used to create user-friendly, interactive programs.

Example 5: FizzBuzz Challenge

THE FIZZBUZZ PROBLEM is a classic coding challenge often used to test basic programming skills. The challenge is to print numbers from 1 to a given limit, but with a twist:

- For numbers divisible by 3, print "Fizz" instead of the number.
- For numbers divisible by 5, print "Buzz".
- For numbers divisible by both 3 and 5, print "FizzBuzz".

Here's the Python implementation using control flow:

```
limit = int(input("Enter the limit for FizzBuzz: "))

for i in range(1, limit + 1):

if i % 3 == 0 and i % 5 == 0:

print("FizzBuzz")

elif i % 3 == 0:

print("Fizz")

elif i % 5 == 0:

print("Buzz")

else:

print(i)
```

In this program:

- The for loop iterates through numbers from 1 to the specified limit.
- The if-elif structure checks for divisibility by 3, 5, or both, printing the appropriate message.
- If none of the conditions are met, the number itself is printed.

Why This Approach Works

- The if-elif structure ensures that each number is checked in the correct order of precedence (divisible by both 3 and 5, then 3, then 5).
- The loop structure makes it easy to apply the same logic to a range of numbers.

THIS IS A SIMPLE BUT effective example of how control flow allows you to solve problems efficiently.

Example 6: Summing Values in Nested Lists

LET'S EXPLORE HOW CONTROL flow can be used to handle more complex data structures like nested lists. Suppose you have a list of lists, where each sublist contains numeric values, and you want to compute the total sum of all values across all sublists.

```
nested_list = [
[1, 2, 3],
[4, 5, 6],
[7, 8, 9]
```

```
]
total_sum = 0
for sublist in nested_list:
for value in sublist:
total_sum += value
print(f"The total sum of all values is: {total_sum}")
```

Here's how it works:

- The outer for loop iterates over each sublist in the main list.
- The inner for loop iterates over each value in the current sublist, adding it to the total_sum.
- After both loops have finished, the program prints the total sum.

Why This Approach Works

- Nested loops allow you to access and process each element in a multi-dimensional data structure.
- By accumulating the sum inside the inner loop, you ensure that all values are counted.

THIS EXAMPLE ILLUSTRATES how loops can be used to perform operations on nested data structures, making it easier to work with matrices or grids of data.

Conclusion

CONTROL FLOW STRUCTURES—SUCH as loops, conditional statements, and loop control mechanisms—are fundamental tools for any Python programmer. They allow you to control the execution of your code, making it more flexible, efficient, and capable of handling complex logic. By mastering these concepts, you can build more interactive, dynamic, and functional programs that respond intelligently to different inputs and conditions. Whether you're validating user input, performing calculations, or interacting with external data, control flow is at the heart of creating efficient and robust Python applications.

Chapter 4: Functions in Python

Defining Functions: The Basics

IN PYTHON, FUNCTIONS are a critical part of writing modular, reusable, and organized code. Functions allow developers to group a series of instructions together and execute them whenever needed, reducing redundancy and improving code maintainability.

What is a Function?

A FUNCTION IN PYTHON is a block of reusable code designed to perform a specific task. Functions help break down large problems into smaller, manageable pieces. Instead of repeating the same code multiple times, you define a function once and call it whenever that specific task needs to be performed.

At its core, a function consists of:

- **A name**: The identifier by which the function can be called.
- **A set of parameters**: These are inputs to the function (optional).
- **A block of code**: The instructions that the function will execute.
- **A return value**: The result that the function outputs (optional).

Defining a Function

IN PYTHON, YOU DEFINE a function using the def keyword. Here's the basic syntax:

```
def function_name(parameters):

# Code block

return value
```

- **function_name**: This is the identifier that you'll use to call the function.
- **parameters**: These are optional inputs you can provide to the function.
- **return**: This keyword optionally sends a value back to the caller of the function. If no return value is specified, the function returns None by default.

Let's take a simple example of a function that adds two numbers:

```
def add_numbers(a, b):

result = a + b

return result
```

In the example above, add_numbers is the function name. The function takes two parameters, a and b, adds them together, and returns the result.

To call the function, you would do the following:

```
sum = add_numbers(10, 20)
```

print(sum) # Output: 30

Why Use Functions?

1. **Code Reusability**: Functions allow you to write code once and reuse it multiple times. Instead of copying and pasting the same block of code, you can simply call the function.
2. **Modularity**: Functions help break down a large problem into smaller parts, making it easier to manage and debug.
3. **Maintainability**: Functions make the code more readable and maintainable. If a bug occurs, you only need to fix it in one place instead of multiple locations.
4. **Abstraction**: Functions allow you to hide the internal implementation details and provide an interface that users can easily interact with.

Function Naming Conventions

WHEN NAMING FUNCTIONS in Python, it is common practice to follow certain conventions:

- Function names should be descriptive and use lowercase letters, with words separated by underscores.

- The function name should reflect its purpose. For example, calculate_area is a good name for a function that computes the area of a shape.

For instance:

def calculate_area(radius):

pi = 3.14159

```
return pi * radius ** 2
```

Parameters and Arguments

FUNCTIONS CAN ACCEPT parameters, which are variables that the function uses to perform its task. When calling the function, you provide actual values for these parameters, known as arguments.

Consider the following function:

```
def greet(name):

print(f"Hello, {name}!")
```

Here, name is a parameter, and when you call the function with an argument, the function will print a greeting with that name:

```
greet("Alice") # Output: Hello, Alice!
```

Default Parameters

PYTHON ALLOWS YOU TO define default values for function parameters. This means if you don't provide an argument for that parameter when calling the function, Python will use the default value.

Here's an example:

```
def greet(name="Guest"):

print(f"Hello, {name}!")
```

Now, if you call the function without passing any arguments, it will use the default value "Guest":

```
greet() # Output: Hello, Guest!
```

However, if you provide an argument, it will override the default value:

```
greet("Bob") # Output: Hello, Bob!
```

Multiple Parameters

A FUNCTION CAN TAKE multiple parameters by separating them with commas. Here's an example:

```
def multiply(a, b, c):

return a * b * c
```

When calling the function, you need to provide all three arguments:

```
result = multiply(2, 3, 4)

print(result) # Output: 24
```

Keyword Arguments

YOU CAN ALSO CALL A function using **keyword arguments**, where the name of the parameter is specified during the function call. This allows you to pass arguments in a different order than the function definition.

For example:

```
def describe_person(name, age, city):

print(f"{name} is {age} years old and lives in {city}.")
```

You can call this function using keyword arguments:

```
describe_person(city="New York", age=30, name="Alice")
```

Output: Alice is 30 years old and lives in New York.

This method improves code readability, especially when functions take many parameters.

Variable-Length Arguments (*args and **kwargs)

PYTHON PROVIDES THE flexibility of allowing functions to take a variable number of arguments using *args and **kwargs.

***args**

*ARGS ALLOWS YOU TO pass a variable number of positional arguments to a function. Here's an example:

```
def add_numbers(*args):

return sum(args)
```

You can now call this function with any number of arguments:

```
print(add_numbers(1, 2, 3)) # Output: 6

print(add_numbers(10, 20)) # Output: 30
```

****kwargs**

**KWARGS ALLOWS YOU TO pass a variable number of keyword arguments. These arguments are passed as a dictionary of key-value pairs:

```
def print_details(**kwargs):

for key, value in kwargs.items():

print(f"{key}: {value}")
```

You can call the function like this:

```
print_details(name="Alice", age=30, city="New York")

# Output:

# name: Alice

# age: 30

# city: New York
```

Return Statement

THE RETURN STATEMENT allows a function to output a value. The function execution ends when a return statement is reached.

Consider this function that returns the square of a number:

```
def square(num):

return num * num
```

If you omit the return statement, the function will return None by default:

```
def no_return():

pass

result = no_return()

print(result) # Output: None
```

Returning Multiple Values

PYTHON FUNCTIONS CAN return multiple values by separating them with commas. These values are returned as a tuple.

Here's an example:

def get_stats(numbers):

return min(numbers), max(numbers), sum(numbers) / len(numbers)

You can unpack these values when calling the function:

minimum, maximum, average = get_stats([10, 20, 30, 40])

print(f"Min: {minimum}, Max: {maximum}, Average: {average}")

Output:

Min: 10, Max: 40, Average: 25.0

Recursion in Functions

FUNCTIONS IN PYTHON can call themselves recursively. Recursion is a powerful technique for solving problems that can be broken down into smaller, similar subproblems.

A classic example of recursion is calculating the factorial of a number:

def factorial(n):

if n == 1:

return 1

else:

```
return n * factorial(n - 1)
```

In this example, the function factorial calls itself to compute the product of all positive integers up to n.

```
print(factorial(5)) # Output: 120
```

Conclusion

FUNCTIONS ARE A FUNDAMENTAL aspect of Python programming. They allow developers to write cleaner, more organized, and reusable code. By understanding how to define functions, pass arguments, and work with return values, you can greatly improve the structure and maintainability of your Python code.

Arguments, Parameters, and Return Values

IN PYTHON, UNDERSTANDING the distinction between arguments and parameters is crucial to effectively defining and using functions. While the terms are often used interchangeably, they refer to different parts of a function's lifecycle. In this section, we'll explore their differences, how they are used, and delve deeper into the power of return values in Python functions.

Parameters vs. Arguments

PARAMETERS are variables listed in the function definition, while **arguments** are the actual values passed to the function when it is called.

For example, in the following function definition, a and b are parameters:

```
def add(a, b):
```

return a + b

When you call the function with specific values:

result = add(10, 20)

The values 10 and 20 are arguments. These arguments are passed to the function and assigned to the parameters a and b.

Positional Arguments

THE MOST COMMON WAY to pass arguments to a function is by **position**. When you call a function, the arguments are mapped to the parameters based on their order.

Example:

def subtract(a, b):

return a - b

result = subtract(10, 5) # 10 is assigned to a, 5 to b

print(result) # Output: 5

In this case, the values 10 and 5 are positional arguments. Python assigns the first value (10) to a and the second value (5) to b.

Keyword Arguments

YOU CAN ALSO PASS ARGUMENTS using **keyword arguments**, where the parameter name is specified in the function call. This allows you to pass values in any order, as long as you specify which value corresponds to which parameter.

Example:

def greet(name, message):

print(f"{message}, {name}!")

greet(message="Welcome", name="Alice") # Output: Welcome, Alice!

Here, the order of the arguments no longer matters because you're explicitly specifying which argument belongs to which parameter by using keywords.

Default Parameters

IN PYTHON, YOU CAN assign **default values** to parameters in the function definition. If an argument is not provided for a parameter with a default value, the default value will be used instead.

Example:

def greet(name="Guest"):

print(f"Hello, {name}!")

greet() # Output: Hello, Guest!

greet("Alice") # Output: Hello, Alice!

In this case, if you call the greet function without passing a name, it defaults to "Guest". However, if you provide a name, that value will override the default.

Combining Positional and Keyword Arguments

PYTHON ALLOWS YOU TO mix positional and keyword arguments in the same function call, but there are some rules to follow. Positional arguments must always come before keyword arguments.

For example, this is valid:

```
def display_info(name, age, city):

print(f"Name: {name}, Age: {age}, City: {city}")

display_info("Alice", age=30, city="New York") # Output: Name: Alice, Age: 30, City: New York
```

However, the following is not valid and will result in an error because the positional argument is placed after the keyword argument:

```
# Invalid function call

display_info(age=30, "Alice", city="New York") # SyntaxError
```

Variable-Length Arguments (*args)

PYTHON OFFERS THE FLEXIBILITY to handle functions with a varying number of arguments using *args. This allows you to pass an arbitrary number of positional arguments to the function.

When you use *args, all the extra positional arguments passed to the function are stored in a tuple. You can then iterate over the tuple or access specific arguments by index.

Example:

```
def print_numbers(*args):

for number in args:

print(number)

print_numbers(1, 2, 3, 4, 5)
```

In this case, the function can accept any number of arguments, and *args collects them into a tuple. You can pass zero, one, or many arguments, and the function will handle them accordingly.

print_numbers(10, 20) # Output: 10, 20

print_numbers(1, 2, 3) # Output: 1, 2, 3

Variable-Length Keyword Arguments (**kwargs)

SIMILAR TO *ARGS, PYTHON provides **kwargs for handling an arbitrary number of keyword arguments. The keyword arguments are passed into the function as a dictionary, where the keys are the parameter names and the values are the corresponding arguments.

Example:

def print_details(**kwargs):

for key, value in kwargs.items():

print(f"{key}: {value}")

print_details(name="Alice", age=30, city="New York")

Here, **kwargs collects all keyword arguments into a dictionary. This approach is especially useful when the number of keyword arguments is dynamic or unknown beforehand.

Output:

name: Alice

age: 30

city: New York

Returning Values from Functions

A FUNCTION IN PYTHON can return a value using the return statement. The return statement ends the function execution and sends the specified value back to the caller.

Example:

def multiply(a, b):

return a * b

result = multiply(10, 5)

print(result) # Output: 50

In this example, the function multiply returns the product of the two arguments, which is then stored in the variable result.

No Return Value

IF A FUNCTION DOES not have a return statement, or if the return statement is used without a value, the function will return None.

Example:

def no_return():

print("This function does not return anything")

result = no_return()

print(result) # Output: None

Here, since there is no return statement, the function returns None.

Returning Multiple Values

PYTHON FUNCTIONS CAN return more than one value by separating them with commas. The values are returned as a tuple, which can then be unpacked into separate variables.

Example:

```
def get_min_max(numbers):

return min(numbers), max(numbers)

min_value, max_value = get_min_max([1, 2, 3, 4, 5])

print(f"Min: {min_value}, Max: {max_value}")
```

The function get_min_max returns both the minimum and maximum values from the list, which are then unpacked into min_value and max_value.

Nested Function Returns

YOU CAN RETURN A FUNCTION from another function, allowing for the creation of higher-order functions or factory functions. This is a powerful feature of Python that promotes modularity and code reuse.

Example:

```
def outer_function(msg):

def inner_function():

print(msg)

return inner_function
```

greet = outer_function("Hello, World!")

greet() # Output: Hello, World!

In this example, outer_function returns inner_function, which captures the argument msg. When the returned function is called later, it remembers the value of msg and prints it.

Lambda Functions

LAMBDA FUNCTIONS ARE anonymous functions that are defined using the lambda keyword. They are used when you need a simple function for a short period of time. Lambda functions can take any number of arguments but have only one expression.

Example:

square = lambda x: x ** 2

print(square(5)) # Output: 25

Here, the lambda function takes one argument, x, and returns the square of x.

Lambda functions are often used in combination with functions like map(), filter(), and sorted() to process lists or other iterable objects.

Example:

numbers = [1, 2, 3, 4, 5]

squares = list(map(lambda x: x ** 2, numbers))

print(squares) # Output: [1, 4, 9, 16, 25]

Scope of Parameters

WHEN YOU PASS ARGUMENTS to a function, the parameters act as local variables within that function. This means they are only accessible within the function's body, and once the function finishes execution, the parameters are discarded.

Example:

def my_function(a):

print(a)

my_function(10) # Output: 10

'a' is not accessible outside of the function

print(a) # NameError: name 'a' is not defined

In this example, the variable a only exists within the function my_function and is not accessible outside of it.

Passing Mutable and Immutable Objects

WHEN PASSING ARGUMENTS to a function, it's essential to understand how Python handles **mutable** and **immutable** objects. Immutable objects like integers, strings, and tuples are passed by value, meaning the original value cannot be changed inside the function. On the other hand, mutable objects like lists and dictionaries are passed by reference, allowing modifications to persist outside the function.

Immutable Example:

DEF MODIFY_STRING(S):

s += " World"

my_string = "Hello"

modify_string(my_string)

print(my_string) # Output: Hello

Mutable Example:

DEF MODIFY_LIST(LST):

lst.append(4)

my_list = [1, 2, 3]

modify_list(my_list)

print(my_list) # Output: [1, 2, 3, 4]

In the second example, the changes made to the list inside the function are reflected outside the function, because lists are mutable.

Conclusion

ARGUMENTS AND PARAMETERS are fundamental to writing flexible and reusable functions in Python. Understanding how to pass arguments—whether by position, keyword, or using *args and **kwargs—allows you to write more robust and versatile code. Additionally, mastering the return value of a function enables you to build more complex programs that can process and return multiple types of data. By using these features effectively, you can greatly improve the modularity, readability, and maintainability of your Python code.

Scope and Lifetime of Variables

UNDERSTANDING THE **scope** and **lifetime** of variables is crucial for managing how and where data is stored and accessed in a Python program. Scope determines the visibility of a variable within different parts of a program, while lifetime refers to the duration for which a variable exists in memory. Together, they play a significant role in ensuring that your code behaves as expected, especially in larger, more complex programs.

What is Scope?

IN PYTHON, SCOPE REFERS to the region of the program where a variable is recognized and can be accessed. Variables can have different scopes depending on where they are defined, and understanding this helps avoid unintended behaviors, such as variable name collisions and incorrect data being accessed or modified.

There are generally four types of scopes in Python:

1. **Local Scope**
2. **Enclosing Scope**
3. **Global Scope**
4. **Built-in Scope**

These scopes are organized in what is known as the **LEGB rule** (Local, Enclosing, Global, Built-in). When a variable is referenced in a Python program, Python looks for it following this order.

Local Scope

A VARIABLE DECLARED inside a function is said to have **local scope**. Such variables can only be accessed within that function and are not visible outside of it. They are created when the function is called and are destroyed once the function terminates.

Example:

def my_function():

x = 10 # Local variable

print(x)

my_function() # Output: 10

print(x) # NameError: name 'x' is not defined

In this example, the variable x is defined within my_function(). It only exists within the function, so when you try to print x outside the function, Python raises a NameError because x does not exist in the global scope.

Shadowing

LOCAL VARIABLES CAN sometimes **shadow** global variables with the same name. When a local variable is declared with the same name as a global variable, the local variable takes precedence within the function's scope, and the global variable is temporarily inaccessible.

Example:

x = 50 # Global variable

def my_function():

x = 10 # Local variable shadows the global one

print(x)

```
my_function() # Output: 10

print(x) # Output: 50
```

In this case, inside the function my_function(), the local variable x takes precedence. However, once the function ends, the global x remains unchanged.

Enclosing Scope (Nonlocal Variables)

ENCLOSING SCOPE refers to the scope of a nested function. When a function is defined inside another function, it can access variables from the outer function, but those variables are not part of the local scope of the nested function. These variables reside in the **enclosing scope** and can be accessed by the nested function.

Example:

```
def outer_function():

x = 10 # Variable in enclosing scope

def inner_function():

print(x) # Accesses variable from enclosing scope

inner_function()

outer_function() # Output: 10
```

Here, the variable x is in the scope of outer_function(), but it is also accessible by inner_function() because of the enclosing scope.

Nonlocal Keyword

IF YOU WANT TO MODIFY a variable from an enclosing scope within a nested function, you can use the nonlocal keyword.

Without this keyword, assigning a value to the variable would create a new local variable inside the nested function.

Example:

```
def outer_function():

x = 10

def inner_function():

nonlocal x # Refers to x in the enclosing scope

x += 5

inner_function()

print(x)

outer_function() # Output: 15
```

Without the nonlocal keyword, the assignment x += 5 would create a new local variable inside inner_function(), leaving the x in outer_function() unchanged.

Global Scope

A VARIABLE DEFINED outside of any function or class has **global scope**. Such variables can be accessed from anywhere in the program, including from within functions, unless shadowed by a local variable with the same name.

Example:

```
x = 100 # Global variable

def my_function():
```

print(x)

my_function() # Output: 100

In this case, the global variable x can be accessed from inside my_function() because it exists in the global scope.

Global Keyword

IF YOU WANT TO MODIFY a global variable from inside a function, you need to use the global keyword. Without it, Python will treat any assignment to the variable as the creation of a new local variable, even if a global variable with the same name exists.

Example:

x = 50 # Global variable

def my_function():

global x # Refers to the global variable

x = 100 # Modifies the global variable

my_function()

print(x) # Output: 100

Without the global keyword, the assignment x = 100 would create a new local variable x, leaving the global x unchanged.

Built-in Scope

THE **built-in scope** is a special scope that contains all the names of Python's built-in functions and exceptions. These names are always available to your program, no matter what other variables or functions you define.

For example, functions like print(), len(), and sum() are all part of Python's built-in scope:

```
print(len([1, 2, 3])) # Output: 3
```

Lifetime of Variables

THE **lifetime** of a variable refers to how long the variable exists in memory during the execution of the program. Variables have different lifetimes depending on their scope.

Local Variables

LOCAL VARIABLES, AS mentioned earlier, are created when a function is called and destroyed when the function ends. Once the function has finished executing, the memory allocated to its local variables is released.

Example:

```
def my_function():

x = 10 # Local variable

print(x)

my_function() # Output: 10

# 'x' no longer exists here
```

In this case, x is a local variable, and its lifetime ends when my_function() completes execution.

Global Variables

GLOBAL VARIABLES, ON the other hand, remain in memory for the entire duration of the program. They are only destroyed when the program terminates or if they are explicitly deleted using the del statement.

Example:

x = 50 # Global variable

def my_function():

print(x)

my_function() # Output: 50

del x # Explicitly delete the global variable

print(x) # NameError: name 'x' is not defined

After calling del x, the global variable x is no longer available, and trying to access it results in a NameError.

Dynamic Nature of Python Variables

IN PYTHON, VARIABLES are **dynamically typed**, meaning you don't need to declare their type explicitly. The type is inferred based on the value assigned to the variable. This flexibility allows Python variables to change types during the execution of a program.

Example:

x = 10 # Integer

print(x)

x = "Hello" # Now x is a string

print(x)

Here, the variable x first holds an integer and later holds a string. Python dynamically adjusts the type of x based on the assigned value.

Variable Scope in Loops

IN PYTHON, VARIABLES declared inside loops behave similarly to those inside functions in terms of scope. For example, variables declared inside a for loop or while loop are treated as local to that loop's execution block but are available even after the loop completes.

Example:

for i in range(3):

num = i * 10

print(num) # Output: 0, 10, 20

print(num) # Output: 20

In this example, num remains accessible even after the loop terminates.

Best Practices for Managing Scope

1. **Avoid Global Variables**: Global variables can make your code harder to debug and maintain because their values can be changed from anywhere in the program. Use local variables whenever possible to limit the scope of data.
2. **Use Clear and Descriptive Variable Names**: Whether

local or global, use descriptive names for your variables to reduce the likelihood of name collisions and make your code easier to understand.

3. **Limit the Use of global and nonlocal**: Although the global and nonlocal keywords can be useful, overusing them can lead to confusing code. It's better to pass data explicitly between functions through parameters and return values.
4. **Document Scope and Lifetime of Variables**: If you're working with complex code that involves nested functions, recursion, or closures, documenting the scope and lifetime of key variables will help others (and your future self) understand how your code works.

Closures and Variable Scope

CLOSURES ARE A POWERFUL feature in Python where inner functions can "remember" variables from their enclosing scope, even after the outer function has finished executing. This is possible because functions in Python are first-class citizens, meaning they can be passed around and referenced even after their creation.

Example:

def outer_function(message):

def inner_function():

print(message) # Remembers 'message' from outer_function's scope

return inner_function

closure = outer_function("Hello, World!")

closure() # Output: Hello, World!

In this case, the inner function inner_function() retains access to the message variable, even though outer_function() has finished executing. This concept of retaining access to variables in the enclosing scope is what makes closures powerful in Python.

Conclusion

UNDERSTANDING THE SCOPE and lifetime of variables is essential for writing clean, efficient, and bug-free Python code. By knowing where and how long variables exist in memory, you can better control the flow of your program and avoid unintended side effects. Following the principles of limiting global scope, using local variables effectively, and leveraging Python's global and nonlocal keywords appropriately can lead to more organized and maintainable code.

Lambda Functions and Anonymous Functions

IN PYTHON, **lambda functions** are anonymous functions defined without a name. These functions are commonly used when you need a small function for a short period of time, often as an argument to higher-order functions like map(), filter(), or reduce(). Lambda functions are concise, consisting of a single expression and can be written in a single line of code. While they serve specific use cases, they play a critical role in simplifying functional-style programming in Python.

Defining a Lambda Function

A LAMBDA FUNCTION IS defined using the lambda keyword, followed by the parameters, a colon, and then the single expression that it evaluates. Unlike a normal function, a lambda function does not use the def keyword or a function name.

Here is the basic syntax of a lambda function:

lambda arguments: expression

For example, a simple lambda function that adds two numbers can be written as:

add = lambda a, b: a + b

Now, you can call the lambda function just like a normal function:

result = add(3, 5)

print(result) # Output: 8

The lambda function above takes two arguments a and b, and returns their sum. You can see how compact this syntax is compared to defining a normal function.

Lambda Functions vs Regular Functions

LAMBDA FUNCTIONS ARE often compared to regular functions defined using the def keyword. The key differences are:

1. **Anonymous**: Lambda functions do not have a name unless you assign them to a variable, whereas regular functions always have a name.
2. **Single Expression**: Lambda functions are limited to a single expression. You cannot have multiple statements inside a lambda, whereas a regular function can contain multiple lines of code.
3. **Use Case**: Lambda functions are typically used for short, simple tasks or for passing as arguments to higher-order

functions. Regular functions are more versatile and used when you need to perform more complex tasks.

Example of a regular function:

def add(a, b):

return a + b

print(add(3, 5)) # Output: 8

Compared to a lambda function:

add = lambda a, b: a + b

print(add(3, 5)) # Output: 8

Use Cases for Lambda Functions

LAMBDA FUNCTIONS ARE primarily used when you need a small function for a limited purpose, especially when you don't want to define a full-fledged function with the def keyword. Some common scenarios where lambda functions are useful include:

1. **Functional Programming**: When using functions like map(), filter(), or reduce() that take other functions as arguments, lambda functions are commonly used to simplify the code.
2. **Short and Simple Functions**: When a function is only required temporarily and does not need a name.
3. **Callbacks**: Lambda functions are often used in callback functions, particularly in graphical user interfaces (GUIs) or event-driven programming.
4. **Sorting and Custom Key Functions**: Lambda functions are frequently used in sorting lists, especially when you

need a custom sort order based on a specific key.

Using Lambda with map()

THE MAP() FUNCTION applies a given function to all the items in an iterable (e.g., a list) and returns a new iterable with the results. Lambda functions are often passed to map() to perform quick transformations on elements in a list.

Example:

```
numbers = [1, 2, 3, 4, 5]

squares = list(map(lambda x: x ** 2, numbers))

print(squares) # Output: [1, 4, 9, 16, 25]
```

In this example, the lambda function lambda x: x ** 2 squares each element in the numbers list, and the result is a new list with the squares of the numbers.

Using Lambda with filter()

THE FILTER() FUNCTION filters elements in an iterable based on a function that returns True or False. Lambda functions are often used with filter() to quickly define the filtering criteria.

Example:

```
numbers = [1, 2, 3, 4, 5, 6]

even_numbers = list(filter(lambda x: x % 2 == 0, numbers))

print(even_numbers) # Output: [2, 4, 6]
```

In this example, the lambda function lambda x: x % 2 == 0 filters the list and returns only the even numbers.

Using Lambda with reduce()

THE REDUCE() FUNCTION, from the functools module, applies a function to the items of an iterable cumulatively, reducing the iterable to a single value. Lambda functions are often used to define the operation that reduce() will apply.

Example:

```
from functools import reduce

numbers = [1, 2, 3, 4, 5]

sum_of_numbers = reduce(lambda a, b: a + b, numbers)

print(sum_of_numbers) # Output: 15
```

In this case, the lambda function lambda a, b: a + b is used to add up all the numbers in the list, resulting in the total sum.

Using Lambda with Sorting

LAMBDA FUNCTIONS ARE often used in sorting when you need to specify a custom sorting criterion. The sorted() function and the sort() method of lists accept a key argument, which can be a lambda function.

Example:

```
students = [

{'name': 'Alice', 'grade': 85},

{'name': 'Bob', 'grade': 90},

{'name': 'Charlie', 'grade': 78}

]
```

Sort students by grade in descending order

sorted_students = sorted(students, key=lambda student: student['grade'], reverse=True)

print(sorted_students)

Output: [{'name': 'Bob', 'grade': 90}, {'name': 'Alice', 'grade': 85}, {'name': 'Charlie', 'grade': 78}]

In this example, the lambda function lambda student: student['grade'] is used as the key for sorting the list of dictionaries by the grade field.

Lambda Functions in List Comprehensions

LAMBDA FUNCTIONS CAN also be combined with list comprehensions to create more compact and readable code. While list comprehensions typically don't require lambda functions, they can be useful in specific situations.

Example:

numbers = [1, 2, 3, 4, 5]

squares = [(lambda x: x ** 2)(x) for x in numbers]

print(squares) # Output: [1, 4, 9, 16, 25]

This example uses a lambda function within a list comprehension to square each number in the list.

Lambda Functions in Dictionary Operations

LAMBDA FUNCTIONS ARE also useful when performing operations on dictionaries, such as sorting or filtering based on keys or values.

Example:

```
prices = {'apple': 3.5, 'banana': 2.0, 'cherry': 4.0}

# Sort by price (value)

sorted_prices = sorted(prices.items(), key=lambda item: item[1])

print(sorted_prices)

# Output: [('banana', 2.0), ('apple', 3.5), ('cherry', 4.0)]
```

In this example, the lambda function lambda item: item[1] is used to sort the dictionary items by their values.

Lambda Functions in Functional Programming

PYTHON SUPPORTS A FUNCTIONAL programming paradigm, and lambda functions are an essential tool in this style of programming. Functional programming emphasizes the use of functions as first-class citizens, meaning functions can be passed around as arguments, returned from other functions, and assigned to variables.

Higher-Order Functions

A **higher-order function** is a function that takes another function as an argument or returns a function as a result. Lambda functions are often passed as arguments to higher-order functions because they provide a concise way to define the logic to be applied.

Example:

```
def apply_function(func, data):

return func(data)
```

```
result = apply_function(lambda x: x * 2, 5)

print(result) # Output: 10
```

In this example, apply_function() accepts a lambda function and applies it to the given data.

Currying

CURRYING is a functional programming technique where a function that takes multiple arguments is transformed into a sequence of functions, each taking a single argument. Lambda functions can be used to implement currying in Python.

Example:

```
def curried_multiply(x):

return lambda y: x * y

multiply_by_2 = curried_multiply(2)

result = multiply_by_2(5)

print(result) # Output: 10
```

In this example, curried_multiply() returns a lambda function that multiplies its argument by x, effectively currying the multiplication operation.

Using Lambda Functions for Callbacks

LAMBDA FUNCTIONS ARE frequently used in event-driven programming or graphical user interfaces (GUIs) as **callbacks**—small functions that are executed in response to user actions like clicking a button or typing text.

Example in a GUI context (using the Tkinter library):

```
import tkinter as tk

def on_click():

print("Button clicked!")

root = tk.Tk()

button = tk.Button(root, text="Click me", command=lambda: on_click())

button.pack()

root.mainloop()
```

Here, the lambda function is used to pass the on_click function to the Button widget's command argument. When the button is clicked, the callback function is executed.

Limitations of Lambda Functions

WHILE LAMBDA FUNCTIONS are powerful and useful in many situations, they do come with some limitations:

1. **Single Expression**: Lambda functions can only contain a single expression. If you need more complex logic, you should use a regular function defined with def.
2. **Reduced Readability**: While lambda functions can make code more concise, they can also reduce readability, especially for developers unfamiliar with their syntax. For complex logic, it's often better to use a named function.
3. **Debugging**: Lambda functions do not have names, which can make debugging more difficult. When an error occurs, the traceback may not provide as much useful

information compared to named functions.

4. **Limited Use Cases**: Lambda functions are best suited for simple, one-off tasks. When your function needs to perform multiple operations or becomes too complex, it's better to define a regular function for clarity and maintainability.

Conclusion

LAMBDA FUNCTIONS ARE an essential tool in Python that provide a compact and efficient way to define small, anonymous functions. They shine in situations where a function is needed for a short time, especially in functional programming contexts like map(), filter(), and reduce(), or when passing simple callbacks in event-driven programs.

Although lambda functions offer concise syntax, they should be used judiciously, keeping in mind their limitations in readability and debugging. For more complex operations, regular named functions are preferable. By understanding when and how to use lambda functions, you can write cleaner, more efficient Python code that embraces functional programming principles while maintaining clarity and maintainability.

Best Practices for Writing Functions

WRITING EFFICIENT AND clean functions is a critical part of becoming a proficient Python programmer. Following best practices in function design ensures that your code is maintainable, reusable, and easy to debug. In this section, we will explore various guidelines and strategies for writing functions that not only work but also follow industry standards in terms of readability, efficiency, and flexibility.

1. Function Names and Naming Conventions

THE FIRST AND PERHAPS most important aspect of function writing is naming. A function's name should be descriptive, concise, and follow consistent naming conventions.

Best Practices for Naming:

- **Use action words**: Since functions perform actions, they should be named using verbs or action-oriented phrases. For example, instead of naming a function data(), prefer names like process_data(), load_data(), or calculate_average() that describe the action being taken.

- **Be descriptive but concise**: Your function name should clearly indicate what the function does. Avoid overly long names, but make sure the name is detailed enough to be meaningful.

- **Follow snake_case**: In Python, the common naming convention for functions is snake_case, where words are separated by underscores (_). For instance, calculate_total, send_email, and update_database are all examples of well-named functions.

EXAMPLE OF A GOOD FUNCTION name:

```
def calculate_discount(price, discount_rate):

return price * (1 - discount_rate)
```

In this example, the function calculate_discount clearly indicates what the function does—calculates a discounted price based on the price and discount rate passed in as arguments.

2. Keep Functions Short and Focused

A WELL-WRITTEN FUNCTION should perform a single task or a small set of related tasks. This principle is often referred to as **single responsibility**—a function should have one clearly defined purpose.

Why Keep Functions Short?

- **Easier to understand**: Short functions are easier to read and understand at a glance. If you can understand what a function does without reading through dozens of lines of code, debugging and maintaining it becomes easier.

- **Reusability**: Functions that perform a single task are easier to reuse in other parts of your code. If a function has multiple responsibilities, it becomes harder to reuse and maintain.

- **Easier to test**: Smaller functions are easier to unit test. When a function is doing too much, testing becomes more complicated because there are more possible inputs, outputs, and edge cases.

EXAMPLE OF A FUNCTION doing too much:

```
def process_and_save_data(data):

# Process the data

processed_data = [x ** 2 for x in data if x > 0]

# Save the processed data to a file
```

```
with open('output.txt', 'w') as f:

for item in processed_data:

f.write(f"{item}\n")
```

This function is responsible for both processing data and saving it to a file, violating the single responsibility principle. Instead, break it into two functions:

```
def process_data(data):

return [x ** 2 for x in data if x > 0]

def save_data_to_file(data, filename):

with open(filename, 'w') as f:

for item in data:

f.write(f"{item}\n")
```

By separating the concerns, the code becomes more modular, reusable, and easier to test.

3. Use Docstrings to Document Functions

DOCUMENTATION IS AN essential part of writing maintainable code, and functions should be documented with **docstrings**. A docstring is a string literal that appears as the first statement in a function, and it explains the purpose of the function, the parameters it takes, and the value it returns.

Python has a standard format for docstrings called **PEP 257**, which encourages consistency in how functions are documented.

Example of a properly documented function:

```
def calculate_area_of_circle(radius):

"""

Calculate the area of a circle given its radius.

Parameters:

radius (float): The radius of the circle.

Returns:

float: The area of the circle.

"""

import math

return math.pi * radius ** 2
```

The docstring here provides a clear explanation of what the function does, what input it expects, and what it returns. This makes it easier for anyone using or maintaining your code to understand how to use the function.

Benefits of Using Docstrings:

- **Clarity**: Explains the purpose of the function without needing to read the code itself.
- **Tools support**: Many IDEs and documentation generation tools, like Sphinx, can automatically extract and display docstrings.
- **Collaboration**: When working in a team, well-documented code helps others quickly understand

your code, reducing onboarding time for new developers.

4. Avoid Side Effects

A FUNCTION SHOULD AVOID **side effects**, which occur when a function changes the state of something outside its scope, such as modifying global variables or altering mutable objects passed as arguments. Functions that rely heavily on side effects can lead to bugs and make the code harder to understand and maintain.

Example of Side Effects:

```
GLOBAL_VAR = 10

def increment_global():

global global_var

global_var += 1

increment_global()

print(global_var) # Output: 11
```

In this case, the function increment_global() modifies a global variable, which can cause unexpected behavior if other parts of the code also modify or rely on this variable.

Avoid Side Effects:

INSTEAD OF MODIFYING global variables or mutable objects directly, try to make your functions return new values and keep the data immutable whenever possible.

Example of avoiding side effects:

def increment(value):

return value + 1

new_value = increment(global_var)

print(new_value) # Output: 11

In this example, the function increment() returns a new value rather than modifying a global variable. This makes the function more predictable and easier to test.

5. Handle Errors Gracefully

GOOD FUNCTIONS SHOULD handle errors gracefully, making the code more robust. Python provides several mechanisms for handling exceptions, including try, except, and finally. When writing functions, always consider what could go wrong and how you can handle it.

Use Exceptions to Handle Errors:

BY USING EXCEPTIONS, you can anticipate and manage errors without crashing the program. This improves the overall user experience and makes debugging easier.

Example of error handling in a function:

def divide_numbers(a, b):

"""

Divide two numbers and handle division by zero.

Parameters:

a (float): The numerator.

b (float): The denominator.

Returns:

float: The result of division, or None if there is an error.

"""

try:

return a / b

except ZeroDivisionError:

print("Error: Cannot divide by zero.")

return None

In this example, the function handles the ZeroDivisionError gracefully and returns None instead of crashing the program.

Propagating Errors:

IN SOME CASES, IT MAY make sense to propagate the error to the caller rather than handling it within the function itself. This can be done using the raise statement, which allows the exception to be handled by the calling code.

def divide_numbers(a, b):

"""

Divide two numbers.

Parameters:

a (float): The numerator.

b (float): The denominator.

Raises:

ZeroDivisionError: If the denominator is zero.

Returns:

float: The result of the division.

"""

if b == 0:

raise ZeroDivisionError("Denominator cannot be zero.")

return a / b

Now, the responsibility of handling the exception is passed to the code that calls the function.

6. Use Type Hints for Better Readability

TYPE HINTS IN PYTHON help clarify what types of arguments a function expects and what type it returns. This makes the code more readable and helps tools like linters and IDEs catch potential bugs early.

Example of Type Hints:

DEF ADD(A: INT, B: int) -> int:

"""

Add two integers.

Parameters:

a (int): The first integer.

b (int): The second integer.

Returns:

int: The sum of the two integers.

"""

return a + b

Type hints are not enforced at runtime, but they improve code clarity and are supported by modern IDEs, which can provide better autocompletion and error detection.

7. Make Use of Default Arguments

DEFAULT ARGUMENTS ALLOW you to provide default values for parameters, making functions more flexible and reducing the need for the caller to provide every argument explicitly.

Example of Default Arguments:

DEF GREET(NAME: STR, message: str = "Hello"):

"""

Greet a person with a message.

Parameters:

name (str): The name of the person.

message (str): The greeting message. Default is "Hello".

"""

```
print(f"{message}, {name}!")
```

By providing a default value for the message parameter, the caller can choose to pass only the name argument if they don't need a custom message:

```
greet("Alice") # Output: Hello, Alice!

greet("Bob", "Good morning") # Output: Good morning, Bob!
```

8. Avoid Using Mutable Default Arguments

ONE OF THE COMMON PITFALLS in Python is using mutable default arguments, like lists or dictionaries. Python only initializes default arguments once when the function is defined, which can lead to unexpected behavior if the default argument is modified.

Problem with Mutable Defaults:

```
DEF APPEND_ITEM(ITEM, my_list=[]):

my_list.append(item)

return my_list

print(append_item(1)) # Output: [1]

print(append_item(2)) # Output: [1, 2] <—Unexpected behavior!
```

In this case, the default list is shared across multiple calls, which is usually not the desired behavior.

Solution:

```
DEF APPEND_ITEM(ITEM, my_list=None):

if my_list is None:

my_list = []

my_list.append(item)

return my_list

print(append_item(1)) # Output: [1]

print(append_item(2)) # Output: [2]
```

By using None as the default argument and initializing the list inside the function, you ensure that a new list is created for each function call.

9. Use Keyword Arguments for Clarity

WHEN A FUNCTION HAS many parameters, using keyword arguments makes the function call more readable and reduces the likelihood of errors due to the incorrect order of arguments.

Example of Using Keyword Arguments:

```
DEF CREATE_ACCOUNT(username, password, email, age):

print(f"Account created for {username} with email {email} and age {age}.")

# Using keyword arguments for clarity

create_account(username="john_doe", password="secure123", email="john@example.com", age=25)
```

Using keyword arguments makes the function call more explicit, improving readability and making the code less error-prone.

Conclusion

WRITING EFFECTIVE PYTHON functions involves more than just getting the code to work. It's about following best practices that make your code readable, maintainable, and efficient. By adhering to naming conventions, keeping functions short and focused, documenting with docstrings, handling errors properly, and using tools like type hints and default arguments, you ensure that your functions not only work but are also easy to understand and reuse in the future. Functions are the building blocks of any program, and mastering how to write them well is a key step in improving as a Python developer.

Chapter 5: Working with Modules and Libraries

Introduction to Python Modules

IN PYTHON, A MODULE is a file containing Python definitions, functions, and statements. The file name of a module is the name of the module with the suffix .py. Modules are an essential part of structuring larger Python programs into smaller, reusable components. By breaking your program into modules, you can manage and maintain it more easily, avoid redundancy, and promote code reuse.

Why Use Modules?

MODULES ALLOW FOR THE organization of code logically. Instead of placing all functions, classes, and variables in one giant script, developers can group related code into separate modules. For example, in a large program, you might have modules for handling database operations, user interface, file input/output, etc.

When you import a module, Python executes the code within that module and makes its functions, classes, and variables available for use in the importing code.

Here's an example:

```
# Save this as my_module.py

def greeting(name):

print(f"Hello, {name}!")
```

Now, in another Python file, you can import and use my_module:

```
# main.py

import my_module

my_module.greeting("Alice")
```

HELLO, ALICE!

This is a basic introduction to how you can split functionality into different modules for better code organization and reuse.

Importing Modules

PYTHON PROVIDES SEVERAL ways to import modules, and each has specific use cases:

1. **Basic Import**: The simplest form of importing modules is using the import statement. When you use this method, all the code in the imported module is executed, and you can access its content using dot notation.

```
import math

print(math.sqrt(16)) # Output: 4.0
```

1. **Importing Specific Items**: You can import specific functions, classes, or variables from a module using the from keyword.

```
from math import sqrt

print(sqrt(25)) # Output: 5.0
```

This approach is useful when you want to keep your code cleaner by importing only what you need, but you should be careful to avoid name collisions, especially in larger projects.

1. **Renaming Modules**: If the name of a module is too long or conflicts with another module, you can give it an alias using the as keyword.

```
import math as m

print(m.sqrt(36)) # Output: 6.0
```

Renaming modules can also be helpful when working with libraries that have long or complex names.

1. **Wildcard Import**: You can import everything from a module using the asterisk (*). However, this is generally discouraged as it can lead to name conflicts and make the code harder to understand.

```
from math import *

print(sqrt(49)) # Output: 7.0
```

Module Search Path

WHEN YOU IMPORT A MODULE, Python searches for it in a sequence of directories. This search path is stored in sys.path, which is a list of strings representing the directories Python searches.

Here's how you can see the module search path:

```
import sys

print(sys.path)
```

The first entry in sys.path is usually the directory containing the script that is being run. Python also searches standard library directories and directories specified by the PYTHONPATH environment variable.

Standard Python Modules

PYTHON COMES WITH A large collection of standard modules that are immediately available. These are known as the standard library. The standard library includes modules for working with operating system functionality, data structures, file input/output, and much more.

Some useful standard modules include:

- os: Provides functions to interact with the operating system.
- sys: Provides access to system-specific parameters and functions.
- math: Provides mathematical functions.
- datetime: Deals with dates and times.

Example of using the os module:

```
import os

# Get the current working directory

print(os.getcwd())

# List the files in the current directory

print(os.listdir())
```

Third-Party Libraries and the Python Package Index (PyPI)

IN ADDITION TO THE standard library, Python has a vast ecosystem of third-party libraries that can be installed via the Python Package Index (PyPI). These libraries allow you to extend Python's capabilities in areas such as web development, data analysis, machine learning, and more.

The most common tool for installing third-party libraries is pip, which is included in modern Python installations.

```
pip install requests
```

This command installs the requests library, which is used for making HTTP requests in Python. Once installed, you can import and use the library in your program:

```
import requests

response = requests.get('https://api.github.com')

print(response.status_code)
```

Creating Your Own Python Module

CREATING A CUSTOM PYTHON module is simple. Just create a .py file with functions, classes, and variables, and it can be imported into another Python file.

Here's an example:

```
# Save this as my_math.py

def add(a, b):

return a + b
```

```
def subtract(a, b):

return a - b
```

Now, import this module in another Python file:

```
# main.py

import my_math

result_add = my_math.add(5, 3)

result_sub = my_math.subtract(5, 3)

print(f"Addition: {result_add}, Subtraction: {result_sub}")
```

This outputs:

```
Addition: 8, Subtraction: 2
```

By modularizing your code this way, you can reuse it across different projects without having to rewrite the same functionality multiple times.

Packages: Organizing Modules into Directories

A PACKAGE IN PYTHON is a way of organizing related modules into a directory hierarchy. A package is simply a directory that contains a special file called __init__.py. This file can be empty, but it must be present for Python to recognize the directory as a package.

Here's an example structure for a package:

```
my_package/

__init__.py
```

module1.py

module2.py

You can import modules from the package like this:

from my_package import module1

module1.some_function()

Or import specific functions from a module in the package:

from my_package.module2 import some_function

some_function()

Packages allow you to structure your code in a way that makes it more scalable and maintainable, especially in large applications.

Best Practices for Working with Modules

1. **Keep Your Modules Small**: Each module should focus on a single responsibility or functionality. This makes your code easier to understand and maintain.
2. **Use Descriptive Names**: Choose module names that clearly describe the purpose of the module. Avoid using generic names like utils or helpers unless it's absolutely necessary.
3. **Avoid Circular Imports**: Circular imports happen when two modules try to import each other. This can lead to errors and makes your code more difficult to debug. If you find yourself in this situation, reconsider the structure of your code.
4. **Use __all__ to Control What Is Imported**: By default, when a module is imported using from module import *, all names that do not start with an underscore (_) are

imported. You can control which names are exported by defining a list called __all__ in your module.

__ALL__ = ['GREETING']

1. **Document Your Modules**: Write docstrings for your modules, functions, and classes. This helps others (and your future self) understand the purpose and usage of your code.

"""

This module contains functions for basic math operations.

"""

def add(a, b):

"""Returns the sum of a and b."""

return a + b

This is how Python modules and packages work.

Standard Libraries and How to Use Them

PYTHON'S STANDARD LIBRARY is a powerful set of modules and packages that comes with every Python installation. It provides a wide range of utilities, from file handling to mathematical computations, system-level interfaces, web interaction, data serialization, and more. The availability of these built-in modules means that many tasks can be accomplished without the need to install additional third-party libraries, making Python an efficient and versatile language for various applications.

What Is the Python Standard Library?

THE PYTHON STANDARD library is a collection of pre-built and optimized modules that are bundled with Python. These modules cover almost every area of development, including:

- File I/O operations
- Networking
- Databases
- Web services
- Cryptography
- Data structures
- Mathematical computations
- And much more

Using the standard library is beneficial because:

1. You don't need to install or manage additional packages.
2. These libraries are highly optimized and maintained by the Python core development team.
3. The libraries are cross-platform, meaning they work on multiple operating systems.

Let's explore some of the most commonly used modules and see how they can simplify tasks.

The os Module: Interacting with the Operating System

THE OS MODULE PROVIDES a way of using operating system-dependent functionality, such as reading or writing to the file system, manipulating environment variables, and interacting with directories.

Basic File and Directory Operations

THE OS MODULE OFFERS functions to create, delete, or rename files and directories. Here are some common examples:

```
import os

# Get the current working directory

cwd = os.getcwd()

print(f"Current working directory: {cwd}")

# List all files and directories in the current directory

files_and_dirs = os.listdir(cwd)

print(f"Files and directories: {files_and_dirs}")

# Create a new directory

os.mkdir('new_directory')

# Rename a directory

os.rename('new_directory', 'renamed_directory')

# Remove a directory

os.rmdir('renamed_directory')
```

Environment Variables

THE OS MODULE CAN ALSO be used to access and modify environment variables, which can be useful when you need to configure your Python application dynamically.

```
import os

# Get an environment variable

home_directory = os.getenv('HOME')

print(f"Home Directory: {home_directory}")

# Set an environment variable

os.environ['MY_VARIABLE'] = 'my_value'

# Print the updated environment variable

print(os.getenv('MY_VARIABLE'))
```

Path Manipulation

THE OS.PATH SUBMODULE provides tools for manipulating file paths. This is extremely useful for creating platform-independent code that works on both Windows and Unix-like systems.

```
import os

# Join path components

file_path = os.path.join('/path', 'to', 'file.txt')

print(f"File path: {file_path}")
```

```
# Check if a file exists

exists = os.path.exists(file_path)

print(f"Does the file exist? {exists}")

# Get the file extension

extension = os.path.splitext(file_path)[1]

print(f"File extension: {extension}")
```

The sys Module: System-Specific Parameters and Functions

THE SYS MODULE PROVIDES access to system-level parameters and functions, such as command-line arguments, interpreter settings, and Python runtime information.

Command-Line Arguments

COMMAND-LINE ARGUMENTS are passed to a Python script via the sys.argv list. The first item in sys.argv is always the name of the script being executed, and subsequent items are the arguments passed to the script.

```
import sys

# Print all command-line arguments

print("Command-line arguments:", sys.argv)

# Access specific argument

if len(sys.argv) > 1:

print(f"First argument: {sys.argv[1]}")
```

Exiting the Script

YOU CAN USE SYS.EXIT() to terminate a Python program. This can be useful in certain cases where an error condition occurs and you need to stop execution immediately.

```
import sys

# Exit the script with a status code

sys.exit("Exiting with an error")
```

Python Version Information

YOU CAN RETRIEVE INFORMATION about the Python interpreter being used with sys.version and sys.version_info.

```
import sys

# Print Python version

print("Python version:", sys.version)

# Check if Python version is greater than 3.6

if sys.version_info >= (3, 6):

print("Python 3.6 or greater is running")

else:

print("Python version is lower than 3.6")
```

The math Module: Mathematical Functions

THE MATH MODULE PROVIDES access to common mathematical functions such as square roots, trigonometric functions, logarithms, and constants like pi.

Common Mathematical Functions

HERE ARE A FEW EXAMPLES of how to use the math module for common operations:

```
import math

# Calculate the square root of 16

print(f"Square root of 16: {math.sqrt(16)}")

# Calculate the sine of an angle (in radians)

angle_radians = math.radians(90)

print(f"Sine of 90 degrees: {math.sin(angle_radians)}")

# Get the value of pi

print(f"Value of pi: {math.pi}")

# Calculate the natural logarithm of a number

print(f"Natural logarithm of 2.718: {math.log(math.e)}")
```

The math module also includes functions for rounding, finding the greatest common divisor, calculating factorials, and more.

The datetime Module: Working with Dates and Times

THE DATETIME MODULE provides classes for manipulating dates and times. This is especially useful for logging, timestamping, and time-based calculations.

Getting the Current Date and Time

YOU CAN USE DATETIME.datetime.now() to get the current date and time.

```
import datetime

# Get the current date and time

now = datetime.datetime.now()

print(f"Current date and time: {now}")

# Get the current date only

today = datetime.date.today()

print(f"Today's date: {today}")
```

Formatting Dates

YOU CAN FORMAT DATES in different ways using the strftime() method, which allows you to specify a format string.

```
# Format date as "Year-Month-Day"

formatted_date = today.strftime("%Y-%m-%d")

print(f"Formatted date: {formatted_date}")
```

```
# Format time as "Hour:Minute:Second"

formatted_time = now.strftime("%H:%M:%S")

print(f"Formatted time: {formatted_time}")
```

Date Arithmetic

THE DATETIME MODULE also supports date arithmetic, which allows you to add or subtract days, months, or years from a given date.

```
# Calculate the date 10 days from now

ten_days_later = today + datetime.timedelta(days=10)

print(f"Date 10 days from now: {ten_days_later}")

# Calculate the date 30 days ago

thirty_days_ago = today - datetime.timedelta(days=30)

print(f"Date 30 days ago: {thirty_days_ago}")
```

The random Module: Generating Random Numbers

THE RANDOM MODULE IS used to generate random numbers, which can be helpful for simulations, games, and testing purposes.

Basic Random Number Generation

```
IMPORT RANDOM

# Generate a random float between 0 and 1

random_float = random.random()
```

```
print(f"Random float: {random_float}")

# Generate a random integer between 1 and 10

random_int = random.randint(1, 10)

print(f"Random integer between 1 and 10: {random_int}")
```

Random Choices from a List

YOU CAN ALSO USE THE random module to randomly select an item from a list or shuffle the order of items in a list.

```
# Randomly choose an item from a list

choices = ['apple', 'banana', 'cherry']

random_choice = random.choice(choices)

print(f"Random choice: {random_choice}")

# Shuffle a list of items

random.shuffle(choices)

print(f"Shuffled list: {choices}")
```

The json Module: Working with JSON Data

THE JSON MODULE PROVIDES functions to encode and decode data in the JavaScript Object Notation (JSON) format. JSON is a popular format for transmitting data between a server and a web client.

Encoding Python Objects as JSON

YOU CAN CONVERT PYTHON objects into JSON strings using the json.dumps() function.

```
import json

# A Python dictionary

data = {

'name': 'Alice',

'age': 30,

'city': 'New York'

}

# Convert the dictionary to a JSON string

json_string = json.dumps(data)

print(f"JSON string: {json_string}")
```

Decoding JSON Strings into Python Objects

YOU CAN ALSO CONVERT a JSON string back into a Python object using json.loads().

```
# A JSON string

json_string = '{"name": "Alice", "age": 30, "city": "New York"}'

# Convert the JSON string to a Python dictionary

data = json.loads(json_string)
```

```
print(f"Python dictionary: {data}")
```

The json module is commonly used when working with web APIs that return or accept data in JSON format.

Conclusion

THE PYTHON STANDARD library is a vast and versatile collection of modules that allows developers to solve complex problems without the need for external dependencies. By leveraging the power of the standard library, you can write efficient, maintainable, and cross-platform code for a wide range of applications.

Understanding and effectively utilizing these standard modules is a key part of mastering Python development. Whether you're interacting with the file system, working with dates and times, performing mathematical calculations, or handling JSON data, the standard library provides the tools you need to accomplish your tasks with ease.

Importing Third-Party Libraries

WHILE PYTHON'S STANDARD library provides an impressive array of built-in functionality, there are countless third-party libraries that expand Python's capabilities even further. These libraries range from highly specialized tools, like those for machine learning and web development, to general utilities that make working with data or performing everyday programming tasks easier. The Python community, through the Python Package Index (PyPI), has created a massive ecosystem of reusable packages that developers can leverage to solve nearly any problem they might face.

What Is PyPI and Why Should You Use It?

THE PYTHON PACKAGE Index (PyPI) is a repository of software packages for Python. It houses thousands of third-party libraries that can be easily installed and used in your Python projects. PyPI is maintained by the Python Software Foundation and serves as the primary source for downloading libraries developed by the Python community.

When you need a library to accomplish a task that isn't covered by the standard library, PyPI is often the best place to look. For example, popular libraries such as requests (for HTTP requests), NumPy (for numerical computations), and pandas (for data manipulation) are all available on PyPI.

Benefits of Using Third-Party Libraries

1. **Increased Functionality**: Third-party libraries extend the base Python language with specialized tools that can dramatically improve your productivity.
2. **Community Contributions**: PyPI libraries are built and maintained by experienced developers from around the world. This collective effort means you can often find high-quality solutions to problems you would otherwise need to develop yourself.
3. **Rapid Development**: Instead of reinventing the wheel, you can use pre-built packages to quickly implement features in your project. This lets you focus on higher-level problems without worrying about the lower-level details.
4. **Regular Updates**: Popular libraries often receive regular updates that improve performance, security, and compatibility with new versions of Python.

Installing Third-Party Libraries with pip

PIP IS THE PACKAGE manager used to install and manage third-party libraries in Python. It is included with most modern Python installations, making it easy to start using libraries from PyPI.

pip install library_name

PIP INSTALL REQUESTS

This will download the latest version of requests from PyPI and install it on your system.

Checking Installed Libraries

PIP LIST

This will output a list of all installed packages along with their respective versions:

Package Version

REQUESTS 2.25.1

numpy 1.19.5

pandas 1.2.1

Upgrading Installed Libraries

LIBRARIES ON PYPI ARE frequently updated to include new features, fix bugs, or patch security vulnerabilities. To upgrade a library to its latest version, you can use the pip install—upgrade command. For example:

```
pip install—upgrade requests
```

This command will check PyPI for the latest version of requests and install it if a newer version is available.

Example: Using requests to Make HTTP Requests

ONE OF THE MOST COMMON tasks in modern programming is working with web APIs. The requests library simplifies this process by providing a simple, intuitive API for making HTTP requests.

Here's a basic example of how to use requests to fetch data from a public API:

```
import requests

# Make a GET request to a public API

response = requests.get('https://api.github.com')

# Check if the request was successful

if response.status_code == 200:

# Print the response content

print(response.json())

else:

print(f"Failed to fetch data. Status code: {response.status_code}")
```

In this example, the requests.get() method is used to send a GET request to the GitHub API. The response is then checked for a successful status code (200), and if the request was successful, the response content is printed.

Virtual Environments: Isolating Your Dependencies

AS YOU BEGIN TO WORK with multiple Python projects, each with its own set of dependencies, it's important to keep these dependencies isolated from one another. This is where virtual environments come into play.

A virtual environment is a self-contained directory that contains its own installation of Python and its own collection of libraries. This allows you to install different versions of libraries for different projects without conflicts.

Creating a Virtual Environment

PYTHON -M VENV MYENV

This will create a virtual environment in a directory called myenv. Inside this directory, you'll find a copy of the Python interpreter and a place to install libraries.

Activating a Virtual Environment

BEFORE YOU CAN START using a virtual environment, you need to activate it. The method for doing this depends on your operating system.

On Windows, run:

myenv\Scripts\activate

•

On macOS or Linux, run:

bash

```
source myenv/bin/activate
```

-

Once the virtual environment is activated, your terminal prompt will change to indicate that you're working inside the virtual environment.

Installing Libraries in a Virtual Environment

AFTER ACTIVATING THE virtual environment, you can install libraries using pip as usual. The difference is that the libraries will be installed inside the virtual environment, rather than system-wide.

```
pip install requests
```

This will install requests only in the current virtual environment. If you deactivate the environment and try to use requests in a different project, it won't be available unless it's installed there as well.

Deactivating a Virtual Environment

DEACTIVATE

Example: Using pandas for Data Manipulation

ANOTHER WIDELY-USED third-party library is pandas, which provides powerful tools for working with structured data, particularly in the form of DataFrames. pandas is commonly used in data analysis, finance, and machine learning projects.

Here's a simple example of how to use pandas to load and manipulate a CSV file:

```
import pandas as pd

# Load a CSV file into a DataFrame

df = pd.read_csv('data.csv')

# Display the first 5 rows of the DataFrame

print(df.head())

# Perform some basic operations

mean_value = df['column_name'].mean()

print(f"Mean value of column_name: {mean_value}")

# Filter rows based on a condition

filtered_df = df[df['column_name'] > 50]

print(filtered_df)
```

In this example, pandas is used to read a CSV file into a DataFrame, a two-dimensional data structure similar to a table in a database. The head() method displays the first five rows of the DataFrame, while other methods like mean() and conditional filtering allow you to perform various operations on the data.

Popular Third-Party Libraries

THERE ARE THOUSANDS of third-party libraries available on PyPI, and the following are just a few of the most popular and widely-used ones across different fields:

1. **NumPy**: Provides support for large, multi-dimensional arrays and matrices, along with a collection of mathematical functions to operate on these arrays.

   ○ Installation: pip install numpy

Usage Example:

python

```
import numpy as np

array = np.array([1, 2, 3, 4])

print(array * 2)
```

○

2. **Flask**: A lightweight web framework for building web applications and APIs.

   ○ Installation: pip install flask

Usage Example:

python

```
from flask import Flask

app = Flask(__name__)
```

```
@app.route('/')
def hello_world():
return 'Hello, World!'
if __name__ == '__main__':
app.run()
```

○

3. **BeautifulSoup**: A library for web scraping that allows you to parse HTML and XML documents and extract useful data.

○ Installation: pip install beautifulsoup4

Usage Example:

```
python
from bs4 import BeautifulSoup
import requests
url = 'https://example.com'
response = requests.get(url)
soup = BeautifulSoup(response.text, 'html.parser')
print(soup.title.text)
```

○

4. **matplotlib**: A plotting library used for creating static, animated, and interactive visualizations in Python.

- Installation: pip install matplotlib

Usage Example:

```python
import matplotlib.pyplot as plt
import numpy as np
x = np.linspace(0, 10, 100)
y = np.sin(x)
plt.plot(x, y)
plt.show()
```

-

5. **Django**: A high-level Python web framework that allows rapid development of secure and maintainable websites.

- Installation: pip install django

Usage Example:

```bash
django-admin startproject myproject
cd myproject
python manage.py runserver
```

-

Keeping Your Project's Dependencies in Sync

WHEN WORKING WITH MULTIPLE libraries in a project, it's often helpful to keep track of the exact versions of each library that you're using. This ensures that your project can be reproduced on other machines with the same dependencies.

pip freeze > requirements.txt

PIP INSTALL -R REQUIREMENTS.txt

This makes it easy to share your project with others and ensure that everyone is using the same environment.

Conclusion

IMPORTING THIRD-PARTY libraries is a fundamental aspect of Python programming. Whether you're building a small utility script or a large-scale application, the vast ecosystem of libraries available through PyPI offers a wealth of functionality that can save you time and effort. By using tools like pip and virtual environments, you can efficiently manage your project's dependencies, avoid conflicts, and keep your development process smooth and scalable.

Building Your Own Python Modules

CREATING YOUR OWN PYTHON modules is a powerful way to organize, reuse, and share your code across multiple projects. By building custom modules, you can structure your application into logical components, each with its own responsibility, making the entire codebase easier to maintain and understand. Modules in Python are simply files containing Python code, and these files can define functions, classes, and variables that can be used elsewhere in your programs.

This section will explore how to create your own modules, how to organize them into packages, and how to ensure that they are reusable across different environments and projects.

Why Create Your Own Modules?

AS PROJECTS GROW IN complexity, keeping all code in a single file becomes unwieldy. Breaking your program into smaller, reusable modules has several advantages:

- **Modularity**: Code is easier to maintain when logically grouped by functionality.
- **Reusability**: Modules can be reused across multiple projects, avoiding code duplication.
- **Testing**: Each module can be tested independently, leading to better code quality.
- **Collaboration**: In team environments, modules allow developers to work on different components in parallel without conflicts.

A well-structured Python project consists of several smaller modules that handle specific responsibilities, from data processing to API communication. Let's walk through how to create your own Python module from scratch.

Creating a Simple Python Module

A PYTHON MODULE IS simply a file with a .py extension. You can define functions, classes, and variables in this file and import them in other files.

For example, let's create a module named math_operations.py that contains functions for basic arithmetic operations.

```
# Save this as math_operations.py

def add(a, b):

"""Return the sum of two numbers."""

return a + b

def subtract(a, b):

"""Return the difference of two numbers."""

return a - b

def multiply(a, b):

"""Return the product of two numbers."""

return a * b

def divide(a, b):

"""Return the quotient of two numbers. Raises an error if division by zero."""

if b == 0:

raise ValueError("Cannot divide by zero")

return a / b
```

In the code above, we've defined four functions—add, subtract, multiply, and divide. These functions perform basic mathematical operations and are now ready to be imported into another Python script.

Importing Your Custom Module

NOW THAT WE HAVE CREATED a module, we can import it into another Python script and use its functions. To import a custom module, simply use the import statement, followed by the module name (without the .py extension).

```
# Save this as main.py

import math_operations

# Using the functions from the custom module

result_add = math_operations.add(10, 5)

result_subtract = math_operations.subtract(10, 5)

result_multiply = math_operations.multiply(10, 5)

result_divide = math_operations.divide(10, 5)

print(f"Addition: {result_add}")

print(f"Subtraction: {result_subtract}")

print(f"Multiplication: {result_multiply}")

print(f"Division: {result_divide}")
```

When you run main.py, it will output the results of the arithmetic operations:

```
Addition: 15
```

Subtraction: 5

Multiplication: 50

Division: 2.0

By importing math_operations, we were able to reuse the functions we defined in that module without having to rewrite them. This demonstrates the power of modular code.

Module Search Path

WHEN PYTHON ENCOUNTERS an import statement, it searches for the specified module in a sequence of locations. This search path is stored in sys.path, a list of directories that Python checks when trying to locate modules. By default, Python looks in the following places:

1. The directory from which the script is being run.
2. The Python standard library directories.
3. Any directories listed in the PYTHONPATH environment variable.

You can view the module search path by printing the sys.path list:

```
import sys

print(sys.path)
```

If you want to import a module from a custom directory, you can append that directory to sys.path at runtime:

```
import sys

sys.path.append('/path/to/your/module')
```

Structuring Your Code with Packages

AS YOUR PROJECT GROWS, you may want to organize related modules into packages. A package is simply a directory that contains one or more Python modules, along with a special file named __init__.py. This __init__.py file can be empty, but it tells Python that the directory should be treated as a package.

Example of a Package Structure

HERE'S AN EXAMPLE OF how you can organize your modules into a package:

my_package/

__init__.py

math_operations.py

string_operations.py

In this example, my_package is a package that contains two modules: math_operations.py and string_operations.py.

Using Packages

TO USE A PACKAGE, YOU can import the individual modules within it. For example, if you want to use the add function from the math_operations module inside my_package, you can do so like this:

from my_package import math_operations

result = math_operations.add(5, 10)

print(result) # Output: 15

You can also import specific functions directly:

```
from my_package.math_operations import add

result = add(5, 10)

print(result) # Output: 15
```

This structure makes it easy to manage a large codebase with multiple modules, keeping everything well-organized.

Namespaces and __all__

IN PYTHON, A MODULE has its own namespace, which means that all functions, variables, and classes within the module are local to that module unless explicitly exported. By default, when you import a module using from module import *, all names that do not start with an underscore (_) are imported.

If you want to control which items are imported when someone uses from module import *, you can define an __all__ list inside your module:

```
# Inside math_operations.py

__all__ = ['add', 'subtract']
```

In this case, only the add and subtract functions will be imported when from math_operations import * is used.

Creating Reusable and Well-Documented Modules

A WELL-DESIGNED MODULE should be reusable and easy to understand. To achieve this, follow these best practices:

1. **Write Descriptive Function Names**: Choose names that clearly indicate the function's purpose. For example,

calculate_area is better than just area.

2. **Use Docstrings**: Every function and class should have a docstring that explains what it does, its parameters, and the expected return value. This makes it easier for others (and your future self) to understand how to use the module.

```
def add(a, b):

"""

Return the sum of two numbers.

Parameters:

a (int or float): The first number.

b (int or float): The second number.

Returns:

int or float: The sum of the two numbers.

"""

return a + b
```

1. **Handle Errors Gracefully**: Use exceptions to handle invalid inputs or error conditions. For example, in the divide function, we used a ValueError to handle division by zero.
2. **Keep Modules Focused**: A module should have a clear purpose and contain functions and classes that are logically related. If a module starts to grow too large, consider splitting it into smaller, more focused modules.
3. **Test Your Module**: Write unit tests to verify that your

module works as expected. Python's built-in unittest module provides a framework for writing tests.

```
import unittest

import math_operations

class TestMathOperations(unittest.TestCase):

def test_add(self):

self.assertEqual(math_operations.add(10, 5), 15)

def test_subtract(self):

self.assertEqual(math_operations.subtract(10, 5), 5)

if __name__ == '__main__':

unittest.main()
```

Running this test script will ensure that your math_operations module behaves as expected.

Sharing Your Module with Others

ONCE YOU'VE CREATED a useful module, you may want to share it with others. There are several ways to distribute Python modules:

1. **Local Sharing**: You can share the .py files directly with others. They can simply copy the files into their projects and import them.
2. **PyPI Distribution**: For broader distribution, you can publish your module on the Python Package Index (PyPI). This allows others to install your module using pip. To publish a package on PyPI, you need to create a

setup.py file that contains metadata about your module (such as its name, version, and author) and use the twine tool to upload it.

Here's an example of a simple setup.py file:

```
from setuptools import setup

setup(

name='math_operations',

version='1.0',

description='A simple module for basic arithmetic operations',

author='Your Name',

author_email='youremail@example.com',

py_modules=['math_operations'],

)
```

Once your setup.py file is ready, you can package and upload your module to PyPI.

Conclusion

BUILDING YOUR OWN PYTHON modules allows you to create reusable, organized, and maintainable code. By structuring your projects into smaller components, you can improve both the development and collaboration process. Whether you're working on a small utility script or a large-scale application, knowing how to create and manage Python modules and packages is a crucial skill for any developer.

As you continue developing in Python, you'll find that creating modules not only simplifies your workflow but also enables you to build more complex and feature-rich applications. With Python's vast ecosystem and support for third-party tools, you can even publish your work to the world, contributing to the Python community at large.

Virtual Environments: Managing Dependencies

IN PYTHON DEVELOPMENT, virtual environments play a crucial role in managing dependencies. They allow developers to create isolated environments for each project, ensuring that the libraries and packages used in one project don't conflict with those used in another. Virtual environments provide a controlled space for Python and its dependencies, making it easier to manage different projects that may require different versions of packages.

This section will explore the importance of virtual environments, how to create and manage them, and how they can help you maintain clean and organized Python projects. We will also look at some tools that assist in working with virtual environments and best practices for managing dependencies efficiently.

Why Use Virtual Environments?

VIRTUAL ENVIRONMENTS allow you to avoid the problem of "dependency hell," which occurs when multiple projects require different versions of the same package. Without virtual environments, if you install a package globally, it might conflict with the needs of another project. This is particularly problematic in production environments where dependencies must be strictly controlled to ensure stability.

Benefits of Virtual Environments

1. **Isolation**: Each project can have its own set of dependencies, preventing version conflicts.
2. **Reproducibility**: It's easier to replicate the environment on another machine, making your projects more portable.
3. **Easy Management**: Virtual environments simplify package management, especially when different projects require different versions of Python or libraries.
4. **Cleaner Global Python Installation**: By keeping all project-specific libraries within their virtual environment, you avoid cluttering your global Python installation.

Creating and Activating a Virtual Environment

CREATING A VIRTUAL environment in Python is simple, thanks to the built-in venv module. This module allows you to create virtual environments that are isolated from the global Python environment.

To create a virtual environment, navigate to your project directory in the terminal or command prompt, and run the following command:

```
python -m venv env
```

Here, env is the name of the virtual environment directory that will be created. You can name it anything, but it's common to use names like env, venv, or .venv.

Once the virtual environment is created, you need to activate it before using it. The method for activating the virtual environment depends on your operating system:

On Windows:

bash

env\Scripts\activate

•

On macOS and Linux:

bash

source env/bin/activate

•

Once the virtual environment is activated, your terminal prompt will change to indicate that you are working within the virtual environment. For example, it might look like this:

(env) $

Installing Packages in a Virtual Environment

ONCE THE VIRTUAL ENVIRONMENT is activated, you can install packages using pip, just as you would normally. However, the packages will be installed only in the virtual environment, not globally. This ensures that each project has its own dependencies without affecting others.

pip install requests

PIP LIST

This will display all the installed packages and their versions. The list will typically start out empty, except for a few standard packages that come pre-installed with Python.

Deactivating the Virtual Environment

DEACTIVATE

After deactivating, the terminal prompt will return to normal, and you'll be back to using the system-wide Python environment. The virtual environment is still available, and you can reactivate it whenever you need to work on the project again.

Using .gitignore with Virtual Environments

WHEN WORKING WITH VERSION control systems like Git, it's important to avoid committing your virtual environment to the repository. This is because the virtual environment can take up a lot of space, and it's not necessary for the project's source code. Instead, you should include a requirements.txt file (discussed later) that specifies the project's dependencies.

To exclude the virtual environment from version control, create a .gitignore file in the root of your project and add the following line:

env/

This tells Git to ignore the env directory, ensuring that the virtual environment is not included in commits.

Reproducing Virtual Environments with requirements.txt

ONE OF THE KEY ADVANTAGES of virtual environments is the ability to reproduce them on another machine. This is especially important for collaboration, deployment, or when you need to reinstall the environment later. To ensure that the same dependencies are installed on other systems, you can create a requirements.txt file that lists all the packages and their versions.

pip freeze > requirements.txt

This command will output a list of all installed packages and their exact versions, and write it to a file named requirements.txt.

Here's an example of what a requirements.txt file might look like:

requests==2.25.1

numpy==1.19.5

pandas==1.2.1

PIP INSTALL -R REQUIREMENTS.txt

This will ensure that the same versions of the libraries are installed, making the environment reproducible.

Using virtualenvwrapper for Easier Virtual Environment Management

MANAGING MULTIPLE VIRTUAL environments manually can become cumbersome, especially if you have many projects that require different environments. virtualenvwrapper is a popular tool that simplifies the process of creating, activating, and managing virtual environments.

pip install virtualenv

Then, install virtualenvwrapper:

On macOS and Linux:

pip install virtualenvwrapper

•

On Windows, you can use virtualenvwrapper-win:

pip install virtualenvwrapper-win

•

Once installed, virtualenvwrapper provides a set of commands for managing virtual environments:

- mkvirtualenv env_name: Creates a new virtual environment.
- workon env_name: Activates a virtual environment.
- deactivate: Deactivates the current virtual environment.
- rmvirtualenv env_name: Deletes a virtual environment.

These commands make it easier to switch between different environments, and they store all virtual environments in a single location, keeping things organized.

Managing Python Versions with pyenv

SOMETIMES, DIFFERENT projects require different versions of Python itself, not just different packages. For example, you might be working on one project that uses Python 3.8 and another that uses Python 3.10. Managing multiple Python versions can be tricky, but pyenv is a tool that makes it easy to install and switch between different Python versions.

pyenv install 3.8.10

pyenv install 3.10.0

You can then set the global Python version or the version for a specific directory:

pyenv global 3.8.10

pyenv local 3.10.0

This allows you to use different versions of Python for different projects, ensuring compatibility with the project's requirements.

Best Practices for Managing Dependencies

MANAGING DEPENDENCIES effectively is crucial for ensuring the stability and maintainability of your projects. Here are some best practices to follow when working with virtual environments and dependencies:

1. **Always Use a Virtual Environment**: Never install project-specific dependencies globally. Always create a virtual environment for each project to isolate its dependencies.
2. **Keep Dependencies to a Minimum**: Avoid installing unnecessary packages. Each dependency adds complexity to the project and increases the risk of version conflicts. Install only the libraries you need.

Use Version Constraints: When specifying dependencies in a requirements.txt file, always include version constraints. This ensures that the same versions of packages are installed each time, preventing unexpected behavior caused by new package updates.

For example:

shell

requests>=2.25.1,<3.0.0

1. This ensures that requests version 2.25.1 or higher is installed, but not version 3.x.x, which might introduce breaking changes.
2. **Regularly Update Dependencies**: Keeping your dependencies up to date is important for security and performance reasons. However, make sure to test your project thoroughly after updating dependencies to ensure that nothing breaks.
3. **Pin Exact Versions for Production**: In production environments, it's a good idea to pin the exact versions of packages in your requirements.txt file. This ensures that the environment is completely reproducible and that no unexpected updates cause issues.

Use pipenv for Advanced Dependency Management: pipenv is a tool that combines pip and virtualenv into a single command-line tool. It also automatically generates Pipfile and Pipfile.lock files, which are more robust than requirements.txt for managing dependencies.

To install pipenv, run:

pip install pipenv

1. Once installed, you can create a virtual environment and manage dependencies with simple commands like pipenv

install and pipenv lock.

Conclusion

VIRTUAL ENVIRONMENTS are a fundamental tool for managing dependencies in Python projects. By isolating project-specific libraries and Python versions, virtual environments prevent conflicts and make it easier to maintain clean, organized projects. Whether you're working on a small script or a large-scale application, using virtual environments ensures that your project's dependencies remain manageable, reproducible, and isolated from other projects.

By following best practices and leveraging tools like virtualenvwrapper, pyenv, and pipenv, you can streamline the process of managing dependencies, reduce potential issues, and keep your development environment clean and efficient. As your projects grow in complexity, mastering virtual environments will become an essential skill that allows you to develop, test, and deploy code more effectively.

Chapter 6: File Handling in Python

Reading and Writing Text Files

IN PYTHON, FILE HANDLING is an essential skill, allowing programs to read from and write to external files. Whether you're processing logs, generating reports, or just saving user input, mastering file operations is a key part of Python programming. Python simplifies file handling by providing built-in functions and methods for working with files in various modes. In this section, we'll cover the basics of reading and writing text files, focusing on best practices and common use cases.

Opening a File

BEFORE READING OR WRITING to a file, it needs to be opened. Python provides the open() function, which is used to open a file and return a file object. The syntax of the open() function is as follows:

file_object = open(file_name, mode)

- file_name: The name of the file you want to open.
- mode: Specifies the mode in which the file is opened. It can be one of the following:
    - 'r': Read mode (default). Opens the file for reading.
    - 'w': Write mode. Opens the file for writing and truncates the file if it already exists.
    - 'a': Append mode. Opens the file for writing and appends data at the end of the file if it exists.

○ 'x': Exclusive creation mode. Creates the file but raises an error if the file already exists.

○ 'b': Binary mode. Used for binary files such as images or executable files.

○ 't': Text mode (default). Used for text files.

For example, to open a file named example.txt in read mode, you would use:

file = open('example.txt', 'r')

Reading from a File

ONCE A FILE IS OPENED in read mode, you can read its contents using several methods:

- read(): Reads the entire content of the file as a single string.
- readline(): Reads one line from the file.
- readlines(): Reads all the lines of the file into a list, where each element is a line.

Example: Reading the Entire File

FILE = OPEN('EXAMPLE.txt', 'r')

content = file.read()

print(content)

file.close()

In this example, the read() method reads the entire content of example.txt, and file.close() ensures that the file is closed after reading to free up system resources.

Example: Reading Line by Line

```
FILE = OPEN('EXAMPLE.txt', 'r')

for line in file:

print(line.strip()) # Strip is used to remove the newline character

file.close()
```

Here, the file is read line by line using a for loop. This method is memory-efficient for large files because it doesn't load the entire file into memory at once.

Writing to a File

WRITING TO A FILE IN Python is equally simple. To write to a file, you need to open it in write ('w'), append ('a'), or exclusive creation ('x') mode. The write() method is used to write text to the file.

Example: Writing to a File

```
FILE = OPEN('OUTPUT.txt', 'w')

file.write('Hello, world!\n')

file.write('This is a test file.\n')

file.close()
```

In this example, the write() method writes two lines to the file output.txt. If the file does not exist, it will be created. If it does exist, its contents will be truncated (deleted) before writing new data.

Example: Appending to a File

FILE = OPEN('OUTPUT.txt', 'a')

file.write('Appending this line to the file.\n')

file.close()

This example demonstrates appending to a file. The existing content of output.txt remains intact, and the new line is added to the end of the file.

File Modes in Detail

PYTHON PROVIDES VARIOUS file modes to control how the file is opened. The most common modes are:

- 'r': Opens the file for reading. If the file does not exist, a FileNotFoundError is raised.

- 'w': Opens the file for writing. If the file exists, its content is truncated. If the file does not exist, it is created.

- 'a': Opens the file for appending. New data is written at the end of the file. If the file does not exist, it is created.

- 'x': Creates a new file for writing. If the file already exists, a FileExistsError is raised.

- 'b': Binary mode. This is used for binary files (e.g., images, audio files). It is used in combination with other modes like 'rb', 'wb', etc.

- 't': Text mode (default). Used for reading and writing text files. It is used in combination with other modes like 'rt', 'wt', etc.

Example: Writing Binary Data

```
FILE = OPEN('IMAGE.jpg', 'wb')

file.write(b'\x89PNG\r\n\x1a\n') # Writing binary data

file.close()
```

This example demonstrates writing binary data to a file. The b prefix before the string indicates that the data is in binary format.

Using the with Statement for File Handling

IN PYTHON, IT'S A BEST practice to use the with statement when working with files. The with statement automatically closes the file after the block of code is executed, even if an exception occurs. This ensures that file resources are properly released.

Example: Reading a File with with

```
WITH OPEN('EXAMPLE.txt', 'r') as file:

content = file.read()

print(content)
```

In this example, the with statement ensures that the file is closed automatically after reading its contents, so there is no need to explicitly call file.close().

Example: Writing to a File with with

WITH OPEN('OUTPUT.TXT', 'w') as file:

file.write('Writing to the file using with statement.\n')

Here, the file is opened for writing, and the with statement guarantees that the file is closed once the block is exited.

Reading Large Files

FOR VERY LARGE FILES, loading the entire file into memory using read() may not be feasible. In such cases, reading the file line by line or in chunks is more efficient.

Example: Reading a File in Chunks

WITH OPEN('LARGE_FILE.txt', 'r') as file:

while True:

chunk = file.read(1024) # Read 1024 bytes at a time

if not chunk:

break

print(chunk)

This example reads the file in 1024-byte chunks, making it suitable for handling large files without consuming too much memory.

Best Practices for File Handling

1. **Always Close Files**: Always ensure that files are closed after you are done with them. The with statement is highly recommended for this purpose.
2. **Use Exception Handling**: When working with file operations, it is a good idea to use exception handling to handle potential errors like file not found or permission issues.
3. **Use Absolute Paths**: To avoid confusion, use absolute file paths when opening files, especially in larger projects.
4. **Work with Binary Files Carefully**: When handling binary files, ensure that you open them in binary mode ('b'). This is important for reading and writing non-text data.
5. **Limit Memory Usage**: When working with large files, read the file in chunks or line by line to minimize memory usage.

Conclusion

FILE HANDLING IS A fundamental aspect of Python programming, and understanding how to read from and write to files is essential for many applications. By using Python's built-in file handling capabilities, you can easily manage data, store output, and read from external sources. Whether you're working with text or binary files, the principles covered in this section provide a solid foundation for effective file management in Python.

Working with CSV Files

COMMA-SEPARATED VALUES (CSV) files are one of the most common file formats used for storing and exchanging data, particularly in fields like data science, web development, and database management. CSV files store tabular data (text and numbers) in plain text form, where each line represents a row and each column is separated by a delimiter, usually a comma. Python provides built-in support for handling CSV files through its csv module, making it simple to read from and write to CSV files.

Introduction to the csv Module

PYTHON'S CSV MODULE provides a convenient way to work with CSV files. The module defines classes and functions for reading from and writing to CSV files. To use the csv module, you need to import it at the start of your script:

```
import csv
```

The two main classes provided by this module are:

- csv.reader: Used for reading CSV files.
- csv.writer: Used for writing to CSV files.

Additionally, Python offers support for handling CSV files through other popular libraries like pandas, which is a powerful tool for data manipulation and analysis. However, this section will focus on the core functionality provided by the built-in csv module.

Reading from a CSV File

READING FROM A CSV file involves opening the file in read mode ('r') and using the csv.reader class to process the contents. The csv.reader class returns an iterable that produces rows from the CSV file as lists.

Example: Reading a CSV File Line by Line

```
IMPORT CSV

with open('data.csv', mode='r') as file:

csv_reader = csv.reader(file)

for row in csv_reader:

print(row)
```

In this example, the csv.reader object reads the file line by line, and each line is printed as a list. Each list element corresponds to a column in the CSV file.

Skipping the Header Row

IF THE CSV FILE HAS a header row (i.e., the first row contains column names), you might want to skip it when processing the data. This can be done by using the next() function to skip the first line.

```
with open('data.csv', mode='r') as file:

csv_reader = csv.reader(file)

header = next(csv_reader) # Skip the header row

print(f"Header: {header}")

for row in csv_reader:

print(row)
```

In this example, the first row of the CSV file is stored in the header variable and skipped in the subsequent loop that processes the rest of the file.

Reading CSV Files with Different Delimiters

CSV FILES MAY USE DIFFERENT delimiters, such as semicolons (;), tabs (\t), or other characters, instead of commas. The csv.reader class allows you to specify the delimiter used in the file.

Example: Reading a CSV File with a Semicolon as Delimiter

```
WITH OPEN('DATA_SEMICOLON.csv', mode='r') as file:

csv_reader = csv.reader(file, delimiter=';')

for row in csv_reader:

print(row)
```

Here, the delimiter argument is set to ';' to handle a CSV file where columns are separated by semicolons rather than commas.

Writing to a CSV File

WRITING TO A CSV FILE is just as simple as reading from one. The csv.writer class is used to write data to a CSV file. You open the file in write mode ('w'), create a csv.writer object, and then use the writerow() or writerows() methods to write data to the file.

Example: Writing Data to a CSV File

```
IMPORT CSV
```

```
data = [
['Name', 'Age', 'Country'],
['Alice', 30, 'USA'],
['Bob', 25, 'Canada'],
['Charlie', 35, 'UK']
]
with open('output.csv', mode='w', newline='') as file:
csv_writer = csv.writer(file)
csv_writer.writerows(data)
```

In this example, the writerows() method is used to write multiple rows at once. The newline='' parameter is passed to prevent Python from adding extra blank lines between rows on some systems.

Writing a Single Row

IF YOU WANT TO WRITE rows one at a time, you can use the writerow() method. This method writes a single row (list) to the file.

```
with open('output_single_row.csv', mode='w', newline='') as file:
csv_writer = csv.writer(file)
csv_writer.writerow(['Name', 'Age', 'Country'])
csv_writer.writerow(['Alice', 30, 'USA'])
csv_writer.writerow(['Bob', 25, 'Canada'])
```

Appending to a CSV File

TO APPEND DATA TO AN existing CSV file without overwriting its contents, you can open the file in append mode ('a'). The new data will be added at the end of the file.

Example: Appending Data to a CSV File

WITH OPEN('OUTPUT.CSV', mode='a', newline='') as file:

csv_writer = csv.writer(file)

csv_writer.writerow(['David', 28, 'Australia'])

In this case, the file is opened in append mode, and the new row is added after the existing data.

Handling Complex CSV Files

SOME CSV FILES MIGHT have more complex structures, such as fields containing commas, line breaks, or quotation marks. The csv module handles these cases using different formatting options. The most commonly used are:

- quotechar: Defines the character used to quote fields that contain the delimiter.

- quoting: Controls when quoting is applied. It can take values like csv.QUOTE_MINIMAL, csv.QUOTE_ALL, csv.QUOTE_NONNUMERIC, and csv.QUOTE_NONE.

Example: Writing CSV with Quoted Fields

WITH OPEN('OUTPUT_QUOTED.csv', mode='w', newline='') as file:

csv_writer = csv.writer(file, quotechar='"', quoting=csv.QUOTE_MINIMAL)

csv_writer.writerow(['Name', 'Description'])

csv_writer.writerow(['Apple', 'A fruit, that is red or green.'])

csv_writer.writerow(['Orange', 'A citrus fruit, often orange.'])

In this example, the quotechar is set to " and quoting=csv.QUOTE_MINIMAL ensures that only fields containing special characters (like commas) are enclosed in quotes.

Using DictReader and DictWriter

THE CSV.DICTREADER and csv.DictWriter classes provide a more convenient way of working with CSV files, especially when your data is structured in key-value pairs (i.e., dictionaries). With DictReader, each row is returned as a dictionary, where the keys are the column names.

Example: Reading a CSV File with DictReader

WITH OPEN('DATA.CSV', mode='r') as file:

csv_reader = csv.DictReader(file)

for row in csv_reader:

print(row['Name'], row['Age'], row['Country'])

In this example, each row is returned as a dictionary, and you can access specific columns by their names.

Example: Writing to a CSV File with DictWriter

WITH OPEN('OUTPUT_DICT.csv', mode='w', newline='') as file:

fieldnames = ['Name', 'Age', 'Country']

csv_writer = csv.DictWriter(file, fieldnames=fieldnames)

csv_writer.writeheader()

csv_writer.writerow({'Name': 'Alice', 'Age': 30, 'Country': 'USA'})

csv_writer.writerow({'Name': 'Bob', 'Age': 25, 'Country': 'Canada'})

In this case, DictWriter is used to write rows as dictionaries, with fieldnames defining the column headers.

Handling Errors in CSV Operations

WHILE WORKING WITH CSV files, you may encounter errors, such as missing files, incorrect file formats, or issues with reading/writing permissions. It's important to handle these errors gracefully using Python's error handling mechanisms like try, except, and finally.

Example: Handling File Not Found Error

TRY:

with open('nonexistent.csv', mode='r') as file:

csv_reader = csv.reader(file)

for row in csv_reader:

print(row)

except FileNotFoundError:

print("The file does not exist.")

In this example, the FileNotFoundError is caught, and an appropriate message is displayed.

Best Practices for Working with CSV Files

1. **Always Use the with Statement**: Using the with statement ensures that files are properly closed after they are read or written, even if an error occurs.
2. **Handle Special Characters**: If your CSV data contains special characters like commas, newlines, or quotes, make sure to handle them using appropriate quoting and delimiter options.
3. **Choose the Right Delimiter**: While the default delimiter for CSV files is a comma, it's important to choose the right delimiter for your data. For instance, use semicolons for European datasets, where commas are often used as decimal points.
4. **Use DictReader and DictWriter When Working with Dictionaries**: These classes make it easier to work with CSV data in dictionary form, which is especially useful when processing data from databases or JSON-like structures.
5. **Handle Errors Gracefully**: When working with file operations, always be prepared for errors like file not found, permission denied, or incorrect file formats. Use exception handling to make your code more robust.

Conclusion

WORKING WITH CSV FILES is a common task in Python programming, and the csv module provides a simple yet powerful interface for handling CSV data. Whether you're reading from large datasets, writing to structured files, or dealing with complex data, mastering CSV file operations will greatly enhance your ability to manage and process information in Python.

JSON Files: Parsing and Writing

JAVASCRIPT OBJECT NOTATION (JSON) has become one of the most popular formats for exchanging data, particularly in web development. JSON is lightweight, easy for humans to read, and easy for machines to parse and generate. Python provides built-in support for working with JSON files through the json module, which allows us to read, write, and manipulate JSON data effortlessly. In this section, we'll explore how to parse JSON data, write to JSON files, handle nested JSON structures, and follow best practices when working with JSON.

What is JSON?

JSON IS A TEXT-BASED format that represents structured data as key-value pairs. It closely resembles Python dictionaries. A typical JSON object looks like this:

```
{
"name": "John",
"age": 30,
"is_student": false,
```

"skills": ["Python", "JavaScript"],

"address": {

"street": "123 Main St",

"city": "Springfield"

}

}

JSON supports a limited number of data types:

- Strings
- Numbers (integer or floating-point)
- Booleans (true or false)
- Arrays (represented as lists in Python)
- Objects (represented as dictionaries in Python)
- Null (null in JSON, equivalent to None in Python)

Reading JSON Files

IN PYTHON, READING a JSON file is straightforward. The json module provides a load() function that reads a JSON object from a file and parses it into a Python data structure.

Example: Reading a JSON File

IMPORT JSON

with open('data.json', 'r') as file:

data = json.load(file)

print(data)

In this example, the json.load() function reads the content of the file data.json and converts it into a Python dictionary. Once loaded, you can access the data using dictionary-style key lookups.

Accessing JSON Data

ONCE YOU'VE LOADED the JSON data into a Python dictionary, you can easily access its elements by referring to the keys, just as you would with any dictionary.

print(data['name']) # Accessing a string value

print(data['skills']) # Accessing a list

print(data['address']['city']) # Accessing nested objects

Writing JSON Files

WRITING TO A JSON FILE involves converting a Python dictionary or list into a JSON string and then writing it to a file. The json module provides the dump() function for this purpose.

Example: Writing a Python Dictionary to a JSON File

IMPORT JSON

data = {

"name": "Jane",

"age": 25,

```
"is_student": True,
"skills": ["Python", "Java"],
"address": {
"street": "456 Oak St",
"city": "Shelbyville"
}
}
with open('output.json', 'w') as file:
json.dump(data, file)
```

In this example, the json.dump() function serializes the Python dictionary data into a JSON string and writes it to the file output.json.

JSON Serialization and Deserialization

THE PROCESS OF CONVERTING a Python object (like a dictionary or list) into a JSON string is called **serialization**. Conversely, **deserialization** refers to the process of converting a JSON string into a Python object. Python's json module handles both serialization and deserialization.

- **Serialization**: json.dumps() and json.dump()
  - json.dumps(): Converts a Python object to a JSON string.
  - json.dump(): Writes a Python object to a JSON file.

- **Deserialization**: json.loads() and json.load()

○ json.loads(): Converts a JSON string into a Python object.

○ json.load(): Reads a JSON object from a file and converts it into a Python object.

Example: Serialization Using json.dumps()

```
IMPORT JSON

data = {

"name": "Alice",

"age": 28,

"is_student": False,

"skills": ["Python", "Django"]

}

json_string = json.dumps(data)

print(json_string)
```

The json.dumps() function converts the Python dictionary into a JSON string. You can also control the formatting of the JSON string by specifying parameters like indent.

Example: Pretty-Printing JSON

YOU CAN IMPROVE THE readability of JSON output by adding indentation and sorting the keys:

```
json_string = json.dumps(data, indent=4, sort_keys=True)

print(json_string)
```

The indent parameter specifies the number of spaces to use for indentation, and sort_keys=True sorts the keys alphabetically in the output.

Handling Nested JSON Structures

JSON DATA OFTEN CONTAINS nested structures, such as lists within objects or objects within lists. Python allows you to access these nested elements using chained indexing.

Example: Accessing Nested JSON Elements

CONSIDER THE FOLLOWING JSON structure:

```
{
"name": "Bob",
"projects": [
{
"title": "Project A",
"description": "A simple project"
},
{
"title": "Project B",
"description": "A more complex project"
```

```
}
]
}
```

You can access nested elements like this:

```
print(data['projects'][0]['title']) # Output: Project A
```

This code snippet accesses the first project's title from the nested list.

Working with Large JSON Files

WHEN WORKING WITH LARGE JSON files, it is inefficient to load the entire file into memory at once, especially if only a portion of the data is needed. In such cases, you can process the file in chunks or read it line by line.

Example: Reading a JSON File Line by Line

```
IMPORT JSON

with open('large_data.json', 'r') as file:

for line in file:

data = json.loads(line)

print(data)
```

This approach reads the file line by line and deserializes each line into a Python object. It's particularly useful for large files where each line contains a separate JSON object.

Updating JSON Data

TO MODIFY JSON DATA, you can simply update the corresponding Python dictionary or list and then write the updated data back to the file.

Example: Updating and Writing JSON Data

```
WITH OPEN('DATA.JSON', 'r') as file:

data = json.load(file)

data['age'] = 35 # Updating the 'age' field

data['skills'].append('Machine Learning') # Adding a new skill

with open('data.json', 'w') as file:

json.dump(data, file, indent=4)
```

In this example, we load the JSON data, update the age field, append a new skill to the skills list, and write the updated data back to the file.

Error Handling in JSON Operations

WHEN WORKING WITH JSON files, you may encounter errors like incorrect file formats or issues with reading/writing permissions. Python provides built-in mechanisms to handle such errors gracefully.

Example: Handling JSON Decode Errors

```
IMPORT JSON

try:
```

```
with open('malformed.json', 'r') as file:

data = json.load(file)

except json.JSONDecodeError as e:

print(f"Error decoding JSON: {e}")
```

This code catches JSONDecodeError, which is raised if the JSON data is malformed or contains invalid syntax.

Converting Between JSON and Other Formats

JSON IS OFTEN USED in web applications to exchange data, but you may need to convert JSON data into other formats such as CSV, XML, or YAML for various use cases.

Example: Converting JSON to CSV

```
IMPORT JSON

import csv

with open('data.json', 'r') as file:

data = json.load(file)

with open('output.csv', 'w', newline='') as csvfile:

writer = csv.writer(csvfile)

writer.writerow(data.keys()) # Writing the header row

writer.writerow(data.values()) # Writing the data row
```

In this example, we load JSON data and convert it into CSV format, writing the keys as headers and the values as rows in a CSV file.

Best Practices for Working with JSON Files

1. **Use the with Statement**: When reading or writing JSON files, always use the with statement to ensure the file is properly closed after the operation.
2. **Pretty-Print JSON for Readability**: When writing JSON files intended for human consumption, use the indent and sort_keys parameters to make the JSON more readable.
3. **Handle Exceptions Gracefully**: Always include error handling to manage issues like malformed JSON or missing files. The json.JSONDecodeError and FileNotFoundError exceptions are commonly encountered when working with JSON files.
4. **Validate JSON Structure**: Before deserializing or manipulating JSON data, ensure it adheres to the expected structure to avoid runtime errors. This can be done through schema validation libraries like jsonschema.
5. **Use Appropriate Data Types**: When serializing data, ensure that only supported types are used (e.g., strings, numbers, lists, and dictionaries). Python objects like sets or tuples need to be converted to JSON-compatible types.
6. **Minimize Memory Usage for Large Files**: For large JSON files, avoid loading the entire file into memory at once. Instead, read and process the data in chunks or line by line.

Conclusion

WORKING WITH JSON FILES in Python is simple and efficient thanks to the json module. Whether you are reading, writing, or manipulating JSON data, Python provides a range of tools to make these tasks straightforward. By following best practices and leveraging Python's built-in functionalities, you can ensure that your programs handle JSON data effectively and efficiently.

Error Handling in File Operations

ERROR HANDLING IS A crucial aspect of working with files in Python. When dealing with files, numerous issues can arise, such as files not being found, lacking permissions to access a file, or encountering data corruption. Proper error handling ensures that your program can gracefully manage such issues without crashing unexpectedly.

Python provides robust mechanisms for handling exceptions that may occur during file operations. The core tool for this is the try-except block, which allows you to catch and respond to exceptions in a controlled manner. Additionally, Python offers several built-in exception types specific to file handling, such as FileNotFoundError, PermissionError, and IOError, which help in identifying and addressing different issues.

Understanding File-Related Exceptions

WHEN WORKING WITH FILES in Python, the following are some common exceptions you might encounter:

1. **FileNotFoundError**: Raised when a file or directory is requested but cannot be found.

2. **PermissionError**: Raised when attempting to open a file or directory without the required permissions.
3. **IOError**: Raised when an input/output operation fails, such as a failed read/write operation.
4. **IsADirectoryError**: Raised when a file operation (like reading) is attempted on a directory, instead of a file.
5. **NotADirectoryError**: Raised when an operation expecting a directory is performed on a file.

Using Try-Except for Error Handling

THE MOST COMMON WAY to handle file-related errors in Python is by using the try-except block. This allows you to attempt an operation and define a fallback action if an error occurs.

Example: Handling FileNotFoundError

TRY:

with open('nonexistent_file.txt', 'r') as file:

content = file.read()

except FileNotFoundError:

print("The file was not found. Please check the file path and try again.")

In this example, Python attempts to open a file named nonexistent_file.txt. Since the file does not exist, the FileNotFoundError exception is caught, and the program prints a helpful message instead of crashing.

Example: Handling Multiple Exceptions

SOMETIMES, MORE THAN one type of exception can occur during a file operation. In such cases, you can handle multiple exceptions using multiple except blocks.

```
try:

with open('restricted_file.txt', 'r') as file:

content = file.read()

except FileNotFoundError:

print("The file was not found.")

except PermissionError:

print("You do not have permission to read this file.")
```

Here, the program handles both FileNotFoundError and PermissionError. If the file does not exist, the appropriate error message is printed. If the file exists but the user lacks the necessary permissions, a different message is displayed.

Catching All Exceptions

IN SOME CASES, YOU may want to catch any kind of exception, regardless of its type. You can do this by using a generic except block. However, it's generally a better practice to catch specific exceptions to avoid masking unexpected issues.

Example: Catching All Exceptions

```
TRY:
```

with open('data.txt', 'r') as file:

content = file.read()

except Exception as e:

print(f"An error occurred: {e}")

In this example, any exception that occurs during the file operation is caught, and the error message is printed. The variable e contains the specific exception message, which helps in identifying the exact issue.

Finally: Ensuring Cleanup

IN SOME CASES, YOU may need to ensure that certain cleanup actions are performed, such as closing a file, regardless of whether an exception occurs. The finally block is used for this purpose. Code within the finally block is guaranteed to execute, even if an error occurs during the try block.

Example: Using Finally to Close a File

TRY:

file = open('data.txt', 'r')

content = file.read()

except FileNotFoundError:

print("The file was not found.")

finally:

file.close()

In this example, the file.close() method is called in the finally block to ensure the file is closed, even if an error occurs while reading the file. This ensures proper resource management.

The with Statement: Simplifying File Handling

WHILE THE FINALLY BLOCK is a good way to ensure that resources are cleaned up, Python provides a more convenient way to handle files using the with statement. The with statement automatically closes the file after the block of code is executed, even if an exception is raised. This makes it easier to write clean, safe code when dealing with files.

Example: Using the with Statement

```
TRY:

with open('data.txt', 'r') as file:

content = file.read()

except FileNotFoundError:

print("The file was not found.")
```

In this example, the file is automatically closed when the with block is exited, so there is no need to explicitly call file.close(). The with statement is the preferred method for working with files in Python because it reduces the likelihood of errors related to file management.

Common File Handling Errors and How to Handle Them

1. FileNotFoundError

THIS ERROR OCCURS WHEN you try to open a file that does not exist. It can be handled by providing the user with a message or prompting them to provide a correct file path.

```
try:

with open('non_existent_file.txt', 'r') as file:

content = file.read()

except FileNotFoundError:

print("File not found. Please check the file name and try again.")
```

2. PermissionError

THIS ERROR OCCURS WHEN you don't have the necessary permissions to access a file. It can be handled by notifying the user or attempting to change the file permissions (if possible).

```
try:

with open('/root/restricted_file.txt', 'r') as file:

content = file.read()

except PermissionError:

print("You do not have permission to access this file.")
```

3. IOError (or OSError)

THIS ERROR IS A MORE general exception related to input/output operations. It could occur when there's an issue with reading or writing a file, like running out of disk space or the file being corrupted.

```
try:

with open('corrupted_file.txt', 'r') as file:

content = file.read()

except IOError:

print("An I/O error occurred while reading the file.")
```

Handling Large Files

WHEN WORKING WITH LARGE files, it's essential to handle errors related to memory usage and ensure that file operations are efficient. Reading a large file all at once can consume a lot of memory and may cause your program to slow down or crash. To avoid this, you can read the file in chunks or process it line by line.

Example: Reading a Large File in Chunks

```
TRY:

with open('large_file.txt', 'r') as file:

while chunk := file.read(1024): # Read 1024 bytes at a time

print(chunk)

except FileNotFoundError:
```

```
print("The file was not found.")

except IOError:

print("An I/O error occurred.")
```

In this example, the file is read 1024 bytes at a time, which reduces the amount of memory used. If any file-related errors occur, they are handled appropriately.

Logging Errors for Debugging

WHEN HANDLING FILE errors, it can be helpful to log the errors for later debugging or auditing purposes. The logging module in Python allows you to log error messages, stack traces, and other information to a file or the console.

Example: Logging File Errors

```
IMPORT LOGGING

logging.basicConfig(filename='file_errors.log',
level=logging.ERROR)

try:

with open('data.txt', 'r') as file:

content = file.read()

except FileNotFoundError as e:

logging.error(f"FileNotFoundError: {e}")

except PermissionError as e:

logging.error(f"PermissionError: {e}")
```

```
except IOError as e:

logging.error(f"IOError: {e}")
```

In this example, any file-related errors are logged to the file_errors.log file. This is useful in production environments where you may need to review errors after the fact.

Custom Exception Handling

IN SOME CASES, YOU might want to raise custom exceptions during file operations. This can be helpful when you want to enforce specific business logic, such as checking the file format or size before processing it.

Example: Raising a Custom Exception

```
CLASS INVALIDFILETYPEERROR(Exception):

pass

def process_file(file_path):

if not file_path.endswith('.txt'):

raise InvalidFileTypeError("Only .txt files are allowed.")

with open(file_path, 'r') as file:

return file.read()

try:

content = process_file('data.json')

except InvalidFileTypeError as e:
```

print(e)

In this example, a custom exception InvalidFileTypeError is raised if the file being processed is not a .txt file. This approach allows you to enforce specific rules or constraints in your application.

Best Practices for Error Handling in File Operations

1. **Always Handle Specific Exceptions**: Catch specific exceptions like FileNotFoundError, PermissionError, or IOError instead of using a blanket except clause. This makes your code more predictable and easier to debug.
2. **Use the with Statement**: Always use the with statement when opening files to ensure they are properly closed after use. This prevents resource leaks and simplifies error handling.
3. **Log Errors**: Use the logging module to log errors instead of printing them. Logging provides more flexibility and control over how errors are captured and stored.
4. **Provide User-Friendly Error Messages**: When an error occurs, display a clear and informative message to the user, especially in production environments where users may not have technical expertise.
5. **Handle Large Files Efficiently**: When dealing with large files, read them in chunks or line by line to avoid excessive memory usage. This is particularly important for applications that process logs or large datasets.
6. **Implement Custom Exceptions When Necessary**: Custom exceptions allow you to define and enforce specific application-level constraints and behaviors during file operations.

Conclusion

ERROR HANDLING IS AN essential aspect of working with file operations in Python. By using try-except blocks, ensuring proper cleanup with finally or the with statement, and logging errors for future analysis, you can build robust file-handling systems. Whether you are working with small files or large datasets, proper error handling ensures that your program remains resilient in the face of unexpected issues.

Best Practices for Managing Files

MANAGING FILES EFFICIENTLY is essential when working on any software project. From handling input/output (I/O) operations to ensuring data integrity, file management plays a significant role in determining the performance and reliability of your application. Whether you are working with text, binary, or large data files, adhering to best practices ensures that your application runs smoothly, remains scalable, and avoids common pitfalls such as data loss, file corruption, and inefficient resource usage.

This section focuses on best practices for managing files in Python, covering key areas like file opening and closing, handling large files, security considerations, and performance optimization.

1. Using the with Statement for File Management

ONE OF THE MOST IMPORTANT practices when managing files is to ensure they are properly closed after use. Leaving files open can cause memory leaks, resource locks, and other system-level issues, especially when working with a large number of files.

The with statement provides a clean, reliable way to handle files. It automatically closes the file once the block of code is executed, even if an exception occurs.

Example: Using the with Statement to Read a File

```
WITH OPEN('EXAMPLE.txt', 'r') as file:

data = file.read()

print(data)
```

In this example, the with statement ensures that the file is closed after the reading operation is complete. This eliminates the need to explicitly call file.close(), reducing the risk of leaving files open unintentionally.

2. Choosing the Right File Mode

WHEN WORKING WITH FILES, it's important to select the correct file mode. Python provides several modes for reading, writing, and appending to files, and choosing the appropriate mode can impact file integrity and performance.

Here are the most commonly used file modes:

- 'r': Read mode. Opens the file for reading. The file must already exist; otherwise, a FileNotFoundError is raised.

- 'w': Write mode. Opens the file for writing. If the file exists, its content is truncated. If it doesn't exist, it is created.

- 'a': Append mode. Opens the file for appending. Data is written to the end of the file without truncating its existing content.

- 'rb' or 'wb': Binary mode for reading ('rb') or writing ('wb') non-text files, such as images or audio files.

Example: Writing to a File in Append Mode

WITH OPEN('LOGFILE.txt', 'a') as log:

log.write('New log entry: Application started\n')

In this example, the file logfile.txt is opened in append mode ('a'), meaning that any new content is added to the end of the file without overwriting existing data.

3. Handling Large Files Efficiently

WORKING WITH LARGE files presents unique challenges, such as memory consumption and processing speed. Reading or writing a large file all at once can consume excessive memory, potentially crashing the program or slowing down the system.

To handle large files efficiently, consider reading and writing them in chunks or processing them line by line.

Example: Reading a File Line by Line

WITH OPEN('LARGE_FILE.txt', 'r') as file:

for line in file:

process_line(line) # Process each line individually

This approach reads the file one line at a time, which is much more memory-efficient than loading the entire file into memory at once.

Example: Reading a File in Chunks

DEF READ_IN_CHUNKS(file_object, chunk_size=1024):

while True:

chunk = file_object.read(chunk_size)

if not chunk:

break

yield chunk

with open('large_file.txt', 'r') as file:

for chunk in read_in_chunks(file):

process_chunk(chunk) # Process each chunk separately

This method reads the file in chunks of 1024 bytes (or any specified chunk size), which helps manage memory consumption when dealing with large data files.

4. Managing File Paths and Cross-Platform Compatibility

WHEN DEALING WITH FILE paths, it's important to ensure cross-platform compatibility. File paths in Windows use backslashes (\), while Unix-based systems like macOS and Linux use forward slashes (/). Python's os module provides a way to manage file paths in a cross-platform manner using os.path or the pathlib module.

Example: Handling File Paths with os.path

IMPORT OS

file_path = os.path.join('folder', 'subfolder', 'file.txt')

with open(file_path, 'r') as file:

data = file.read()

In this example, os.path.join() creates a file path that works across different operating systems, ensuring that the path separator is correctly used based on the platform.

Example: Using pathlib for File Path Operations

FROM PATHLIB IMPORT Path

file_path = Path('folder') / 'subfolder' / 'file.txt'

with file_path.open('r') as file:

data = file.read()

The pathlib module is a modern approach to managing file paths, offering a cleaner syntax and additional features like checking file existence, creating directories, and more.

5. Security Considerations in File Handling

WHEN WORKING WITH FILES, it's important to ensure that your application is secure. Some common security concerns include unauthorized file access, overwriting critical system files, or processing malicious files uploaded by users.

Here are a few best practices to follow:

- **Validate File Inputs**: Always validate user inputs when dealing with file paths. Never blindly trust external inputs, as this could lead to path traversal attacks or other security vulnerabilities.

```
import os

user_input = '../../etc/passwd' # Malicious input

base_path = '/safe/directory'

file_path = os.path.join(base_path,
os.path.normpath(user_input))

if os.path.commonpath([base_path, file_path]) == base_path:

with open(file_path, 'r') as file:

data = file.read()

else:

print("Invalid file path!")
```

In this example, os.path.normpath() is used to sanitize the input file path, ensuring that malicious inputs like ../../ (which attempts to traverse directories) are normalized and prevented.

- **Set Correct File Permissions**: Ensure that files are only accessible to users or processes with the necessary permissions. On Unix-based systems, you can use os.chmod() to set the correct permissions.

```
import os

# Set file to be read-only for the owner, no permissions for others
```

```
os.chmod('data.txt', 0o400)
```

- **Avoid Writing to System Files**: When working with critical files (e.g., system configuration files), always check that the path does not point to a system file that could be accidentally overwritten.

6. Error Handling in File Operations

HANDLING ERRORS GRACEFULLY is essential when working with files. Common errors such as missing files, permission issues, and I/O failures should be anticipated and managed using exception handling techniques.

Example: Handling File Not Found and Permission Errors

```
TRY:

with open('important_file.txt', 'r') as file:

data = file.read()

except FileNotFoundError:

print("The file does not exist.")

except PermissionError:

print("You do not have permission to read this file.")

except Exception as e:

print(f"An unexpected error occurred: {e}")
```

In this example, different exceptions are caught and handled appropriately. FileNotFoundError handles cases where the file doesn't exist, while PermissionError deals with access issues. A generic except block is included to catch any other unexpected errors.

7. Managing Temporary Files

SOMETIMES, YOU NEED to create temporary files to store intermediate results or cache data. Python's tempfile module provides a secure and efficient way to create temporary files and directories. Temporary files are automatically deleted when they are no longer needed.

Example: Creating a Temporary File

```
IMPORT TEMPFILE

with tempfile.NamedTemporaryFile(delete=True) as temp_file:

temp_file.write(b'Some temporary data')

temp_file.seek(0)

print(temp_file.read())
```

In this example, a temporary file is created using tempfile.NamedTemporaryFile(). The file is deleted when the with block is exited, ensuring that no leftover files remain.

8. File Compression and Decompression

WHEN WORKING WITH LARGE files, it may be beneficial to compress them to save disk space and reduce file transfer times. Python's gzip and zipfile modules allow you to work with compressed files in various formats.

Example: Compressing and Decompressing a File with gzip

```
IMPORT GZIP

# Compressing a file

with open('data.txt', 'rb') as f_in:

with gzip.open('data.txt.gz', 'wb') as f_out:

f_out.writelines(f_in)

# Decompressing a file

with gzip.open('data.txt.gz', 'rb') as f_in:

with open('decompressed_data.txt', 'wb') as f_out:

f_out.write(f_in.read())
```

In this example, the file data.txt is compressed into a .gz format, and then decompressed back to its original form.

9. Performance Optimization in File Operations

WHEN WORKING WITH LARGE datasets or performing multiple file operations, performance optimization becomes essential. Here are some tips for optimizing file handling:

- **Buffered I/O**: Reading and writing files in large blocks (buffering) can significantly improve performance compared to line-by-line processing.
- **Asynchronous File Operations**: For I/O-bound applications, consider using asynchronous file operations with asyncio or multithreading to speed up file processing without blocking the main thread.

- **Caching**: If you need to access the same file repeatedly, consider caching the file contents in memory to avoid repeated disk reads.

Example: Using Buffered I/O for Performance

```
WITH OPEN('LARGE_FILE.txt', 'r', buffering=8192) as file:

while chunk := file.read(8192):

process_chunk(chunk)
```

In this example, the file is read in 8192-byte chunks, which reduces the number of I/O operations and improves performance.

Conclusion

MANAGING FILES EFFECTIVELY in Python involves much more than simply reading and writing data. By following best practices such as using the with statement, choosing the correct file modes, handling errors gracefully, and optimizing for performance, you can ensure that your file-handling operations are efficient, secure, and scalable. Proper file management not only improves the performance of your application but also enhances its reliability and user experience.

Chapter 7: Object-Oriented Programming (OOP) in Python

Classes and Objects: Core Concepts

OBJECT-ORIENTED PROGRAMMING (OOP) is one of the most important paradigms in Python and is widely used in both small and large projects. It allows developers to model real-world entities as objects and their behaviors through classes. Understanding the core concepts of classes and objects is essential to leveraging the full power of Python in an organized and scalable manner.

What Is OOP?

OBJECT-ORIENTED PROGRAMMING is a way of organizing and structuring code by treating data and behavior as entities. In OOP, data is represented by objects, and behaviors are encapsulated in functions called methods, all of which are defined within a class. OOP focuses on the following fundamental principles:

1. **Encapsulation**: Grouping data (attributes) and functions (methods) that operate on the data within a class. This makes the internal workings of objects hidden from the outside, protecting the data from accidental modifications.
2. **Abstraction**: Simplifying complex systems by modeling real-world objects. Abstraction hides the complexities of how objects interact while exposing essential functionality to the user.
3. **Inheritance**: Creating new classes based on existing

classes to reuse code and extend functionality. This allows a subclass to inherit methods and properties from a parent class.

4. **Polymorphism**: Defining methods in such a way that they can be used interchangeably with objects of different classes. It allows different types of objects to be treated as instances of a common superclass.

Let's start by looking at how classes and objects fit into the OOP paradigm.

Defining a Class

A CLASS IN PYTHON IS a blueprint for creating objects. It defines the properties and behaviors (attributes and methods) that objects created from the class will have. The class keyword is used to define a class.

Here's an example of a simple class called Car:

```
class Car:

# Constructor to initialize attributes

def __init__(self, make, model, year):

self.make = make

self.model = model

self.year = year

# Method to display car details

def display_info(self):

print(f"This car is a {self.year} {self.make} {self.model}.")
```

In the above example, the class Car has three attributes: make, model, and year. It also has one method display_info, which prints the car details.

Creating an Object

AN OBJECT IS AN INSTANCE of a class. Once a class is defined, you can create multiple objects from it. Each object represents an individual instance of the class, with its own attributes and behaviors.

Here's how you can create an object of the Car class:

my_car = Car("Toyota", "Corolla", 2020)

In this example, my_car is an object of the Car class. You can now access its attributes and call its methods.

my_car.display_info() # Output: This car is a 2020 Toyota Corolla.

The __init__ Method (Constructor)

THE __INIT__ METHOD is a special method in Python classes known as a constructor. It is called automatically when an object is created, and it is used to initialize the attributes of the class.

In the previous example, __init__ takes three parameters—make, model, and year—and assigns them to the object's attributes.

Here's a slightly more complex example that adds more functionality:

class Car:

def __init__(self, make, model, year, fuel_type):

self.make = make

self.model = model

self.year = year

self.fuel_type = fuel_type

self.mileage = 0 # Setting a default attribute

def drive(self, distance):

self.mileage += distance

print(f"Driving {distance} miles. Total mileage is now {self.mileage} miles.")

def display_info(self):

print(f"This car is a {self.year} {self.make} {self.model}, and it runs on {self.fuel_type}.")

MY_CAR = CAR("HONDA", "Civic", 2022, "Petrol")

my_car.display_info() # Output: This car is a 2022 Honda Civic, and it runs on Petrol.

my_car.drive(100) # Output: Driving 100 miles. Total mileage is now 100 miles.

Attributes and Methods

- **Attributes**: These are variables that hold data specific to an object. In our example, make, model, year, and fuel_type are attributes.

- **Methods**: Functions defined inside a class that describe the behaviors of an object. For example, display_info and drive are methods that define the actions that a Car object can perform.

YOU CAN ACCESS OR MODIFY attributes directly using dot notation:

print(my_car.mileage) # Output: 100

my_car.mileage = 150 # Changing the mileage directly

print(my_car.mileage) # Output: 150

Class and Instance Variables

- **Instance Variables**: These are unique to each object. In the Car class, make, model, year, and mileage are instance variables, which means each object of the class can have different values for these attributes.

- **Class Variables**: These are shared across all instances of a class. You define class variables directly inside the class but outside of any methods. For example:

CLASS CAR:

wheels = 4 # This is a class variable

def __init__(self, make, model, year):

self.make = make

self.model = model

self.year = year

All Car objects share the class variable 'wheels'

```
car1 = Car("Ford", "Fiesta", 2019)

car2 = Car("Tesla", "Model S", 2023)

print(car1.wheels) # Output: 4

print(car2.wheels) # Output: 4
```

Encapsulation

ENCAPSULATION REFERS to bundling the data (attributes) and methods that operate on the data within a class and restricting access to some of the object's components. This is done by making attributes or methods private using underscores (_ or __).

For example:

```
class Car:

def __init__(self, make, model, year):

self.make = make

self.model = model

self.__year = year # Private attribute

def display_info(self):

print(f"This car is a {self.__year} {self.make} {self.model}.")
```

Here, the year attribute is private and cannot be accessed directly:

```
my_car = Car("BMW", "X5", 2021)

my_car.__year # This will raise an AttributeError
```

However, you can still access the private attribute using a method:

```
my_car.display_info() # Output: This car is a 2021 BMW X5.
```

Encapsulation ensures that data is safe from unintended or malicious modification.

Getters and Setters

TO ACCESS PRIVATE ATTRIBUTES safely, Python uses getter and setter methods. A getter retrieves the value of a private attribute, while a setter updates its value.

Here's how you can define them:

```
class Car:

def __init__(self, make, model, year):

self.make = make

self.model = model

self.__year = year # Private attribute

def get_year(self):

return self.__year # Getter method

def set_year(self, year):

if year > 1885: # Simple validation

self.__year = year

else:

print("Invalid year.")
```

You can now safely get and set the year attribute:

```
my_car = Car("Chevy", "Impala", 1967)

print(my_car.get_year()) # Output: 1967

my_car.set_year(2020) # Changing the year to 2020

print(my_car.get_year()) # Output: 2020
```

Getters and setters are a key part of encapsulation, allowing controlled access to an object's attributes.

Conclusion

CLASSES AND OBJECTS are the building blocks of object-oriented programming in Python. By defining a class, you create a template from which objects can be made. These objects have attributes that store data and methods that define their behavior. Key principles like encapsulation, class variables, and instance variables play a vital role in organizing and structuring your code.

With a solid understanding of classes, you can move on to more advanced topics like inheritance, polymorphism, and design patterns that will enhance your ability to write clean, scalable, and efficient Python programs.

Constructors and Destructors

CONSTRUCTORS AND DESTRUCTORS are integral parts of object-oriented programming in Python. They provide a mechanism for initializing and cleaning up objects. Understanding how constructors and destructors work is crucial for writing efficient, well-structured code. This section explores these concepts in depth and demonstrates their significance in the context of object creation and memory management.

Constructors

A CONSTRUCTOR IS A special type of method in a class that gets called automatically whenever a new object is created. In Python, the constructor is implemented using the __init__ method. This method is used to initialize the object's attributes and perform any setup actions necessary when the object is instantiated.

The __init__ Method

THE __INIT__ METHOD is called immediately after the object is created. It allows you to define and initialize the attributes that will be associated with the object. It can accept parameters, allowing different objects to be initialized with different values.

Let's look at an example:

```
class Person:

def __init__(self, name, age):

# Instance variables

self.name = name

self.age = age

def introduce(self):

print(f"Hello, my name is {self.name} and I am {self.age} years old.")

# Creating an object of the Person class

person1 = Person("Alice", 30)
```

person1.introduce() # Output: Hello, my name is Alice and I am 30 years old.

In this example, the __init__ method accepts two parameters (name and age) and assigns them to the object's attributes. Every time a new Person object is created, these attributes are initialized through the constructor.

Default Values in the Constructor

IT IS POSSIBLE TO ASSIGN default values to the parameters of the __init__ method. This allows you to create objects without having to provide all the arguments:

```
class Car:

def __init__(self, make, model, year=2020):

self.make = make

self.model = model

self.year = year

def car_info(self):

print(f"This car is a {self.year} {self.make} {self.model}.")

# Creating an object with the default year

car1 = Car("Toyota", "Corolla")

car1.car_info() # Output: This car is a 2020 Toyota Corolla.

# Creating an object with a specified year

car2 = Car("Honda", "Civic", 2022)
```

car2.car_info() # Output: This car is a 2022 Honda Civic.

In the above example, the year parameter has a default value of 2020. When creating a Car object, you can omit the year argument, and the default value will be used.

Constructor Overloading

PYTHON DOES NOT SUPPORT constructor overloading in the traditional sense (like other programming languages such as Java or C++), but you can achieve similar behavior by using default arguments or by checking the number of arguments passed.

Here's an example of how you can simulate constructor overloading:

```
class Rectangle:

def __init__(self, length=0, width=0):

if length == 0 and width == 0:

self.length = 1

self.width = 1 # Default values for both length and width

else:

self.length = length

self.width = width

def area(self):

return self.length * self.width

# Creating rectangles with different sets of parameters
```

```
rect1 = Rectangle()
print(f"Area of default rectangle: {rect1.area()}") # Output: 1
rect2 = Rectangle(5, 10)
print(f"Area of 5x10 rectangle: {rect2.area()}") # Output: 50
```

In this case, depending on the parameters passed, the constructor behaves differently. It assigns default values if no parameters are provided, simulating constructor overloading.

Destructors

DESTRUCTORS IN PYTHON are used for clean-up operations before an object is destroyed. A destructor is defined by the __del__ method, which is called when an object is about to be destroyed, either when it goes out of scope or when the program terminates.

Unlike constructors, destructors are less commonly used in Python due to Python's built-in garbage collection mechanism, which automatically manages memory. However, destructors can be useful in situations where explicit clean-up actions are required, such as closing database connections or releasing file handles.

The __del__ Method

THE __DEL__ METHOD is automatically invoked when an object is no longer needed. Here's an example of how destructors work:

```
class FileHandler:
def __init__(self, filename):
```

```
self.file = open(filename, 'w')

print(f"File {filename} opened.")

def write_data(self, data):

self.file.write(data)

def __del__(self):

self.file.close()

print("File closed.")

# Creating an object of the FileHandler class

file_handler = FileHandler('test.txt')

file_handler.write_data('Hello, world!')

# Destructor will be called when file_handler goes out of scope or program ends
```

In this example, the FileHandler class opens a file in the constructor and writes data to it. When the object is destroyed (either when the program ends or when the object goes out of scope), the destructor (__del__) is called, which closes the file.

Explicit Object Deletion

WHILE PYTHON HANDLES memory management automatically, you can explicitly delete objects using the del statement. When del is used, the object is immediately destroyed, and the __del__ method is called:

```
class Sample:
```

```
def __init__(self):
print("Object created.")
def __del__(self):
print("Object destroyed.")
# Creating and deleting an object
obj = Sample()
del obj # Output: Object destroyed.
```

In the above code, when the del statement is executed, the destructor is invoked, and the object is destroyed.

Resource Management with Destructors

DESTRUCTORS CAN BE used to manage resources, such as database connections, network sockets, or files. However, because Python has built-in garbage collection, it's often more efficient to use context managers (with statements) for managing resources.

Here's an example of how destructors can be used for resource management:

```
class DatabaseConnection:
def __init__(self, db_name):
self.db_name = db_name
print(f"Connecting to database {db_name}...")
self.connection = None # Simulated connection
def open_connection(self):
```

```
self.connection = True

print(f"Connection to {self.db_name} opened.")

def __del__(self):

if self.connection:

print(f"Closing connection to {self.db_name}...")

self.connection = False

# Creating a DatabaseConnection object

db = DatabaseConnection('my_database')

db.open_connection()

# Destructor will close the connection when the object is destroyed
```

In this example, the connection to the database is opened in the constructor, and when the object is destroyed, the destructor ensures the connection is closed.

Destructors vs Context Managers

ALTHOUGH DESTRUCTORS are useful, they are not the most reliable way to manage resources like files or network connections in Python because they are not guaranteed to be called when expected (e.g., in cases of unexpected termination). For better resource management, Python provides context managers (with statement), which handle resources more explicitly.

Here's an example of using a context manager instead of a destructor:

```
# Using a context manager for file handling
```

```
with open('test.txt', 'w') as file:
file.write('Hello, world!')
# The file is automatically closed when the with block is exited
```

In this case, when the with block is exited, the file is automatically closed, ensuring proper resource management. Context managers are the preferred method in Python for handling resources.

The super() Function and Constructors in Inheritance

WHEN DEALING WITH INHERITANCE, constructors can become more complex. The super() function is used to call the constructor of the parent class in child classes. This allows the child class to inherit and initialize the attributes and methods of the parent class while adding its own functionality.

Here's an example:

```
class Animal:
def __init__(self, species):
self.species = species
print(f"{species} is an animal.")
class Dog(Animal):
def __init__(self, breed):
super().__init__('Dog')
self.breed = breed
def bark(self):
```

```
print(f"The {self.breed} is barking.")

# Creating a Dog object

my_dog = Dog('Golden Retriever')

my_dog.bark() # Output: The Golden Retriever is barking.
```

In this example, the Dog class calls the constructor of the Animal class using super(), ensuring that the species attribute is initialized.

Conclusion

CONSTRUCTORS AND DESTRUCTORS are essential components of object-oriented programming in Python. The constructor (__init__) is used to initialize an object's attributes and ensure that it is set up properly. Destructors (__del__), while less commonly used, provide a way to clean up resources when an object is no longer needed.

Although destructors are useful in certain scenarios, Python's garbage collection and context managers offer more reliable and efficient ways to manage resources. Nonetheless, understanding constructors and destructors is fundamental to writing robust, object-oriented code.

In more complex inheritance scenarios, constructors can be combined with the super() function to ensure proper initialization of both parent and child classes. By mastering these concepts, you can create well-structured and efficient Python programs that make the most of object-oriented principles.

Inheritance: Reusing Code Efficiently

INHERITANCE IS ONE of the four pillars of Object-Oriented Programming (OOP), alongside encapsulation, abstraction, and polymorphism. It allows a new class (called a subclass or child class) to inherit the attributes and methods of an existing class (called a superclass or parent class). By leveraging inheritance, you can reuse code, avoid redundancy, and extend the functionality of an existing class without modifying it.

Inheritance encourages the design of a hierarchical structure in programming, where child classes can extend or override the behavior of their parent classes. This section covers the core concepts of inheritance, various types of inheritance in Python, method overriding, and the best practices for using inheritance effectively.

The Basics of Inheritance

IN PYTHON, INHERITANCE is implemented by passing the parent class as a parameter to the child class when defining it. The child class inherits all the attributes and methods of the parent class. Here's a simple example of inheritance:

```
class Animal:

def __init__(self, name):

self.name = name

def speak(self):

print(f"{self.name} makes a sound.")

# Child class inheriting from Animal
```

```
class Dog(Animal):

def __init__(self, name, breed):

super().__init__(name) # Call the parent class constructor

self.breed = breed

def speak(self):

print(f"{self.name}, the {self.breed}, barks.")

# Creating objects of the child class

dog = Dog("Rex", "Golden Retriever")

dog.speak() # Output: Rex, the Golden Retriever, barks.
```

In this example, the Dog class inherits from the Animal class. The Dog class adds a new attribute (breed) and overrides the speak method to provide its own implementation, while still inheriting the core functionality of the Animal class.

Types of Inheritance

PYTHON SUPPORTS DIFFERENT types of inheritance, each offering flexibility in how you design your class hierarchies. The main types of inheritance are:

1. **Single Inheritance**: A child class inherits from only one parent class.
2. **Multiple Inheritance**: A child class inherits from more than one parent class.
3. **Multilevel Inheritance**: A child class inherits from a parent class, which itself inherits from another parent class.

4. **Hierarchical Inheritance**: Multiple child classes inherit from the same parent class.
5. **Hybrid Inheritance**: A combination of more than one type of inheritance.

Single Inheritance

SINGLE INHERITANCE is the simplest form of inheritance, where a child class derives from a single parent class. Here's an example:

```
class Vehicle:

def __init__(self, make, model):

self.make = make

self.model = model

def display_info(self):

print(f"Vehicle Make: {self.make}, Model: {self.model}")

class Car(Vehicle):

def __init__(self, make, model, doors):

super().__init__(make, model)

self.doors = doors

def car_info(self):

print(f"Car: {self.make} {self.model}, Doors: {self.doors}")

# Creating an object of the Car class

car = Car("Toyota", "Camry", 4)
```

car.display_info() # Output: Vehicle Make: Toyota, Model: Camry

car.car_info() # Output: Car: Toyota Camry, Doors: 4

In this example, the Car class inherits from the Vehicle class. It reuses the display_info method of the Vehicle class and adds its own car_info method. This is a classic case of single inheritance.

Multiple Inheritance

MULTIPLE INHERITANCE allows a class to inherit from more than one parent class. This can be powerful, but it also introduces complexity, especially when the parent classes have methods with the same name (this is where the method resolution order, or MRO, comes into play). Here's an example:

```
class Engine:

def __init__(self, horsepower):

self.horsepower = horsepower

def start_engine(self):

print(f"Engine with {self.horsepower} horsepower started.")

class Wheels:

def __init__(self, wheel_count):

self.wheel_count = wheel_count

def roll(self):

print(f"Vehicle is rolling on {self.wheel_count} wheels.")

class Car(Engine, Wheels):
```

```
def __init__(self, horsepower, wheel_count, make, model):

Engine.__init__(self, horsepower)

Wheels.__init__(self, wheel_count)

self.make = make

self.model = model

def display_info(self):

print(f"Car Make: {self.make}, Model: {self.model}, Horsepower: {self.horsepower}, Wheels: {self.wheel_count}")

# Creating an object of the Car class

car = Car(150, 4, "Honda", "Civic")

car.display_info() # Output: Car Make: Honda, Model: Civic, Horsepower: 150, Wheels: 4

car.start_engine() # Output: Engine with 150 horsepower started.

car.roll() # Output: Vehicle is rolling on 4 wheels.
```

In this example, the Car class inherits from both Engine and Wheels. It combines the functionality of both parent classes and extends it with its own attributes and methods. While multiple inheritance is flexible, care must be taken to avoid conflicts between parent classes.

Multilevel Inheritance

IN MULTILEVEL INHERITANCE, a class is derived from another class, which is itself derived from another class. This creates a chain of inheritance, where each level inherits the properties and methods of the level above. Here's an example:

```
class LivingBeing:

def breathe(self):

print("Breathing...")

class Animal(LivingBeing):

def walk(self):

print("Walking on four legs...")

class Dog(Animal):

def bark(self):

print("Barking...")

# Creating an object of the Dog class

dog = Dog()

dog.breathe() # Output: Breathing...

dog.walk() # Output: Walking on four legs...

dog.bark() # Output: Barking...
```

In this example, Dog is a subclass of Animal, and Animal is a subclass of LivingBeing. The Dog class inherits the behaviors of both the Animal and LivingBeing classes, showcasing how inheritance chains work in multilevel inheritance.

Hierarchical Inheritance

HIERARCHICAL INHERITANCE occurs when multiple child classes inherit from the same parent class. Each child class has its own unique behaviors but shares common attributes or methods from the parent class. Here's an example:

```
class Shape:

def __init__(self, color):

self.color = color

def display_color(self):

print(f"The shape is {self.color}.")

class Circle(Shape):

def area(self, radius):

return 3.1416 * radius ** 2

class Square(Shape):

def area(self, side):

return side ** 2

# Creating objects of the Circle and Square classes

circle = Circle("red")

square = Square("blue")

circle.display_color() # Output: The shape is red.
```

print(f"Circle Area: {circle.area(5)}") # Output: Circle Area: 78.54

square.display_color() # Output: The shape is blue.

print(f"Square Area: {square.area(4)}") # Output: Square Area: 16

In this example, both Circle and Square inherit from the Shape class. They share the display_color method but have their own unique area methods.

Hybrid Inheritance

HYBRID INHERITANCE is a combination of more than one type of inheritance. It allows for complex hierarchies and is used in situations where multiple inheritance types are required to fulfill design needs. Here's an example that combines multilevel and multiple inheritance:

class Animal:

def speak(self):

print("Animal makes a sound.")

class Bird(Animal):

def fly(self):

print("Bird is flying.")

class Parrot(Bird):

def talk(self):

print("Parrot is talking.")

class Dog(Animal):

def bark(self):

print("Dog is barking.")

Parrot inherits from Bird, which in turn inherits from Animal (Multilevel)

parrot = Parrot()

parrot.speak() # Output: Animal makes a sound.

parrot.fly() # Output: Bird is flying.

parrot.talk() # Output: Parrot is talking.

Dog inherits from Animal (Single Inheritance)

dog = Dog()

dog.speak() # Output: Animal makes a sound.

dog.bark() # Output: Dog is barking.

In this example, Parrot inherits from Bird, which inherits from Animal, showing multilevel inheritance, while Dog inherits directly from Animal, demonstrating single inheritance.

Method Overriding

METHOD OVERRIDING IS a feature in object-oriented programming where a subclass provides a specific implementation of a method that is already defined in its parent class. Overriding allows the child class to modify or extend the behavior of the parent class.

To override a method, simply define a method with the same name in the child class. Here's an example:

```
class Parent:

def introduce(self):

print("I am the parent.")

class Child(Parent):

def introduce(self):

print("I am the child.")

# Creating objects of Parent and Child classes

parent = Parent()

child = Child()

parent.introduce() # Output: I am the parent.

child.introduce() # Output: I am the child.
```

In this example, the Child class overrides the introduce method of the Parent class. When the method is called on a Child object, the overridden method in the child class is executed.

The super() Function in Method Overriding

WHEN A CHILD CLASS overrides a method, there are cases where you might want to still call the parent class's version of the method in addition to the child class's implementation. This is done using the super() function, which allows you to call methods from the parent class.

Here's an example:

```
class Person:

def introduce(self):

print("Hello, I am a person.")

class Student(Person):

def introduce(self):

super().introduce() # Call the parent class method

print("I am also a student.")

# Creating an object of the Student class

student = Student()

student.introduce()

# Output:

# Hello, I am a person.

# I am also a student.
```

In this example, the Student class overrides the introduce method but still calls the introduce method of the Person class using super(). This allows for both the parent class and child class methods to be executed.

Conclusion

INHERITANCE IS A POWERFUL feature of object-oriented programming that allows for efficient code reuse and the creation of more complex class hierarchies. By using inheritance, you can avoid code duplication and create relationships between classes that model real-world scenarios. Understanding the different types of inheritance, method overriding, and the role of the super() function will help you write more organized, maintainable, and scalable Python programs.

Inheritance is not just about reusing code but about building a logical, extensible structure that reflects the relationships between different objects in your application. By mastering inheritance, you will be better equipped to tackle complex programming challenges and design more elegant software systems.

Polymorphism and Encapsulation

POLYMORPHISM AND ENCAPSULATION are two foundational principles of Object-Oriented Programming (OOP). These concepts provide flexibility, abstraction, and security in how data is managed and how objects interact within a program. While they are often used in conjunction with other OOP principles like inheritance, each plays a specific role in how object-oriented systems are designed and executed.

Polymorphism

POLYMORPHISM ALLOWS objects of different types to be treated as objects of a common supertype. It is the ability of a function or a method to process objects differently based on their type or class. In Python, polymorphism allows functions and methods to operate on objects of different classes that share a common interface, without knowing the exact type of the object.

Polymorphism in Python is achieved primarily through two mechanisms:

1. **Method Overriding**: Inheritance allows child classes to override methods of the parent class, enabling

polymorphic behavior.

2. **Duck Typing**: Python's dynamic typing system supports polymorphism by allowing objects of different types to be passed to a function, as long as they support the same interface (method names and signatures).

Method Overriding and Polymorphism

METHOD OVERRIDING IS one of the most common ways polymorphism is implemented in object-oriented languages. When a child class provides a specific implementation of a method that is already defined in its parent class, polymorphism allows the method to behave differently depending on the object it is called on.

Here's an example demonstrating polymorphism using method overriding:

```
class Animal:

def speak(self):

print("The animal makes a sound.")

class Dog(Animal):

def speak(self):

print("The dog barks.")

class Cat(Animal):

def speak(self):

print("The cat meows.")
```

```
# Function demonstrating polymorphism
def animal_sound(animal):
animal.speak()
# Passing different objects to the same function
dog = Dog()
cat = Cat()
animal_sound(dog) # Output: The dog barks.
animal_sound(cat) # Output: The cat meows.
```

In this example, the animal_sound function accepts any object that inherits from the Animal class. The function calls the speak method on the object passed to it, but because the Dog and Cat classes have overridden the speak method, the behavior changes depending on the type of the object. This is polymorphism in action—one interface (speak) but different underlying implementations depending on the object type.

Duck Typing in Python

DUCK TYPING IS AN INFORMAL approach to polymorphism in Python. The name comes from the saying: "If it looks like a duck and quacks like a duck, it probably is a duck." Python's dynamic typing system allows you to pass objects to a function without concern for their type, as long as they support the expected methods.

Here's an example of duck typing:

```
class Duck:
```

```
def sound(self):

print("Quack!")

class Car:

def sound(self):

print("Vroom!")

# Function demonstrating duck typing

def make_sound(obj):

obj.sound()

duck = Duck()

car = Car()

make_sound(duck) # Output: Quack!

make_sound(car) # Output: Vroom!
```

In this case, the make_sound function doesn't care whether the object passed to it is a Duck or a Car; it only cares that the object has a sound method. Both objects provide a sound method, so the function works for both types.

Polymorphism with Built-In Functions

POLYMORPHISM IS NOT limited to custom classes. Many built-in functions in Python, like len, max, and min, demonstrate polymorphic behavior by working on different types of data.

Here's an example:

```
print(len("Hello")) # Output: 5
```

print(len([1, 2, 3, 4])) # Output: 4

print(len({"name": "Alice", "age": 30})) # Output: 2

In this example, the len function works on a string, a list, and a dictionary, all of which are different data types. This is a form of polymorphism where the same function can operate on different types of objects.

Encapsulation

ENCAPSULATION IS THE OOP principle that restricts access to certain components of an object, making some of its attributes and methods private, while exposing others publicly. This helps prevent accidental or unauthorized modification of data and ensures that an object maintains control over its own state.

In Python, encapsulation is achieved through naming conventions and access control for attributes and methods. While Python does not enforce strict access control (as some languages like Java do), it follows a philosophy of "we are all consenting adults," meaning that access restrictions are more of a convention than a hard rule.

Public, Protected, and Private Attributes

PYTHON USES NAMING conventions to indicate the visibility and access level of attributes and methods:

- **Public Attributes**: Attributes that are accessible from outside the class. They are defined without any leading underscores.

- **Protected Attributes**: Attributes intended to be accessed only within the class and its subclasses. They are indicated by a single leading underscore (_).

- **Private Attributes**: Attributes intended to be accessed only within the class itself. They are indicated by a double leading underscore (__).

Here's an example:

```
class Person:

def __init__(self, name, age):

self.name = name # Public attribute

self._age = age # Protected attribute

self.__ssn = "123-45-6789" # Private attribute

def display_info(self):

print(f"Name: {self.name}, Age: {self._age}, SSN: {self.__ssn}")

person = Person("Alice", 30)

# Accessing public and protected attributes

print(person.name) # Output: Alice

print(person._age) # Output: 30

# Attempting to access a private attribute directly will result in an error

# print(person.__ssn) # AttributeError

# However, the private attribute can still be accessed indirectly
```

person.display_info() # Output: Name: Alice, Age: 30, SSN: 123-45-6789

In this example, the name attribute is public and can be accessed from outside the class, while the _age attribute is protected and can also be accessed from outside, although it is intended to be used only by the class or its subclasses. The __ssn attribute is private and cannot be accessed directly outside the class.

Getters and Setters

TO PROVIDE CONTROLLED access to private attributes, Python uses getter and setter methods. A getter retrieves the value of an attribute, while a setter updates the attribute's value, often with validation.

Here's how getters and setters work:

```
class BankAccount:

def __init__(self, balance):

self.__balance = balance # Private attribute

# Getter method

def get_balance(self):

return self.__balance

# Setter method

def set_balance(self, amount):

if amount >= 0:

self.__balance = amount
```

```
else:
print("Invalid amount. Balance cannot be negative.")
# Creating an object of BankAccount
account = BankAccount(1000)
# Using the getter method to access the private attribute
print(account.get_balance()) # Output: 1000
# Using the setter method to update the private attribute
account.set_balance(500)
print(account.get_balance()) # Output: 500
# Attempting to set a negative balance
account.set_balance(-100) # Output: Invalid amount. Balance cannot be negative.
```

In this example, the __balance attribute is private, and direct access to it is restricted. Instead, the getter and setter methods are used to retrieve and update the balance. The setter also includes validation to prevent the balance from being set to a negative value.

Name Mangling in Python

PYTHON USES A TECHNIQUE called name mangling to make private attributes less accessible. When an attribute name is prefixed with a double underscore (__), Python changes its name internally to include the class name. This makes it harder to accidentally override or access private attributes, although they can still be accessed through special syntax.

Here's an example:

```
class Employee:
def __init__(self, name, salary):
self.name = name
self.__salary = salary # Private attribute
def display_salary(self):
print(f"Salary: {self.__salary}")
employee = Employee("John", 50000)
# Attempting to access the private attribute directly will result in an error
# print(employee.__salary) # AttributeError
# Accessing the private attribute using name mangling
print(employee._Employee__salary) # Output: 50000
```

In this example, Python internally renames the __salary attribute to _Employee__salary, which makes it less likely to be accidentally accessed. While this doesn't provide absolute protection, it serves as a deterrent against unintentional access.

Encapsulation and Polymorphism in Practice

ENCAPSULATION AND POLYMORPHISM often work together in real-world applications. Encapsulation ensures that objects manage their own state and provide a controlled interface for interaction, while polymorphism allows these objects to be used interchangeably in functions or methods that expect certain behaviors.

Here's an example that combines encapsulation and polymorphism:

```
class Shape:

def __init__(self, color):

self._color = color # Protected attribute

def get_color(self):

return self._color

def area(self):

raise NotImplementedError("Subclasses must implement this method.")

class Circle(Shape):

def __init__(self, radius, color):

super().__init__(color)

self._radius = radius # Protected attribute

def area(self):

return 3.1416 * self._radius ** 2

class Rectangle(Shape):

def __init__(self, width, height, color):

super().__init__(color)
```

```
self._width = width
self._height = height
def area(self):
return self._width * self._height
# Polymorphic function to calculate area
def calculate_area(shape):
print(f"The area of the shape is {shape.area()} square units.")
# Creating different shapes
circle = Circle(5, "red")
rectangle = Rectangle(4, 6, "blue")
# Calculating the area of different shapes
calculate_area(circle) # Output: The area of the shape is 78.54 square units.
calculate_area(rectangle) # Output: The area of the shape is 24 square units.
```

In this example, encapsulation is used to protect the attributes of the Shape, Circle, and Rectangle classes. The polymorphic calculate_area function can accept any object that inherits from Shape, and the actual implementation of the area method is determined by the specific subclass (Circle or Rectangle).

Conclusion

POLYMORPHISM AND ENCAPSULATION are key concepts in object-oriented programming that allow for flexible, maintainable, and secure code. Polymorphism enables the same function or method to operate on different types of objects, providing versatility and reusability in your code. Encapsulation ensures that the internal state of an object is protected and can only be accessed or modified in controlled ways, improving data security and reducing the risk of unintended side effects.

Together, these principles empower you to design robust object-oriented systems where objects can interact seamlessly while maintaining the integrity and security of their internal states. Mastering these concepts is essential for writing clean, efficient, and scalable Python programs.

Advanced OOP Concepts: Abstract Classes and Multiple Inheritance

ADVANCED OBJECT-ORIENTED Programming (OOP) in Python builds on core principles like inheritance, polymorphism, and encapsulation. Two critical concepts at the advanced level are abstract classes and multiple inheritance. These concepts offer flexibility, modularity, and extensibility in software design, allowing developers to create highly reusable, scalable, and maintainable systems. In this section, we will explore these advanced concepts, their significance, and practical use in building sophisticated Python applications.

Abstract Classes

AN ABSTRACT CLASS IS a blueprint for other classes. It cannot be instantiated directly, and its purpose is to define a common interface for subclasses. Abstract classes can include abstract methods, which are methods that must be implemented by any class that inherits from the abstract class. They can also include concrete methods, which are fully implemented and can be used by subclasses.

Abstract classes are particularly useful when defining classes that share a common interface but differ in their specific implementations. By enforcing that certain methods must be implemented in child classes, you ensure that subclasses adhere to a consistent structure.

Using the abc Module

IN PYTHON, ABSTRACT classes are created using the abc (Abstract Base Class) module. The ABC class in this module serves as the base class for all abstract classes, and the @abstractmethod decorator is used to define abstract methods.

Here's an example of an abstract class:

```
from abc import ABC, abstractmethod

class Shape(ABC):

@abstractmethod

def area(self):

pass

@abstractmethod

def perimeter(self):

pass
```

In this example, the Shape class is an abstract class because it inherits from ABC. The methods area and perimeter are abstract methods, meaning any subclass that inherits from Shape must implement these methods.

Concrete Subclasses

ONCE YOU'VE DEFINED an abstract class, you can create concrete subclasses that inherit from it and implement its abstract methods. Here's an example:

```
class Rectangle(Shape):

def __init__(self, width, height):

self.width = width

self.height = height

def area(self):

return self.width * self.height

def perimeter(self):

return 2 * (self.width + self.height)

class Circle(Shape):

def __init__(self, radius):

self.radius = radius

def area(self):

return 3.1416 * self.radius ** 2

def perimeter(self):

return 2 * 3.1416 * self.radius
```

In this example, Rectangle and Circle are concrete classes that inherit from the abstract class Shape. Both subclasses implement the area and perimeter methods as required by the abstract class.

Attempting to Instantiate an Abstract Class

BECAUSE ABSTRACT CLASSES are meant to serve as blueprints, they cannot be instantiated directly. If you attempt to create an instance of an abstract class, Python will raise a TypeError:

```
shape = Shape() # This will raise a TypeError
```

This error ensures that the abstract class is used only as a base class for other classes, and not as a standalone class.

Benefits of Abstract Classes

ABSTRACT CLASSES PROVIDE several benefits in Python programming:

1. **Code Reusability**: Abstract classes allow you to define common behavior in one place and reuse it across multiple subclasses.
2. **Consistency**: By enforcing the implementation of specific methods, abstract classes ensure that all subclasses provide the required functionality.
3. **Polymorphism**: Abstract classes promote polymorphism by allowing objects of different types to be treated uniformly as long as they share a common interface.

Here's an example of using polymorphism with abstract classes:

```
def display_shape_info(shape):
```

print(f"Area: {shape.area()}, Perimeter: {shape.perimeter()}")

rectangle = Rectangle(5, 10)

circle = Circle(7)

display_shape_info(rectangle) # Output: Area: 50, Perimeter: 30

display_shape_info(circle) # Output: Area: 153.9379, Perimeter: 43.9824

In this example, the display_shape_info function can accept any object that is a subclass of Shape. This demonstrates the polymorphic behavior enabled by abstract classes.

Multiple Inheritance

MULTIPLE INHERITANCE is a feature in object-oriented programming that allows a class to inherit from more than one parent class. In Python, a child class can inherit methods and attributes from multiple parent classes, enabling you to combine functionality from different sources.

Multiple inheritance can be extremely useful, but it also introduces complexities, such as the potential for method conflicts when two parent classes define methods with the same name. Python resolves these conflicts using the Method Resolution Order (MRO).

Example of Multiple Inheritance

HERE'S AN EXAMPLE THAT demonstrates multiple inheritance:

class Engine:

def start_engine(self):

```
print("Engine started.")

class Wheels:

def roll(self):

print("Wheels rolling.")

class Car(Engine, Wheels):

def drive(self):

print("Car is driving.")

# Creating an object of the Car class

car = Car()

car.start_engine() # Output: Engine started.

car.roll() # Output: Wheels rolling.

car.drive() # Output: Car is driving.
```

In this example, the Car class inherits from both Engine and Wheels. It gains the start_engine method from Engine and the roll method from Wheels. Multiple inheritance allows the Car class to combine functionality from both parent classes.

Method Resolution Order (MRO)

WHEN A CLASS INHERITS from multiple parents, Python uses the Method Resolution Order (MRO) to determine the order in which methods should be inherited. Python follows the "C3 linearization algorithm" to calculate the MRO. You can view the MRO for a class using the mro() method:

```
print(Car.mro())
```

This will output a list of the classes that Python will check, in order, when searching for a method in the Car class.

Diamond Problem

THE DIAMOND PROBLEM is a common issue in languages that support multiple inheritance. It occurs when a class inherits from two classes that share a common parent. This can create ambiguity when determining which method to inherit from the common parent.

Here's an example of the diamond problem:

```
class A:

def greet(self):

print("Hello from A")

class B(A):

def greet(self):

print("Hello from B")

class C(A):

def greet(self):

print("Hello from C")

class D(B, C):

pass

# Creating an object of class D
```

d = D()

d.greet() # Output: Hello from B

In this example, class D inherits from both B and C, which in turn inherit from A. When D calls the greet method, Python follows the MRO and resolves the method from B first, even though both B and C inherit from A. This resolves the diamond problem by ensuring a consistent order for method resolution.

Using super() with Multiple Inheritance

IN CASES OF MULTIPLE inheritance, using the super() function can help manage method calls by ensuring that the MRO is respected. The super() function automatically follows the MRO to determine which method to call next.

Here's an example:

class A:

def greet(self):

print("Hello from A")

class B(A):

def greet(self):

super().greet()

print("Hello from B")

class C(A):

def greet(self):

```
super().greet()
print("Hello from C")
class D(B, C):
def greet(self):
super().greet()
print("Hello from D")
# Creating an object of class D
d = D()
d.greet()
```

Output:

Hello from A

Hello from C

Hello from B

Hello from D

In this example, the super() function ensures that the greet method from each parent class is called in the correct order according to the MRO.

Mixins and Multiple Inheritance

A COMMON USE CASE FOR multiple inheritance is the implementation of mixins. A mixin is a class that provides additional functionality to a class through inheritance but is not intended to be instantiated on its own. Mixins allow you to "mix" specific functionality into multiple classes without duplicating code.

Here's an example of a mixin:

```
class LogMixin:

def log(self, message):

print(f"Log: {message}")

class Animal:

def speak(self):

pass

class Dog(Animal, LogMixin):

def speak(self):

self.log("The dog barks.")

print("Woof!")

# Creating an object of the Dog class

dog = Dog()

dog.speak()
```

Output:

```
Log: The dog barks.

Woof!
```

In this example, the LogMixin class provides logging functionality that can be "mixed" into the Dog class. The Dog class inherits from both Animal and LogMixin, allowing it to use the log method without duplicating code.

Best Practices for Using Multiple Inheritance

WHILE MULTIPLE INHERITANCE can be a powerful tool, it should be used judiciously. Here are some best practices to keep in mind:

1. **Use Mixins for Specific Functionality**: Mixins are a good way to add specific, reusable functionality to multiple classes without introducing complexity. Avoid using multiple inheritance for general-purpose classes, as it can lead to confusing hierarchies.
2. **Avoid Deep Inheritance Chains**: Deep inheritance chains can make code difficult to understand and maintain. Limit the depth of inheritance hierarchies to avoid complexity.
3. **Understand the MRO**: Always be aware of the method resolution order when working with multiple inheritance. The MRO determines how methods are inherited and can introduce unexpected behavior if not understood correctly.
4. **Use Composition Over Inheritance**: In many cases, it's better to use composition (having one class contain an instance of another) rather than inheritance. This can make your design more modular and flexible.

Conclusion

ABSTRACT CLASSES AND multiple inheritance are advanced OOP concepts that offer powerful ways to structure and organize your code in Python. Abstract classes provide a template for other classes, ensuring consistency and enforcing a specific interface. Multiple inheritance allows classes to inherit functionality from multiple sources, making it possible to build complex, reusable, and flexible systems.

When used appropriately, these concepts can greatly enhance the modularity and maintainability of your code. However, it's important to balance their use with best practices, such as keeping inheritance hierarchies shallow and using composition where appropriate, to avoid complexity and confusion. By mastering these advanced OOP techniques, you can write more robust and scalable Python applications.

Chapter 8: Error Handling and Exceptions

Introduction to Error Handling

ERROR HANDLING IN PYTHON is a critical aspect of writing robust, reliable programs. At its core, error handling allows developers to anticipate, catch, and manage errors or exceptions that may occur during the execution of a program. Instead of your program crashing or halting when an unexpected event occurs, you can gracefully handle these issues and continue execution or exit in a controlled manner.

Errors and exceptions are unavoidable in any programming language, and Python is no different. The beauty of Python lies in its simplicity and the clarity with which it handles exceptions. Error handling involves recognizing potential problems in your code and using specific constructs like try, except, and finally to manage these issues.

Types of Errors in Python

PYTHON HANDLES TWO main categories of errors: **syntax errors** and **exceptions**.

Syntax errors: These occur when the Python interpreter encounters an invalid line of code. These are often easy to detect and resolve because the interpreter will flag the offending line with a detailed error message.

python

```
if x > 10:
```

print("x is greater than 10"

The error message would look like this:

arduino

File "<stdin>", line 2

print("x is greater than 10"

^

SyntaxError: unexpected EOF while parsing

- In this case, the missing closing parenthesis causes a syntax error.

Exceptions: These are errors that occur during the execution of a program. Unlike syntax errors, exceptions are only raised when the interpreter encounters a problematic situation while running the code. Common exceptions include ZeroDivisionError, FileNotFoundError, and TypeError. Each of these exceptions provides a way for the program to detect and respond to unexpected conditions.

For example:

python

x = 10 / 0

This will result in the following exception:

vbnet

ZeroDivisionError: division by zero

-

Basic Error Handling Using try and except

PYTHON PROVIDES A POWERFUL construct for handling exceptions in the form of the try and except blocks. The basic idea is simple: place any code that might raise an exception within a try block, and define an except block to catch and handle the exception if one occurs.

Here's an example:

```
try:

num = int(input("Enter a number: "))

result = 10 / num

print(f"Result is: {result}")

except ZeroDivisionError:

print("You cannot divide by zero!")

except ValueError:

print("Invalid input! Please enter a valid number.")
```

In this example:

- The try block attempts to execute the code that could raise exceptions.
- The except ZeroDivisionError block catches the ZeroDivisionError if the user tries to divide by zero and handles it by printing an error message.
- The except ValueError block handles invalid input (e.g., if the user enters a non-numeric value).

This approach ensures that the program doesn't crash when an exception occurs and that the user is informed of the problem in a user-friendly manner.

Catching Multiple Exceptions

IN THE ABOVE EXAMPLE, we handled different types of exceptions using multiple except blocks. This is a common pattern when you're dealing with multiple potential issues. You can also handle multiple exceptions within a single except block by passing them as a tuple.

```
try:

num = int(input("Enter a number: "))

result = 10 / num

except (ZeroDivisionError, ValueError):

print("An error occurred: either division by zero or invalid input.")
```

In this case, both ZeroDivisionError and ValueError are handled by the same except block, and the error message is more general. This can be useful when you want to group multiple exceptions under a common handling strategy.

Catching All Exceptions

YOU CAN CATCH ANY EXCEPTION using a generic except block, without specifying an error type. However, this should be used with caution, as it may obscure the real nature of the problem.

```
try:

# some operation that may raise an exception
```

```
result = 10 / int(input("Enter a number: "))

except:

print("An error occurred.")
```

While this might seem convenient, it's often not the best practice. Catching all exceptions without specifying the type makes it harder to debug, and you may inadvertently hide errors that you actually want to handle differently. A better approach is to catch specific exceptions and handle them accordingly.

else and finally Clauses

IN ADDITION TO TRY and except, Python provides else and finally clauses for more fine-grained control over error handling.

else clause: This block will execute only if no exceptions were raised in the try block. It's useful for placing code that should only run when everything went smoothly.

```
python

try:

result = 10 / int(input("Enter a number: "))

except ZeroDivisionError:

print("You cannot divide by zero.")

else:

print(f"The result is: {result}")
```

- In this example, the else block runs only if no exceptions were raised in the try block. If an exception occurs, the else block is skipped.

finally clause: This block of code will run regardless of whether an exception was raised or not. It's often used to clean up resources, like closing files or network connections, that were opened during the try block.

python

```
try:

file = open("example.txt", "r")

content = file.read()

except FileNotFoundError:

print("File not found!")

finally:

file.close()

print("File closed.")
```

- In this case, the finally block ensures that the file is closed whether or not an exception was raised during the file reading process. This is particularly important when working with external resources like files, databases, or network connections.

Raising Exceptions

IN PYTHON, YOU CAN manually raise exceptions using the raise keyword. This is useful when you want to enforce certain conditions in your code and trigger an exception if those conditions are not met.

For example, let's say you want to restrict the input to positive numbers only. You can raise a ValueError if the user enters a negative number.

```
def check_positive(number):

if number < 0:

raise ValueError("Negative numbers are not allowed.")

return number

try:

num = int(input("Enter a positive number: "))

check_positive(num)

except ValueError as e:

print(e)
```

In this case, if the user enters a negative number, a ValueError will be raised with a custom error message, which is then caught and printed in the except block.

Custom Exceptions

PYTHON ALLOWS YOU TO define your own custom exceptions by subclassing the built-in Exception class. This is useful when you want to create more meaningful and specific exceptions in your code.

```
class NegativeNumberError(Exception):
```

```
"""Custom exception for negative numbers."""

pass

def check_positive(number):

if number < 0:

raise NegativeNumberError("Negative numbers are not allowed.")

return number

try:

num = int(input("Enter a positive number: "))

check_positive(num)

except NegativeNumberError as e:

print(e)
```

In this example, the NegativeNumberError class is a custom exception that inherits from Python's built-in Exception class. It behaves just like a standard exception but is more descriptive and specific to the use case.

Best Practices for Error Handling

1. **Be specific**: Always catch the specific exceptions you expect, rather than using a catch-all approach with except. This makes your code easier to debug and understand.
2. **Use meaningful error messages**: Provide helpful error messages that make it clear to the user or developer what went wrong and how to fix it.
3. **Avoid silencing exceptions**: Don't use a bare except

clause unless you're intentionally trying to suppress all errors. This can lead to bugs that are difficult to trace.
4. **Clean up resources**: Use the finally block to ensure that resources like files or network connections are properly closed, even if an error occurs.
5. **Use logging**: For complex applications, consider using Python's built-in logging module to track errors and exceptions rather than printing error messages directly.
6. **Raising custom exceptions**: When appropriate, define and raise custom exceptions to make your error handling more readable and maintainable.

ERROR HANDLING IS A vital part of any Python application. By anticipating and managing potential errors in your code, you can create programs that are not only more reliable but also more user-friendly.

try, except, finally: The Building Blocks

ERROR HANDLING IN PYTHON revolves around three fundamental building blocks: try, except, and finally. These constructs provide a robust framework for managing errors that may arise during the execution of a program. While errors are inevitable, handling them gracefully can significantly improve the resilience of your code, allowing it to continue running or exit cleanly without unexpected crashes.

The try Block

THE TRY BLOCK CONTAINS the code that might raise an exception. The Python interpreter attempts to execute the statements within the try block. If no exceptions occur, the program continues normally, and the except block is skipped.

However, if an error does occur, control is immediately passed to the except block, where you can manage the exception.

Here is a simple structure of how the try block works:

```
try:

# Code that might raise an exception

risky_code()

except SomeException:

# Code that runs if an exception occurs

handle_exception()
```

In this case, if risky_code() raises a SomeException, the code inside the except block will execute. Otherwise, the program will continue past the try block without any interruption.

For example, consider a scenario where a user is asked to input a number, and you want to ensure the input is valid. If the user enters a non-numeric value, an exception will be raised. Here's how you can handle that:

```
try:

num = int(input("Enter a number: "))

print(f"The number is: {num}")

except ValueError:

print("That's not a valid number!")
```

In this example, the ValueError is caught when the user enters an invalid number, and the program prints an error message instead of crashing.

The except Block

THE EXCEPT BLOCK HANDLES exceptions raised by the try block. You can specify which exception to catch, and Python will compare the exception raised to those listed in your except clauses. If the exception matches, the corresponding block of code runs.

Python allows you to catch specific exceptions by name. This approach ensures that you only catch errors you expect, making your program more reliable and debuggable. For example:

```
try:

num = 10 / int(input("Enter a number to divide by: "))

print(f"The result is: {num}")

except ZeroDivisionError:

print("You cannot divide by zero!")

except ValueError:

print("Please enter a valid integer.")
```

In this example, two specific exceptions are handled: ZeroDivisionError for when the user tries to divide by zero and ValueError for when the input is not a valid integer. This way, different errors receive appropriate error messages.

Catching Multiple Exceptions

IN SITUATIONS WHERE multiple types of exceptions might be raised, you can handle them all using a single except block by passing them as a tuple. This approach simplifies the code when multiple exceptions require the same handling:

```
try:

num = 10 / int(input("Enter a number: "))

except (ZeroDivisionError, ValueError):

print("Error: Invalid input or division by zero.")
```

Here, both ZeroDivisionError and ValueError are handled by the same block, and the error message is general enough to apply to either situation.

The Generic except Block

SOMETIMES, YOU MAY not know all the possible exceptions that could be raised, or you may want to catch every possible error that occurs. In such cases, you can use a generic except block that catches any exception:

```
try:

risky_code()

except:

print("An error occurred!")
```

While this method can be useful for preventing your program from crashing, it is not recommended in most cases. A generic except block can make it difficult to diagnose problems, as it doesn't provide any information about what kind of exception was raised. If you use a generic except, it's a good idea to log or print the actual error message using the Exception object, like this:

```
try:

risky_code()

except Exception as e:

print(f"An error occurred: {e}")
```

This approach ensures that you're still catching all errors, but it also gives you access to the specific exception message for debugging purposes.

The else Clause

PYTHON PROVIDES AN else clause that works with the try block. The code inside the else clause is executed only if no exceptions are raised in the try block. This is useful for cases where you want to run certain code only when the try block executes successfully.

```
try:

num = int(input("Enter a number: "))

except ValueError:

print("Invalid input!")

else:

print(f"You entered {num}")
```

In this example, if the user inputs a valid number, the else block will run, printing the number. If an exception occurs (e.g., the user inputs a non-numeric value), the except block will execute instead, and the else block will be skipped.

The else clause provides clarity in your code by separating the logic for handling exceptions from the code that runs when everything works as expected. It helps avoid placing unnecessary code inside the try block, making your program easier to read and debug.

The finally Clause

THE FINALLY CLAUSE is a special block of code that is always executed, regardless of whether an exception was raised or not. This makes it ideal for cleaning up resources like closing files, network connections, or freeing up memory. The finally block ensures that certain actions are taken, even if an error occurs or the program exits unexpectedly.

Here's the structure of a try, except, and finally block:

try:

code that might raise an exception

except SomeException:

code that runs if an exception occurs

finally:

code that always runs, whether an exception occurs or not

For example, when working with files, you should always close the file after you're done with it, regardless of whether an error occurred during file operations:

```
try:
file = open("example.txt", "r")
content = file.read()
except FileNotFoundError:
print("File not found!")
finally:
file.close()
print("File closed.")
```

In this case, even if the file is not found and an exception is raised, the finally block ensures that the file is closed (assuming it was opened successfully). This helps prevent resource leaks and ensures that your program cleans up after itself.

Combining else and finally

YOU CAN USE BOTH THE else and finally clauses in the same try block. The else block will run if no exceptions are raised, and the finally block will run regardless of what happens in the try block:

```
try:
num = int(input("Enter a number: "))
except ValueError:
print("Invalid input!")
else:
```

```
print(f"You entered {num}")

finally:

print("End of program.")
```

In this example, the program prints "End of program" whether or not an exception occurs, and the else block only runs if no exceptions are raised.

Nested try Blocks

IN MORE COMPLEX SCENARIOS, you may encounter situations where you need to nest try blocks inside each other. This is particularly useful when you need to handle different types of exceptions at different levels of your program. Here's an example of nested try blocks:

```
try:

num = int(input("Enter a number: "))

try:

result = 10 / num

print(f"Result is {result}")

except ZeroDivisionError:

print("You cannot divide by zero!")

except ValueError:

print("Please enter a valid number.")

finally:
```

```
print("End of program.")
```

In this example, the outer try block catches the ValueError if the user inputs an invalid number, while the inner try block catches the ZeroDivisionError if the user tries to divide by zero. The finally block ensures that "End of program" is printed regardless of any exceptions.

Re-raising Exceptions

SOMETIMES YOU MAY WANT to handle an exception temporarily but still let it propagate up to the calling code. In such cases, you can use the raise keyword inside an except block to re-raise the exception:

```
try:

num = int(input("Enter a number: "))

except ValueError:

print("Caught an invalid input!")

raise # Re-raises the exception to propagate it
```

By re-raising the exception, you're allowing the calling code to handle it further or terminate the program if necessary. This is useful when you need to log or modify the exception but don't want to swallow it entirely.

Conclusion

ERROR HANDLING IN PYTHON is a powerful tool for writing resilient, robust programs. The combination of try, except, else, and finally provides a flexible framework for managing exceptions and ensuring that your code behaves predictably under all circumstances. By catching specific exceptions, cleaning up resources, and using the finally block to guarantee the execution of essential cleanup tasks, you can write programs that gracefully handle errors and keep running even in the face of unexpected events.

Raising and Catching Custom Exceptions

IN PYTHON, ERROR HANDLING is not just limited to using predefined exceptions like ZeroDivisionError, ValueError, or FileNotFoundError. Python provides the flexibility to create custom exceptions, allowing developers to define their own specific error types. This ability is particularly useful in large projects where it becomes necessary to communicate more detailed error messages or enforce specific conditions within the code. By raising and catching custom exceptions, you can create a more meaningful and descriptive error-handling mechanism tailored to the needs of your application.

Why Create Custom Exceptions?

CUSTOM EXCEPTIONS ALLOW you to express unique problems in your program more clearly. While Python's built-in exceptions cover many common cases, they are often too generic for certain situations. For example, suppose you are writing a banking application, and you want to flag errors related to insufficient funds, invalid transactions, or unauthorized access. Using generic exceptions like ValueError might work, but it wouldn't provide specific feedback. Creating your own InsufficientFundsError or UnauthorizedAccessError exceptions, on the other hand, gives you control over the error messages and how they are handled.

Custom exceptions help achieve the following:

1. **Readability**: Custom exceptions provide more clarity and context to the errors that occur. They communicate what went wrong without requiring a detailed explanation in comments or documentation.
2. **Modularity**: If your project grows, specific errors will require special handling. Custom exceptions make the error-handling code modular and extendable.
3. **Separation of Concerns**: Using custom exceptions, you can handle application-specific errors separately from generic programming errors.
4. **Better Debugging**: When debugging complex applications, custom exceptions provide a better understanding of where and why the error occurred. It eliminates ambiguity and leads to quicker resolutions.

Creating a Custom Exception Class

CREATING A CUSTOM EXCEPTION in Python is simple. All you need to do is define a new class that inherits from Python's built-in Exception class or one of its subclasses. You can also add additional functionality to your custom exception by overriding certain methods or including custom attributes.

Here's a basic example of creating a custom exception:

class InsufficientFundsError(Exception):

"""Exception raised for errors in the withdrawal process due to insufficient funds."""

pass

This simple custom exception class InsufficientFundsError can now be raised in situations where a user tries to withdraw more money than their account balance permits. Here's how it might be used:

```
class BankAccount:

def __init__(self, balance):

self.balance = balance

def withdraw(self, amount):

if amount > self.balance:

raise InsufficientFundsError(f"Insufficient funds: Tried to withdraw {amount}, but only {self.balance} is available.")

self.balance -= amount

return self.balance

try:

account = BankAccount(100)

account.withdraw(150)

except InsufficientFundsError as e:

print(e)
```

In this example, if the user tries to withdraw more than the available balance, the custom exception InsufficientFundsError is raised with a clear error message. The except block then catches the exception and prints the error.

Custom Exception with Additional Attributes

IN MANY CASES, CUSTOM exceptions can be enhanced by including additional information about the error. For instance, you might want to pass extra details such as an error code, error message, or other relevant data when raising an exception.

Here's an example of a custom exception with additional attributes:

```
class InvalidTransactionError(Exception):

"""Exception raised for invalid transactions."""

def __init__(self, transaction_id, message="Invalid transaction occurred."):

self.transaction_id = transaction_id

self.message = message

super().__init__(self.message)

def __str__(self):

return f'Transaction ID {self.transaction_id}: {self.message}'
```

In this example, InvalidTransactionError accepts an additional parameter, transaction_id, which uniquely identifies the transaction that caused the error. The exception class also overrides the __str__() method to display a custom error message when the exception is printed.

Here's how it might be used in a program:

```
class PaymentProcessor:

def process_payment(self, transaction_id, amount):
```

if amount <= 0:

raise InvalidTransactionError(transaction_id, "Transaction amount must be positive.")

Process payment logic here

try:

processor = PaymentProcessor()

processor.process_payment("TX123", -50)

except InvalidTransactionError as e:

print(e)

Output:

Transaction ID TX123: Transaction amount must be positive.

This example demonstrates how adding custom attributes and methods to exceptions can make error messages more informative and specific, making it easier to diagnose problems in larger applications.

Raising Custom Exceptions

RAISING A CUSTOM EXCEPTION is similar to raising any other built-in exception. The raise statement is used to trigger an exception, optionally providing a message that describes the error.

Here's another scenario where custom exceptions might be useful: Imagine you're building a user authentication system. You can define custom exceptions for different error conditions, such as invalid passwords, unauthorized access, or inactive accounts.

```
class InvalidPasswordError(Exception):
"""Exception raised when the user enters an invalid password."""
def __init__(self, message="Password is incorrect."):
self.message = message
super().__init__(self.message)
class UnauthorizedAccessError(Exception):
"""Exception raised when the user tries to access a restricted area."""
def __init__(self, username, message="User is not authorized to access this area."):
self.username = username
self.message = message
super().__init__(self.message)
# Example usage:
def authenticate_user(username, password):
if password != "correct_password":
raise InvalidPasswordError()
if username != "admin":
raise UnauthorizedAccessError(username)
try:
authenticate_user("user", "wrong_password")
except InvalidPasswordError as e:
```

```
print(e)

except UnauthorizedAccessError as e:

print(f"{e.username}: {e}")
```

In this example, InvalidPasswordError is raised when the password is incorrect, and UnauthorizedAccessError is raised when the user is not authorized. The custom error messages make it clear why authentication failed, and they differentiate between the two types of errors.

Handling Custom Exceptions

ONCE A CUSTOM EXCEPTION is raised, it can be caught and handled just like any other exception using the try and except blocks. Here's an example that shows how multiple custom exceptions can be caught and handled in a single program:

```
class InactiveAccountError(Exception):

"""Exception raised for inactive user accounts."""

def __init__(self, username):

self.username = username

self.message = f"Account for {self.username} is inactive."

super().__init__(self.message)

def process_user_login(username, password):

if username == "inactive_user":

raise InactiveAccountError(username)

if password != "correct_password":
```

```
raise InvalidPasswordError()
print("Login successful.")
try:
process_user_login("inactive_user", "correct_password")
except InactiveAccountError as e:
print(e)
except InvalidPasswordError as e:
print(e)
```

In this scenario, if the account is inactive, the InactiveAccountError exception is raised with a personalized message, and it is caught in the except block. Handling multiple custom exceptions ensures that your program can respond appropriately to different types of errors.

Best Practices for Custom Exceptions

WHEN CREATING CUSTOM exceptions, it is important to follow some best practices to ensure that your code remains maintainable and understandable.

1. **Use Descriptive Names**: Make sure your custom exception names clearly describe the error they represent. This makes it easier for others (or yourself) to understand the code.
2. **Inherit from the Built-in Exception Class**: Always subclass the Exception class or one of its descendants. This ensures that your custom exceptions behave like standard Python exceptions.

3. **Add Custom Messages**: When creating a custom exception, provide meaningful messages that give context to the error. This can save time when debugging or when dealing with log files.
4. **Avoid Overusing Custom Exceptions**: While custom exceptions can be helpful, avoid defining too many of them. Overusing custom exceptions can clutter your code and make it harder to manage. Stick to creating custom exceptions only when you have specific error conditions that aren't well-represented by Python's built-in exceptions.
5. **Document Your Custom Exceptions**: Clearly document the purpose of your custom exceptions, especially in larger projects. This helps other developers understand when and how these exceptions should be raised and handled.
6. **Use Custom Exceptions for Business Logic**: Reserve custom exceptions for application-specific issues. For example, exceptions like InsufficientFundsError, UnauthorizedAccessError, or InvalidTransactionError are domain-specific and relate directly to the business logic of your application. Avoid using custom exceptions for low-level errors like file I/O or database connectivity issues; built-in exceptions are sufficient in these cases.

Custom Exception Hierarchies

IN COMPLEX APPLICATIONS, you may want to define multiple related custom exceptions. In such cases, it's a good idea to organize them into an exception hierarchy by creating a base exception class and then subclassing it for more specific errors.

Here's an example:

```
class ApplicationError(Exception):

"""Base class for all custom exceptions in the application."""

pass

class DatabaseError(ApplicationError):

"""Exception raised for database-related errors."""

def __init__(self, message="A database error occurred."):

self.message = message

super().__init__(self.message)

class NetworkError(ApplicationError):

"""Exception raised for network-related errors."""

def __init__(self, message="A network error occurred."):

self.message = message

super().__init__(self.message)
```

In this example, ApplicationError serves as the base class for all custom exceptions related to the application. Both DatabaseError and NetworkError inherit from ApplicationError, and they each have their own unique error messages. This structure makes it easier to handle specific errors and general application errors in a consistent manner.

Conclusion

CUSTOM EXCEPTIONS PROVIDE an essential mechanism for managing application-specific errors. By defining your own exceptions, you can communicate error conditions more clearly and ensure that your code is both readable and maintainable. Custom exceptions allow you to create modular and scalable error-handling systems that are tailored to the unique requirements of your application. Whether you're building a small utility or a large enterprise system, leveraging custom exceptions ensures that your programs remain robust and easy to debug.

Debugging Strategies in Python

DEBUGGING IS A CRUCIAL part of the software development process, and Python provides a variety of tools and techniques to make this task easier. The aim of debugging is to identify and fix bugs, or errors, in your code that can cause incorrect behavior or crashes. Debugging isn't just about finding the problems—it's about understanding the flow of your program, how it handles data, and ensuring that it performs as expected. This section explores various strategies and tools for debugging Python programs effectively.

Common Debugging Techniques

BEFORE DIVING INTO the more advanced tools and techniques, let's start with some common strategies that help in identifying bugs early in the development process.

1. Print Statements

ONE OF THE SIMPLEST and most effective debugging techniques is using print() statements to output the current state of your variables or to track the flow of your program. While this is not the most sophisticated debugging method, it often provides quick insights into where things might be going wrong.

For example, if you're unsure why a variable isn't holding the expected value, you can add a print() statement just before or after the variable's assignment to check its value.

```
def calculate_total(prices):

total = 0

for price in prices:

total += price

print(f"Current total: {total}") # Debugging print statement

return total

prices = [10, 20, 30]

print(f"Final total: {calculate_total(prices)}")
```

In this example, adding the print() statement inside the loop allows you to see how total is updated as each price is added, helping you identify any issues with the calculation logic.

2. Using Assertions

AN ASSERT STATEMENT is another useful debugging tool that allows you to check whether a condition is true. If the condition evaluates to False, Python will raise an AssertionError, effectively pausing the program and notifying you of the problem.

Assertions are particularly useful for catching logic errors early in the development process. They can be used to ensure that certain conditions hold true during program execution, such as input validation or maintaining program invariants.

```
def withdraw(balance, amount):
```

```
assert balance >= amount, "Insufficient funds"

return balance - amount

balance = 100

withdraw(balance, 150) # This will raise an AssertionError
```

In this case, if the withdrawal amount exceeds the available balance, an AssertionError is raised with a custom message indicating the problem. Assertions are meant for debugging and should not be used in production code for error handling, as they can be disabled globally by running Python in optimized mode (python -O).

3. Traceback Analysis

PYTHON'S ERROR MESSAGES, known as tracebacks, provide invaluable information about the point at which an error occurred. The traceback shows the sequence of function calls that led to the error, allowing you to trace back through the stack to find the source of the problem.

Consider the following example:

```
def divide(a, b):

return a / b

def calculate_average(numbers):

total = sum(numbers)

return divide(total, len(numbers))

numbers = [10, 20, 30]

print(calculate_average(numbers)) # Works fine
```

print(calculate_average([])) # Raises ZeroDivisionError

The second call to calculate_average([]) raises a ZeroDivisionError because the list is empty, and the program tries to divide by zero. The traceback will show you that the error originated in the divide() function, which was called by calculate_average().

By examining the traceback, you can quickly identify where the error occurred and start investigating why it happened. It's important to read tracebacks carefully, as they often provide all the information you need to resolve the issue.

4. Code Reviews

ONE OF THE MOST EFFECTIVE debugging strategies is conducting code reviews. By having another set of eyes look at your code, you can catch bugs that you might have missed due to familiarity with the code. A fresh perspective often reveals logic errors, potential edge cases, or overlooked conditions.

Code reviews also promote better coding practices and help ensure that your code is maintainable and well-structured, which can prevent bugs from being introduced in the first place.

5. Understanding Edge Cases

EDGE CASES ARE SCENARIOS that occur at the extreme limits of input data or program execution, and they often reveal bugs that go unnoticed in normal use cases. Identifying and testing edge cases is a critical part of debugging.

For example, consider a function that calculates the average of a list of numbers. While it might work correctly with a typical list of positive numbers, edge cases such as an empty list, very large numbers, or negative values can reveal problems.

```
def calculate_average(numbers):

if not numbers:

raise ValueError("Cannot calculate average of an empty list")

return sum(numbers) / len(numbers)

# Test with normal data

print(calculate_average([10, 20, 30])) # Works fine

# Test edge cases

print(calculate_average([])) # Raises ValueError

print(calculate_average([-10, -20])) # Should handle negative numbers
```

In this case, an empty list is an edge case that would cause a division by zero error if not properly handled. By identifying and testing such edge cases, you can prevent these types of bugs from occurring in production.

Debugging with Python's Built-in Tools

PYTHON PROVIDES SEVERAL built-in tools that make debugging more systematic and efficient. While print() statements and assertions are useful for small programs or quick checks, more complex projects require more sophisticated techniques.

6. Using the pdb Module

PYTHON'S BUILT-IN DEBUGGER, pdb, is a powerful tool that allows you to step through your code, examine variable values, and control program execution interactively. This gives you far more control than simply printing out values.

To start a pdb session, you can insert the following line of code at the point where you want to start debugging:

import pdb; pdb.set_trace()

This will pause the execution of your program at that point, and you'll be dropped into the interactive pdb prompt, where you can issue various commands to inspect and manipulate your code. Some useful commands include:

- n (next): Move to the next line of code.
- s (step): Step into a function call.
- c (continue): Continue execution until the next breakpoint.
- p variable: Print the value of a variable.

Here's an example:

def divide(a, b):

import pdb; pdb.set_trace()

return a / b

print(divide(10, 2))

When you run this program, it will pause at the pdb.set_trace() line. You can then use the p command to inspect variables, step through the code, or continue execution. pdb is especially useful for tracking down bugs in larger programs where print statements would be cumbersome.

7. Using Breakpoints

IN PYTHON 3.7 AND LATER, the breakpoint() function simplifies the process of using the debugger. Instead of importing pdb and setting pdb.set_trace(), you can simply call breakpoint() at the desired location:

```
def divide(a, b):

breakpoint()

return a / b

print(divide(10, 0))
```

When you run this code, it will pause at the breakpoint() line, allowing you to inspect variables and step through the program just as you would with pdb.set_trace().

8. Logging for Debugging

LOGGING IS AN ESSENTIAL tool for debugging, especially in production environments where using a debugger or print statements isn't feasible. Python's built-in logging module allows you to record messages at different severity levels, such as DEBUG, INFO, WARNING, ERROR, and CRITICAL.

Unlike print statements, logging allows you to output messages to different destinations (such as files or remote servers) and control the verbosity of the output by adjusting the logging level.

Here's an example of using the logging module for debugging:

```
import logging

logging.basicConfig(level=logging.DEBUG)
```

```
def divide(a, b):
logging.debug(f"Dividing {a} by {b}")
if b == 0:
logging.error("Cannot divide by zero")
raise ValueError("Division by zero")
return a / b
try:
print(divide(10, 0))
except ValueError as e:
logging.exception("Caught an exception")
```

This example uses logging.debug() to print a debug message before attempting the division and logging.error() to log an error when division by zero is attempted. The logging.exception() call inside the except block logs the traceback of the caught exception. Logging can be configured to send output to files, rotate logs, and format messages for better readability.

9. Profiling and Performance Debugging

SOMETIMES, DEBUGGING isn't just about finding logical errors—it's about improving the performance of your code. Python provides several tools for profiling your code, which helps you understand which parts of your program are consuming the most resources.

The cProfile module is a built-in tool that allows you to profile your code and identify bottlenecks. Here's a simple example of how to use cProfile:

```
python -m cProfile my_script.py
```

This will print a detailed report showing how much time each function in your program took to execute, allowing you to pinpoint areas that need optimization.

10. Using faulthandler for Crashes

THE FAULTHANDLER MODULE is another useful debugging tool in Python. It provides detailed reports of low-level crashes (e.g., segmentation faults), which are not typically caught by the standard Python exception mechanism. You can enable faulthandler with the following code:

```
import faulthandler

faulthandler.enable()
```

This is particularly useful when debugging C extensions or dealing with crashes that occur in low-level Python code.

Debugging in Larger Projects

AS YOUR PROJECTS GROW in size and complexity, debugging can become more challenging. To manage this complexity, it's important to adopt a systematic approach to debugging:

1. **Reproduce the Bug**: The first step in debugging any issue is reproducing the problem. If you can consistently reproduce the bug, you can apply various debugging tools

and techniques to isolate and fix the issue.

2. **Minimize the Problem Space**: Once you've reproduced the bug, try to narrow down the parts of the code where the bug might exist. You can do this by commenting out parts of the code, running tests on individual components, or using print statements or breakpoints to focus on a specific section of the code.
3. **Divide and Conquer**: If you're working with a large codebase, break the problem down into smaller, more manageable parts. This is where modular design and writing testable, self-contained functions become important.
4. **Test and Verify**: After identifying and fixing the bug, run tests to ensure that the problem is resolved and that no new issues have been introduced. Automated tests (e.g., unit tests) are particularly helpful for this purpose.

Conclusion

DEBUGGING IS AN INEVITABLE part of programming, but with the right strategies and tools, it can be a systematic and manageable process. From using print statements and assertions for quick checks to leveraging more advanced tools like pdb and logging, Python provides a rich set of resources to help you track down and fix bugs. By mastering these debugging techniques, you'll not only improve your problem-solving skills but also ensure that your code is more reliable, maintainable, and efficient.

Logging for Better Error Tracking

LOGGING IS A VITAL tool for both debugging and monitoring applications. While debugging tools help developers to track down issues during development, logging is indispensable in production environments where developers cannot interact directly with the running program. Logs provide insights into the internal workings of an application, capturing errors, warnings, and general information about the program's state over time.

In Python, the built-in logging module is a powerful and flexible system that allows developers to output messages to different destinations, including the console, files, or remote servers. These log messages can be filtered by severity levels and formatted to provide meaningful context. By implementing a structured logging system, you can gain better visibility into the behavior of your programs and handle errors in a more systematic way.

Why Use Logging?

BEFORE DIVING INTO how to use the logging module, it's important to understand why logging is so critical in software development and error tracking:

1. **Monitoring and Auditing**: Logging allows you to track the state and performance of your application over time. It enables you to monitor the system in real-time and review historical logs for troubleshooting purposes.
2. **Error Tracking**: When exceptions or errors occur, logs provide a detailed trail that can help you understand what happened just before the error. This context is often crucial for diagnosing and resolving the issue.
3. **Debugging**: In production environments, using a debugger or print statements is not practical. Logs provide a non-intrusive way to capture information about the application's state, allowing you to debug problems without pausing or halting the program.
4. **Scalability**: As applications grow in complexity, a proper

logging system can handle large volumes of log data efficiently, allowing developers to track multiple subsystems or services simultaneously.

5. **Security**: Logs can also provide valuable information about security-related incidents. They can capture failed login attempts, suspicious activities, or unauthorized access, helping to identify and respond to potential threats.
6. **Compliance**: In some industries, maintaining logs is a regulatory requirement. Logging helps to keep a record of system events that may be required for compliance audits or legal inquiries.

Logging Basics

TO GET STARTED WITH logging in Python, you need to import the logging module. Here's a basic example of how to use the module to log messages:

```
import logging

logging.basicConfig(level=logging.DEBUG)

logging.debug("This is a debug message")

logging.info("This is an info message")

logging.warning("This is a warning message")

logging.error("This is an error message")

logging.critical("This is a critical message")
```

In this example, the basicConfig() function is used to configure the logging system. The level parameter sets the logging level, which controls the severity of the messages that will be captured. The default levels, in increasing order of severity, are:

- **DEBUG**: Detailed information, typically of interest only when diagnosing problems.

- **INFO**: Confirmation that things are working as expected.

- **WARNING**: An indication that something unexpected happened, or indicative of some problem in the near future (e.g., 'disk space low'). The software is still working as expected.

- **ERROR**: A more serious problem, the software has not been able to perform some function.

- **CRITICAL**: A very serious error, indicating that the program itself may be unable to continue running.

By default, the basicConfig() method outputs messages to the console, but this can be customized to write logs to files or other destinations.

Formatting Log Messages

LOGS ARE MOST USEFUL when they contain sufficient context about the error or event. You can use custom formats to include information such as the timestamp, log level, filename, line number, or function name in the log message.

Here's how you can customize the log message format:

```
import logging
```

```
logging.basicConfig(
level=logging.DEBUG,
format="%(asctime)s - %(name)s - %(levelname)s - %(message)s"
)
logging.debug("This is a debug message")
```

In this example, the log messages will include the timestamp (asctime), the name of the logger (name), the log level (levelname), and the actual message (message).

Here's an example of the output:

2024-10-22 10:42:31,265 - root - DEBUG - This is a debug message

Common format specifiers include:

- %(asctime)s: The timestamp of the log message.
- %(levelname)s: The log level (e.g., DEBUG, INFO, etc.).
- %(name)s: The name of the logger.
- %(message)s: The actual log message.
- %(filename)s: The file where the log call originated.
- %(lineno)d: The line number where the log call occurred.

Logging to Files

LOGGING TO THE CONSOLE is useful for development, but in production, you'll often want to write log messages to a file for later analysis. You can easily configure Python's logging module to write to a file by specifying the filename parameter in the basicConfig() method:

```
import logging

logging.basicConfig(

filename="app.log",

level=logging.INFO,

format="%(asctime)s - %(levelname)s - %(message)s"

)

logging.info("Application started")

logging.warning("Low disk space warning")

logging.error("An error occurred")
```

Now, instead of printing to the console, log messages will be written to the app.log file in the current directory. If you want to rotate log files (to avoid creating excessively large log files), you can use the RotatingFileHandler provided by the logging module.

```
from logging.handlers import RotatingFileHandler

handler = RotatingFileHandler("app.log", maxBytes=2000, backupCount=5)

logging.basicConfig(
```

```
handlers=[handler],
level=logging.DEBUG,
format="%(asctime)s - %(levelname)s - %(message)s"
)
```

In this example, the log file will be rotated once it reaches 2000 bytes, and up to 5 backup files will be kept. This ensures that your log files don't grow indefinitely.

Loggers, Handlers, and Formatters

THE LOGGING MODULE is designed around the concepts of loggers, handlers, and formatters, which together create a flexible and configurable logging system.

- **Loggers**: Loggers are the objects that your application uses to log messages. Each logger has a name (often the name of the module or application). Loggers can have multiple handlers attached, each of which handles the logging output differently.

- **Handlers**: Handlers are responsible for sending the log messages to their intended destination. For example, you can have handlers that send log messages to the console, a file, or even a remote server. Common handlers include StreamHandler (for console output) and FileHandler (for writing logs to files).

- **Formatters**: Formatters define the layout of the log messages, such as how much detail to include and in what order. You can attach different formatters to different handlers to customize the output for each destination.

Here's an example that demonstrates the use of custom loggers, handlers, and formatters:

```
import logging

# Create a custom logger

logger = logging.getLogger("my_logger")

# Create handlers

console_handler = logging.StreamHandler()

file_handler = logging.FileHandler("file.log")

# Set log levels for handlers

console_handler.setLevel(logging.WARNING)

file_handler.setLevel(logging.ERROR)

# Create formatters and add them to the handlers

console_format = logging.Formatter("%(name)s - %(levelname)s -
%(message)s")

file_format = logging.Formatter("%(asctime)s - %(name)s -
%(levelname)s - %(message)s")

console_handler.setFormatter(console_format)

file_handler.setFormatter(file_format)

# Add the handlers to the logger

logger.addHandler(console_handler)
```

```
logger.addHandler(file_handler)

# Log messages

logger.warning("This is a warning")

logger.error("This is an error")
```

In this example:

- A custom logger named my_logger is created.
- Two handlers are attached: one for the console (which logs only warnings and above) and one for a file (which logs only errors and above).
- Each handler has its own formatter, and the messages will be formatted differently depending on where they are output (console or file).

Logging Exceptions

IN MANY CASES, YOU'LL want to log exceptions along with the traceback information to understand where and why the error occurred. The logging module makes this easy with the exception() method, which automatically logs the exception information, including the traceback, when called inside an except block.

```
import logging

logging.basicConfig(level=logging.ERROR,
format="%(asctime)s - %(message)s")

try:

1 / 0
```

except ZeroDivisionError:

logging.exception("Exception occurred")

Output:

2024-10-22 10:45:12,345 - Exception occurred

Traceback (most recent call last):

File "example.py", line 5, in <module>

1 / 0

ZeroDivisionError: division by zero

Using logging.exception() ensures that both the custom error message and the full traceback are captured in the log, making it much easier to diagnose the problem.

Using Log Levels Effectively

CHOOSING THE APPROPRIATE log level for each message is important to ensure that your logs remain useful and manageable. Here's a general guideline for when to use each log level:

- **DEBUG**: Use for detailed diagnostic information, such as the values of variables or the internal state of the application. This level should be used sparingly in production environments, as it can generate large volumes of data.

- **INFO**: Use for general information about the application's operation, such as startup messages, configuration details, or successful completion of tasks.

This level provides a high-level overview of the system's behavior.

• **WARNING**: Use for situations that aren't necessarily errors but indicate that something unexpected has occurred or that there may be a problem in the near future. For example, a low disk space warning or a deprecated API call.

• **ERROR**: Use for serious problems that require immediate attention, such as failed database connections or uncaught exceptions. Errors typically indicate that part of the application cannot continue.

• **CRITICAL**: Use for the most severe issues, such as a complete application failure or critical security breaches. These messages should be rare and indicate that immediate action is required.

Best Practices for Logging

1. **Use Appropriate Log Levels**: Ensure that you are using the correct log levels for your messages. Avoid logging everything as DEBUG or ERROR, as this can lead to confusion and make it harder to spot actual problems.
2. **Log at Strategic Points**: Place log statements at critical points in your application, such as during initialization, error handling, and major state transitions. Logging too much can overwhelm your log files, while logging too little can leave you without the necessary information to diagnose problems.
3. **Avoid Logging Sensitive Information**: Be mindful of the information you include in your logs, especially in

production environments. Avoid logging sensitive data such as passwords, personal information, or API keys.

4. **Rotate Log Files**: Use log rotation to ensure that your log files don't grow indefinitely. This helps keep the log data manageable and prevents storage issues.
5. **Use Structured Logging**: Structured logging outputs logs in a format (like JSON) that is easily machine-readable. This is especially useful when dealing with large-scale systems or microservices, where logs need to be aggregated and analyzed.
6. **Monitor Logs**: Use log monitoring tools to aggregate and analyze your logs. Tools like ELK Stack (Elasticsearch, Logstash, Kibana), Graylog, or Splunk can help you search and visualize log data in real-time, allowing you to identify patterns, anomalies, or security incidents.

Conclusion

LOGGING IS AN ESSENTIAL tool for tracking, debugging, and monitoring your applications, especially in production environments where direct access is limited. By leveraging Python's logging module, you can capture critical information about your program's execution and respond to issues more effectively. Logging provides a historical record that is invaluable for diagnosing problems, improving performance, and ensuring the stability of your software.

Chapter 9: Working with Data Structures

Lists, Sets, and Dictionaries: Review and Advanced Usage

IN PYTHON, DATA STRUCTURES like lists, sets, and dictionaries are fundamental tools for organizing, storing, and retrieving data efficiently. While these are often considered basic concepts, their advanced features and usage can help optimize performance and code readability, especially when working with larger or more complex data sets. Let's delve deeper into each of these data structures, explore their intricacies, and examine some practical examples of how they can be used effectively.

Lists: The Workhorse of Data Structures

A **list** in Python is a collection of items that can be ordered, changed (mutable), and allow duplicate values. Lists are versatile and used for storing a sequence of elements, which can be of different data types. Lists are declared using square brackets [].

```
# Basic list declaration

my_list = [1, 2, 3, 4, 5]

# Mixed data types in a list

mixed_list = [1, "Hello", 3.14, True]

# Accessing elements

print(my_list[0]) # Output: 1

print(mixed_list[1]) # Output: Hello
```

Modifying elements

my_list[2] = 10

print(my_list) # Output: [1, 2, 10, 4, 5]

Advanced List Operations

WHILE BASIC OPERATIONS like indexing and modifying lists are straightforward, some advanced list operations provide powerful functionality:

List Comprehensions: List comprehensions provide a concise way to create lists. They are particularly useful when you want to create a new list by performing an operation on each element of an existing list.

python

List comprehension example

squares = [x ** 2 for x in range(10)]

print(squares) # Output: [0, 1, 4, 9, 16, 25, 36, 49, 64, 81]

1.

Slicing: Slicing allows you to access a subset of the list using the start:end:step syntax.

python

List slicing

sliced_list = my_list[1:4] # Start at index 1, go up to (but not including) index 4

print(sliced_list) # Output: [2, 10, 4]

1.

In-Place Reversal and Sorting: You can reverse and sort a list in place, modifying the original list:

python

Sorting a list in place

my_list.sort()

print(my_list) # Output: [1, 2, 4, 5, 10]

Reversing a list in place

my_list.reverse()

print(my_list) # Output: [10, 5, 4, 2, 1]

1.

Nested Lists: Python lists can be nested within each other, allowing for multi-dimensional arrays.

python

Creating a 2D list (list of lists)

matrix = [[1, 2, 3], [4, 5, 6], [7, 8, 9]]

print(matrix[1][2]) # Output: 6

1.

Sets: Unordered Collections of Unique Items

A **set** is an unordered collection of unique elements. Sets are useful when you need to eliminate duplicate values and perform membership tests efficiently. Sets are declared using curly braces {} or the set() constructor.

Creating a set

```
my_set = {1, 2, 3, 4, 4, 5}

print(my_set) # Output: {1, 2, 3, 4, 5} (no duplicates)

# Adding and removing elements

my_set.add(6)

print(my_set) # Output: {1, 2, 3, 4, 5, 6}

my_set.remove(2)

print(my_set) # Output: {1, 3, 4, 5, 6}
```

Advanced Set Operations

SET UNION: Combines two sets and returns all unique elements.

python

```
set_a = {1, 2, 3}

set_b = {3, 4, 5}

union_set = set_a.union(set_b)

print(union_set) # Output: {1, 2, 3, 4, 5}
```

1.

Set Intersection: Returns only the elements present in both sets.

python

```
intersection_set = set_a.intersection(set_b)

print(intersection_set) # Output: {3}
```

1.

Set Difference: Returns the elements that are in one set but not in another.

python

difference_set = set_a.difference(set_b)

print(difference_set) # Output: {1, 2}

1.

Set Symmetric Difference: Returns the elements that are in either set, but not in both.

python

sym_diff_set = set_a.symmetric_difference(set_b)

print(sym_diff_set) # Output: {1, 2, 4, 5}

1.

Dictionaries: Key-Value Pairs

A **dictionary** is a collection of key-value pairs, where each key is associated with a value. Dictionaries are unordered and mutable. Keys must be unique and immutable, meaning you can use strings, numbers, or tuples as dictionary keys. Dictionaries are declared using curly braces {} with key-value pairs separated by colons.

Creating a dictionary

my_dict = {

"name": "Alice",

"age": 30,

"city": "New York"

}

Accessing values by key

print(my_dict["name"]) # Output: Alice

Modifying a value

my_dict["age"] = 31

print(my_dict) # Output: {'name': 'Alice', 'age': 31, 'city': 'New York'}

Adding a new key-value pair

my_dict["email"] = "alice@example.com"

print(my_dict) # Output: {'name': 'Alice', 'age': 31, 'city': 'New York', 'email': 'alice@example.com'}

Advanced Dictionary Operations

DICTIONARY COMPREHENSION: Similar to list comprehensions, dictionary comprehensions allow for the creation of dictionaries in a concise way.

python

Dictionary comprehension

square_dict = {x: x ** 2 for x in range(5)}

print(square_dict) # Output: {0: 0, 1: 1, 2: 4, 3: 9, 4: 16}

1.

Merging Dictionaries: In Python 3.9 and later, you can merge dictionaries using the | operator.

python

```
dict_a = {"a": 1, "b": 2}

dict_b = {"b": 3, "c": 4}

merged_dict = dict_a | dict_b

print(merged_dict) # Output: {'a': 1, 'b': 3, 'c': 4}
```

1.

Iterating Through Dictionaries: You can iterate over dictionary keys, values, or key-value pairs.

python

```
# Iterating through keys

for key in my_dict:

print(key)

# Iterating through values

for value in my_dict.values():

print(value)

# Iterating through key-value pairs

for key, value in my_dict.items():

print(f"{key}: {value}")
```

1.

Handling Missing Keys with get(): When accessing dictionary values, using get() prevents key errors by returning None or a default value if the key is not found.

python

Using get() to avoid key errors

print(my_dict.get("name")) # Output: Alice

print(my_dict.get("address", "Not Found")) # Output: Not Found

1.

Conclusion

LISTS, SETS, AND DICTIONARIES form the cornerstone of data handling in Python. Understanding how to use these data structures effectively can significantly improve the performance and readability of your code. Whether it's list comprehensions, set operations, or dictionary comprehensions, Python provides a robust toolkit for managing data collections. By mastering these tools and learning how to apply them in more advanced ways, you can write more efficient and powerful Python programs.

Stacks and Queues: Implementing in Python

STACKS AND QUEUES ARE two fundamental data structures in computer science. Both structures provide a way to store and manage data, but they operate in different ways. A stack follows the **Last-In-First-Out (LIFO)** principle, while a queue follows the **First-In-First-Out (FIFO)** principle. These data structures are integral to solving many computational problems, and Python offers various ways to implement them.

Stacks: Last-In-First-Out (LIFO)

A **stack** is a linear data structure that allows elements to be added and removed only from one end, known as the **top** of the stack.

This means the most recently added item is the first to be removed, following the LIFO principle.

Basic Operations in a Stack

1. **Push**: Add an element to the top of the stack.
2. **Pop**: Remove and return the element from the top of the stack.
3. **Peek**: View the element at the top of the stack without removing it.
4. **IsEmpty**: Check if the stack is empty.

Implementing a Stack in Python

PYTHON DOES NOT HAVE a built-in stack data structure, but we can use a **list** to implement it, where append() adds an item to the top of the stack (push operation), and pop() removes the item from the top (pop operation).

```
# Stack implementation using Python list

class Stack:

def __init__(self):

self.stack = []

# Push operation

def push(self, item):

self.stack.append(item)

# Pop operation

def pop(self):
```

```
if not self.is_empty():
return self.stack.pop()
return "Stack is empty"
# Peek operation
def peek(self):
if not self.is_empty():
return self.stack[-1]
return "Stack is empty"
# Check if stack is empty
def is_empty(self):
return len(self.stack) == 0
# Display stack
def display(self):
return self.stack
# Example usage
my_stack = Stack()
my_stack.push(10)
my_stack.push(20)
my_stack.push(30)
print(my_stack.display()) # Output: [10, 20, 30]
```

print(my_stack.pop()) # Output: 30

print(my_stack.display()) # Output: [10, 20]

In this simple implementation, we use Python's list as the underlying data structure for the stack. The append() method adds an element to the top of the stack, and the pop() method removes it. The peek() method allows us to inspect the top element without removing it, and is_empty() checks if the stack contains any elements.

Practical Use Cases of Stacks

1. **Expression Evaluation**: Stacks are often used in the evaluation of expressions, especially when dealing with postfix or prefix notation.
2. **Backtracking Algorithms**: Many algorithms use stacks to keep track of their state, such as when solving puzzles like mazes or navigating trees.
3. **Undo Mechanism in Software**: Most applications that provide an "undo" feature (like text editors) rely on a stack to store the previous states of the data.

Balancing Parentheses with a Stack

A COMMON PROBLEM THAT can be solved using a stack is checking for balanced parentheses in an expression. Let's implement a solution:

def is_balanced(expression):

stack = Stack()

for char in expression:

```
if char in "({[":
stack.push(char)
elif char in ")}]":
if stack.is_empty():
return False
top = stack.pop()
if not matches(top, char):
return False
return stack.is_empty()
def matches(opening, closing):
openings = "({["
closings = ")}]"
return openings.index(opening) == closings.index(closing)
# Example usage
expression = "{[()()]}"
print(is_balanced(expression)) # Output: True
```

In this function, we iterate through each character in the string. If the character is an opening parenthesis, it gets pushed onto the stack. When we encounter a closing parenthesis, we check whether it matches the top element of the stack. If not, the parentheses are unbalanced.

Queues: First-In-First-Out (FIFO)

A **queue** is another linear data structure, but unlike a stack, it operates based on the **FIFO** principle. In a queue, the first element added is the first one to be removed.

Basic Operations in a Queue

1. **Enqueue**: Add an element to the end of the queue.
2. **Dequeue**: Remove and return the element from the front of the queue.
3. **Peek**: View the element at the front of the queue without removing it.
4. **IsEmpty**: Check if the queue is empty.

Implementing a Queue in Python

WHILE LISTS CAN BE used for queues as well, using the collections.deque class is more efficient for this purpose, as it provides faster append() and popleft() operations.

```
from collections import deque

# Queue implementation using deque

class Queue:

def __init__(self):

self.queue = deque()

# Enqueue operation

def enqueue(self, item):

self.queue.append(item)
```

```
# Dequeue operation
def dequeue(self):
if not self.is_empty():
return self.queue.popleft()
return "Queue is empty"
# Peek operation
def peek(self):
if not self.is_empty():
return self.queue[0]
return "Queue is empty"
# Check if queue is empty
def is_empty(self):
return len(self.queue) == 0
# Display queue
def display(self):
return list(self.queue)
# Example usage
my_queue = Queue()
my_queue.enqueue(10)
my_queue.enqueue(20)
```

```
my_queue.enqueue(30)

print(my_queue.display()) # Output: [10, 20, 30]

print(my_queue.dequeue()) # Output: 10

print(my_queue.display()) # Output: [20, 30]
```

In this implementation, we use Python's deque from the collections module to implement the queue. The append() method adds elements to the rear, and the popleft() method removes elements from the front.

Practical Use Cases of Queues

1. **Task Scheduling**: Queues are often used in operating systems for task scheduling and resource management.
2. **Breadth-First Search (BFS)**: Queues are used in graph traversal algorithms like BFS, where nodes are processed level by level.
3. **Printer Queue**: In real-world applications like printer jobs, queues help manage tasks in the order they are received.

Circular Queue

A **circular queue** is a more advanced type of queue where the end of the queue connects back to the front, forming a circle. This allows for efficient memory usage when dealing with fixed-size arrays.

Let's implement a circular queue:

```
class CircularQueue:
```

```
def __init__(self, size):
self.size = size
self.queue = [None] * size
self.front = self.rear = -1
# Enqueue operation
def enqueue(self, item):
if (self.rear + 1) % self.size == self.front:
return "Queue is full"
elif self.front == -1:
self.front = self.rear = 0
else:
self.rear = (self.rear + 1) % self.size
self.queue[self.rear] = item
# Dequeue operation
def dequeue(self):
if self.front == -1:
return "Queue is empty"
temp = self.queue[self.front]
if self.front == self.rear:
self.front = self.rear = -1
```

```
else:
self.front = (self.front + 1) % self.size
return temp
# Display queue
def display(self):
if self.front == -1:
return "Queue is empty"
if self.rear >= self.front:
return self.queue[self.front:self.rear + 1]
else:
return self.queue[self.front:] + self.queue[:self.rear + 1]
# Example usage
cq = CircularQueue(5)
cq.enqueue(10)
cq.enqueue(20)
cq.enqueue(30)
print(cq.display()) # Output: [10, 20, 30]
print(cq.dequeue()) # Output: 10
print(cq.display()) # Output: [20, 30]
```

In a circular queue, both the front and rear pointers are adjusted using the modulo operator to wrap around the array when the end of the queue is reached. This ensures that we can reuse space in the array once items are dequeued.

Conclusion

STACKS AND QUEUES ARE versatile data structures that can be implemented in Python in various ways. Understanding their core principles—LIFO for stacks and FIFO for queues—allows for solving a variety of problems, from simple data management to complex algorithmic challenges. Mastering the implementation and application of stacks and queues is crucial for optimizing performance in both everyday coding tasks and more advanced computational problems.

Trees and Graphs: An Overview

TREES and **graphs** are two fundamental data structures in computer science, often used to represent hierarchical or interconnected data. Both structures are crucial for various algorithms and problem-solving techniques. While trees are a specialized form of graphs with hierarchical organization, graphs are more general and can represent more complex relationships.

Trees: A Hierarchical Data Structure

A **tree** is a data structure made up of **nodes** that are connected by **edges**. A tree is hierarchical in nature, meaning it has a **root node** at the top, with child nodes branching out from the root. Each node in a tree has exactly one parent, except the root, which has no parent.

Basic Terminology

- **Root**: The topmost node in a tree, which has no parent.
- **Child**: A node that has a parent above it.
- **Parent**: A node that has one or more children.
- **Leaf**: A node with no children (a terminal node).
- **Depth**: The distance from the root to a node.
- **Height**: The maximum depth of any node in the tree.

Types of Trees

1. **Binary Tree**: A tree in which each node has at most two children, referred to as the **left child** and **right child**.
2. **Binary Search Tree (BST)**: A binary tree where the left child of a node contains a value less than the parent, and the right child contains a value greater than the parent. This structure allows efficient searching, insertion, and deletion.
3. **Balanced Tree**: A tree in which the height difference between the left and right subtrees of any node is minimal, allowing efficient operations like search, insert, and delete.
4. **AVL Tree**: A self-balancing binary search tree where the height difference between the left and right subtrees is at most 1. AVL trees maintain balance through rotations after insertions and deletions.
5. **Heap**: A specialized binary tree where the parent node is greater than (max-heap) or less than (min-heap) its

children, ensuring efficient retrieval of the maximum or minimum element.

Implementing a Binary Search Tree (BST) in Python

THE BINARY SEARCH TREE (BST) is one of the most commonly used tree structures due to its efficient performance in search operations. Let's implement a basic BST with operations like insertion, search, and traversal.

```
class Node:

def __init__(self, key):

self.left = None

self.right = None

self.value = key

class BinarySearchTree:

def __init__(self):

self.root = None

# Inserting a new node into the tree

def insert(self, key):

if self.root is None:

self.root = Node(key)

else:

self._insert_recursive(self.root, key)
```

```
def _insert_recursive(self, node, key):
if key < node.value:
if node.left is None:
node.left = Node(key)
else:
self._insert_recursive(node.left, key)
elif key > node.value:
if node.right is None:
node.right = Node(key)
else:
self._insert_recursive(node.right, key)
# Searching for a value in the tree
def search(self, key):
return self._search_recursive(self.root, key)
def _search_recursive(self, node, key):
if node is None or node.value == key:
return node
if key < node.value:
return self._search_recursive(node.left, key)
return self._search_recursive(node.right, key)
```

```
# Inorder traversal of the tree
def inorder(self, node):
if node:
self.inorder(node.left)
print(node.value, end=' ')
self.inorder(node.right)
# Example usage
bst = BinarySearchTree()
bst.insert(50)
bst.insert(30)
bst.insert(70)
bst.insert(20)
bst.insert(40)
bst.insert(60)
bst.insert(80)
bst.inorder(bst.root) # Output: 20 30 40 50 60 70 80
```

This basic implementation of a Binary Search Tree (BST) includes the insert(), search(), and inorder() traversal methods. The insert() method adds elements to the tree in such a way that maintains the BST property, where the left child is smaller than the parent and the right child is larger. The search() method looks for a specific value, and the inorder() method prints the values of the tree in ascending order.

Tree Traversal

TREE TRAVERSAL IS THE process of visiting all nodes in a tree in a specific order. There are three primary types of tree traversal:

Inorder Traversal (Left, Root, Right): Visits the left subtree, the root, and then the right subtree. In a BST, this traversal visits the nodes in ascending order.

```
python

def inorder(node):

if node:

inorder(node.left)

print(node.value)

inorder(node.right)
```

1.

Preorder Traversal (Root, Left, Right): Visits the root first, then the left subtree, followed by the right subtree. Preorder traversal is often used to create a copy of the tree.

```
python

def preorder(node):

if node:

print(node.value)
```

preorder(node.left)

preorder(node.right)

1.

Postorder Traversal (Left, Right, Root): Visits the left subtree, the right subtree, and finally the root. Postorder traversal is useful for deleting nodes or evaluating expressions.

python

def postorder(node):

if node:

postorder(node.left)

postorder(node.right)

print(node.value)

1.

Graphs: A Generalized Structure

A **graph** is a more generalized structure than a tree. While a tree is a type of graph with hierarchical structure and no cycles, a graph can represent any relationship between nodes, including cycles and multiple connections between nodes. A graph consists of **vertices** (nodes) and **edges** (connections between the nodes).

Types of Graphs

1. **Directed Graph (Digraph)**: In a directed graph, edges have a direction. If there is an edge from node A to node B, you can travel from A to B, but not necessarily from B to A.

2. **Undirected Graph**: In an undirected graph, edges do not have directions. You can travel between nodes in both directions along an edge.
3. **Weighted Graph**: In a weighted graph, each edge has a weight or cost associated with it. This type of graph is useful for problems like finding the shortest path.
4. **Cyclic and Acyclic Graphs**: A **cyclic graph** contains at least one cycle, where a path returns to the same vertex. An **acyclic graph** has no cycles. Trees are examples of acyclic graphs.

Graph Representation in Python

GRAPHS CAN BE REPRESENTED in several ways:

1. **Adjacency Matrix**: A 2D matrix where each cell (i, j) indicates whether there is an edge between vertex i and vertex j.
2. **Adjacency List**: A dictionary where each vertex has a list of adjacent vertices. This is a more space-efficient way to represent sparse graphs.

Let's implement a basic graph using an adjacency list:

```
class Graph:

def __init__(self):

self.graph = {}

# Add edge to the graph

def add_edge(self, u, v):

if u not in self.graph:
```

```
self.graph[u] = []
self.graph[u].append(v)
# Breadth-First Search (BFS)
def bfs(self, start):
visited = set()
queue = [start]
visited.add(start)
while queue:
vertex = queue.pop(0)
print(vertex, end=' ')
for neighbor in self.graph.get(vertex, []):
if neighbor not in visited:
queue.append(neighbor)
visited.add(neighbor)
# Depth-First Search (DFS)
def dfs(self, vertex, visited=None):
if visited is None:
visited = set()
visited.add(vertex)
print(vertex, end=' ')
```

```
for neighbor in self.graph.get(vertex, []):
if neighbor not in visited:
self.dfs(neighbor, visited)
# Example usage
g = Graph()
g.add_edge(0, 1)
g.add_edge(0, 2)
g.add_edge(1, 2)
g.add_edge(2, 0)
g.add_edge(2, 3)
g.add_edge(3, 3)
print("Breadth-First Search:")
g.bfs(2) # Output: 2 0 3 1
print("\nDepth-First Search:")
g.dfs(2) # Output: 2 0 1 3
```

In this graph implementation, we represent the graph using an adjacency list (a dictionary where the keys are vertices and the values are lists of adjacent vertices). We also implement two common graph traversal algorithms:

1. **Breadth-First Search (BFS)**: This traversal starts at the root (or any arbitrary node) and explores all its neighbors at the present depth before moving on to nodes at the

next depth level. BFS uses a queue to track nodes.

2. **Depth-First Search (DFS)**: This traversal starts at the root and explores as far as possible along each branch before backtracking. DFS uses recursion or a stack to track nodes.

Shortest Path in a Graph

FINDING THE SHORTEST path in a graph is a common problem. One of the most widely used algorithms for this purpose is **Dijkstra's Algorithm**, which finds the shortest path between two nodes in a weighted graph.

```
import heapq

def dijkstra(graph, start):

distances = {vertex: float('infinity') for vertex in graph}

distances[start] = 0

priority_queue = [(0, start)]

while priority_queue:

current_distance, current_vertex = heapq.heappop(priority_queue)

if current_distance > distances[current_vertex]:

continue

for neighbor, weight in graph[current_vertex]:

distance = current_distance + weight

if distance < distances[neighbor]:
```

```
distances[neighbor] = distance

heapq.heappush(priority_queue, (distance, neighbor))

return distances

# Example weighted graph

graph = {

'A': [('B', 1), ('C', 4)],

'B': [('A', 1), ('C', 2), ('D', 5)],

'C': [('A', 4), ('B', 2), ('D', 1)],

'D': [('B', 5), ('C', 1)]

}

print(dijkstra(graph, 'A')) # Output: {'A': 0, 'B': 1, 'C': 3, 'D': 4}
```

Conclusion

TREES AND GRAPHS ARE powerful data structures that provide the foundation for solving many computational problems, from organizing data hierarchically to modeling complex networks. Understanding their structure, implementation, and application is crucial for working on advanced algorithms and efficiently solving real-world problems.

Searching and Sorting Algorithms

SEARCHING AND SORTING algorithms are fundamental concepts in computer science and are widely used in many areas, from databases and file systems to algorithms for more complex data processing tasks. These algorithms provide efficient methods to retrieve or arrange data in a meaningful way, which is critical for optimizing performance, particularly when dealing with large datasets. In this section, we will explore some of the most common and important searching and sorting algorithms.

Searching Algorithms

SEARCHING ALGORITHMS are designed to retrieve data from a collection based on a search query. The efficiency of these algorithms depends on the structure of the data and the type of search operation being performed.

Linear Search

LINEAR SEARCH is the simplest searching algorithm, where each element of the collection is checked sequentially until the target element is found or the list is exhausted. It works on both sorted and unsorted data.

```
def linear_search(arr, target):

for i in range(len(arr)):

if arr[i] == target:

return i

return -1

# Example usage

arr = [10, 20, 30, 40, 50]

result = linear_search(arr, 30)

print(result) # Output: 2
```

While linear search is straightforward to implement, it is inefficient for large datasets because it checks each element individually. The time complexity of linear search is **O(n)**, where n is the number of elements in the array.

Binary Search

BINARY SEARCH is a more efficient algorithm, but it requires the data to be sorted. It works by dividing the dataset in half and determining whether the target element lies in the left or right half. This process is repeated until the target is found or the dataset is reduced to an empty set. The time complexity of binary search is **O(log n)**.

```
def binary_search(arr, target):

low = 0

high = len(arr) - 1

while low <= high:

mid = (low + high) // 2

if arr[mid] == target:

return mid

elif arr[mid] < target:

low = mid + 1

else:

high = mid - 1

return -1
```

```
# Example usage

arr = [10, 20, 30, 40, 50]

result = binary_search(arr, 30)

print(result) # Output: 2
```

Binary search is much more efficient than linear search for large datasets, but its limitation is that the dataset must be sorted beforehand. Sorting a dataset takes additional time, usually **O(n log n)** with efficient sorting algorithms, so the overall performance depends on the situation.

Hash-Based Search

HASHING IS A TECHNIQUE that allows for efficient searching in constant time, **O(1)**, on average. Hash-based searches use a **hash function** to map data into specific positions (or "buckets") in a hash table. When searching for an element, the hash function is applied, and the element is retrieved from its corresponding bucket.

Python's built-in dictionaries (dict) and sets (set) use hashing internally, providing efficient search operations.

```
# Example using a Python dictionary (hash table)

hash_table = {

"apple": 1,

"banana": 2,

"cherry": 3
```

```
}
# Searching for a key
result = hash_table.get("banana")
print(result) # Output: 2
```

The major drawback of hashing is the possibility of **collisions**, where multiple elements are mapped to the same position. Collision handling techniques such as chaining or open addressing are used to manage these conflicts.

Sorting Algorithms

SORTING ALGORITHMS are used to arrange data in a specific order, usually ascending or descending. Sorting is important because many algorithms, such as binary search, require sorted data to function efficiently. Let's explore some popular sorting algorithms, ranging from basic to more advanced techniques.

Bubble Sort

BUBBLE SORT is a simple sorting algorithm where adjacent elements are compared, and if they are in the wrong order, they are swapped. This process is repeated until the entire list is sorted. Although easy to understand, bubble sort is inefficient for large datasets due to its high time complexity of **O(n^2)**.

```
def bubble_sort(arr):
n = len(arr)
for i in range(n):
for j in range(0, n-i-1):
```

```
if arr[j] > arr[j+1]:
arr[j], arr[j+1] = arr[j+1], arr[j]
# Example usage
arr = [64, 34, 25, 12, 22, 11, 90]
bubble_sort(arr)
print(arr) # Output: [11, 12, 22, 25, 34, 64, 90]
```

Bubble sort is not practical for large datasets due to its quadratic time complexity. However, it is useful for teaching purposes and small datasets.

Insertion Sort

INSERTION SORT is another simple sorting algorithm where elements are sorted one at a time by comparing them with the already sorted portion of the list and inserting them in the correct position. The time complexity is **O(n^2)** in the worst case but can be more efficient for small or nearly sorted datasets.

```
def insertion_sort(arr):
for i in range(1, len(arr)):
key = arr[i]
j = i - 1
while j >= 0 and key < arr[j]:
arr[j + 1] = arr[j]
j -= 1
```

```
arr[j + 1] = key

# Example usage

arr = [64, 34, 25, 12, 22, 11, 90]

insertion_sort(arr)

print(arr) # Output: [11, 12, 22, 25, 34, 64, 90]
```

Insertion sort is more efficient than bubble sort for small or nearly sorted datasets, as it only requires a few comparisons and shifts in such cases.

Merge Sort

MERGE SORT is a divide-and-conquer algorithm that divides the dataset into smaller sublists, sorts each sublist recursively, and then merges the sorted sublists back together. The time complexity of merge sort is **O(n log n)**, making it one of the more efficient sorting algorithms for larger datasets.

```
def merge_sort(arr):

if len(arr) > 1:

mid = len(arr) // 2

left_half = arr[:mid]

right_half = arr[mid:]

merge_sort(left_half)

merge_sort(right_half)

i = j = k = 0
```

```
while i < len(left_half) and j < len(right_half):

if left_half[i] < right_half[j]:

arr[k] = left_half[i]

i += 1

else:

arr[k] = right_half[j]

j += 1

k += 1

while i < len(left_half):

arr[k] = left_half[i]

i += 1

k += 1

while j < len(right_half):

arr[k] = right_half[j]

j += 1

k += 1

# Example usage

arr = [64, 34, 25, 12, 22, 11, 90]

merge_sort(arr)

print(arr) # Output: [11, 12, 22, 25, 34, 64, 90]
```

Merge sort is stable and efficient, especially for larger datasets, but it requires additional memory space for the sublists, which is its main drawback compared to other in-place sorting algorithms.

Quick Sort

QUICK SORT is another divide-and-conquer algorithm but is generally faster than merge sort because it works in place (without needing extra memory). It selects a "pivot" element and partitions the array into elements less than the pivot and elements greater than the pivot. The process is repeated for each partition. Its average time complexity is **O(n log n)**, but in the worst case, it can degrade to **O(n^2)** if the pivot is poorly chosen.

```
def quick_sort(arr):

if len(arr) <= 1:

return arr

else:

pivot = arr[len(arr) // 2]

left = [x for x in arr if x < pivot]

middle = [x for x in arr if x == pivot]

right = [x for x in arr if x > pivot]

return quick_sort(left) + middle + quick_sort(right)

# Example usage

arr = [64, 34, 25, 12, 22, 11, 90]

sorted_arr = quick_sort(arr)
```

print(sorted_arr) # Output: [11, 12, 22, 25, 34, 64, 90]

Quick sort is generally the preferred sorting algorithm for most practical purposes due to its speed and in-place nature. However, it can be inefficient in some edge cases where the pivot is poorly chosen, leading to imbalanced partitions.

Heap Sort

HEAP SORT is another comparison-based sorting algorithm. It first transforms the array into a **heap** data structure, where the largest element is at the root (in the case of a max-heap). The largest element is then swapped with the last element of the array, and the heap is rebalanced. The process is repeated until the entire array is sorted. The time complexity of heap sort is **O(n log n)**.

```
def heapify(arr, n, i):

largest = i

left = 2 * i + 1

right = 2 * i + 2

if left < n and arr[left] > arr[largest]:

largest = left

if right < n and arr[right] > arr[largest]:

largest = right

if largest != i:

arr[i], arr[largest] = arr[largest], arr[i]

heapify(arr, n, largest)
```

```
def heap_sort(arr):
n = len(arr)
for i in range(n // 2 - 1, -1, -1):
heapify(arr, n, i)
for i in range(n - 1, 0, -1):
arr[i], arr[0] = arr[0], arr[i]
heapify(arr, i, 0)
# Example usage
arr = [64, 34, 25, 12, 22, 11, 90]
heap_sort(arr)
print(arr) # Output: [11, 12, 22, 25, 34, 64, 90]
```

Heap sort is efficient and uses **O(1)** extra space, making it an in-place sorting algorithm. However, it is not stable (it does not preserve the relative order of equal elements) and is generally slower than quick sort in practice.

Conclusion

SEARCHING AND SORTING algorithms form the backbone of efficient data manipulation in computer science. Understanding these algorithms and knowing when to apply each is critical for optimizing performance in a wide range of applications. From the simplicity of linear search and bubble sort to the efficiency of binary search and quick sort, these algorithms provide essential tools for handling data in both small and large-scale problems.

Practical Examples with Complex Data Structures

IN THIS SECTION, WE will dive into practical applications of complex data structures such as trees, graphs, and heaps, demonstrating how they can be employed in real-world problem-solving. These examples will combine the power of different data structures and algorithms to provide efficient solutions for various computational challenges.

Example 1: Building an Autocomplete System Using Tries

A **Trie** is a tree-like data structure that is commonly used for storing strings in a way that enables fast prefix-based searches. This is particularly useful for implementing an autocomplete system, where given a prefix, we want to quickly retrieve all possible words that match that prefix.

Implementing a Trie

```
CLASS TRIENODE:
def __init__(self):
self.children = {}
self.is_end_of_word = False
class Trie:
def __init__(self):
self.root = TrieNode()
# Insert a word into the trie
```

```
def insert(self, word):
node = self.root
for char in word:
if char not in node.children:
node.children[char] = TrieNode()
node = node.children[char]
node.is_end_of_word = True
# Search for a word in the trie
def search(self, word):
node = self.root
for char in word:
if char not in node.children:
return False
node = node.children[char]
return node.is_end_of_word
# Find words with a given prefix
def starts_with(self, prefix):
node = self.root
for char in prefix:
if char not in node.children:
```

```
return []
node = node.children[char]
# Collect all words starting with the given prefix
return self._collect_words(node, prefix)
def _collect_words(self, node, prefix):
words = []
if node.is_end_of_word:
words.append(prefix)
for char, child_node in node.children.items():
words += self._collect_words(child_node, prefix + char)
return words
# Example usage
trie = Trie()
trie.insert("apple")
trie.insert("app")
trie.insert("apricot")
trie.insert("banana")
# Autocomplete words starting with "app"
print(trie.starts_with("app")) # Output: ['apple', 'app']
```

In this example, we implemented a Trie data structure for storing words and performing fast lookups based on prefixes. This type of system is useful in search engines or any application that requires real-time word suggestions.

Real-World Use Case

AUTOCOMPLETE SYSTEMS are commonly used in search engines, messaging apps, and text editors. When a user begins typing a word, the system suggests possible completions. By using a Trie, these suggestions can be generated quickly, even for large datasets. The efficiency of the Trie lies in its ability to group words by their common prefixes, allowing the search space to be reduced drastically as the user types more characters.

Example 2: Social Network Friend Recommendations Using Graphs

SOCIAL NETWORKS CAN be modeled as **graphs**, where each node represents a user, and edges represent friendships between users. One practical problem is to recommend friends to a user based on mutual connections.

Implementing a Graph for Friend Recommendations

CLASS GRAPH:

def __init__(self):

self.graph = {}

def add_user(self, user):

if user not in self.graph:

self.graph[user] = []

```
def add_friendship(self, user1, user2):
self.graph[user1].append(user2)
self.graph[user2].append(user1)
def get_friends(self, user):
return self.graph.get(user, [])
# Recommend friends based on mutual connections
def recommend_friends(self, user):
if user not in self.graph:
return []
friends = set(self.get_friends(user))
recommended_friends = {}
# For each friend of the user, check their friends
for friend in friends:
for mutual_friend in self.get_friends(friend):
if mutual_friend != user and mutual_friend not in friends:
recommended_friends[mutual_friend] =
recommended_friends.get(mutual_friend, 0) + 1
# Sort recommendations by the number of mutual friends
return sorted(recommended_friends.keys(), key=lambda x:
-recommended_friends[x])
# Example usage
```

```
network = Graph()
network.add_user("Alice")
network.add_user("Bob")
network.add_user("Charlie")
network.add_user("David")
network.add_user("Eve")
network.add_friendship("Alice", "Bob")
network.add_friendship("Alice", "Charlie")
network.add_friendship("Bob", "David")
network.add_friendship("Charlie", "Eve")
# Recommend friends for Alice based on mutual connections
print(network.recommend_friends("Alice")) # Output: ['David', 'Eve']
```

In this example, we built a graph where each user has a list of their friends. The recommend_friends() function recommends friends based on the number of mutual connections between the users. This is a simplified version of a real-world recommendation system used by social networks like Facebook or LinkedIn.

Real-World Use Case

IN SOCIAL NETWORKING platforms, friend recommendation algorithms suggest new connections to users based on various factors, such as the number of mutual friends. Graph-based algorithms efficiently identify these potential connections, making the system scalable even for millions of users. These recommendations help users expand their social circles, making the platform more engaging.

Example 3: Job Scheduling Using Heaps (Priority Queue)

IN MANY SYSTEMS, JOBS or tasks must be scheduled based on priority. A **Priority Queue** is a data structure that allows us to insert elements and retrieve the one with the highest priority efficiently. Heaps are commonly used to implement priority queues.

Implementing a Priority Queue with a Heap

```
IMPORT HEAPQ

class JobScheduler:

def __init__(self):

self.jobs = []

# Add a job to the scheduler with a given priority

def add_job(self, job_name, priority):

heapq.heappush(self.jobs, (-priority, job_name)) # Use negative priority for max-heap behavior

# Get the next job with the highest priority

def get_next_job(self):

if not self.jobs:

return None
```

```
return heapq.heappop(self.jobs)[1]

# Example usage

scheduler = JobScheduler()

scheduler.add_job("Job1", 3)

scheduler.add_job("Job2", 1)

scheduler.add_job("Job3", 5)

scheduler.add_job("Job4", 2)

# Get jobs by priority

print(scheduler.get_next_job()) # Output: Job3 (highest priority)

print(scheduler.get_next_job()) # Output: Job1
```

In this implementation, we use Python's heapq module to implement a priority queue for scheduling jobs. The jobs are stored as a heap, where the job with the highest priority is always retrieved first.

Real-World Use Case

PRIORITY QUEUES ARE essential in operating systems for job scheduling, where different processes are assigned priorities, and the system ensures that higher-priority tasks are executed before lower-priority ones. Similarly, in cloud computing environments, job scheduling is used to manage resources efficiently, ensuring that critical tasks receive precedence over less important ones.

Example 4: Shortest Path in a Weighted Graph Using Dijkstra's Algorithm

IN MANY REAL-WORLD scenarios, such as finding the shortest route in a transportation network or minimizing cost in logistics, we need to compute the shortest path between nodes in a weighted graph. Dijkstra's algorithm is one of the most popular algorithms for this purpose.

Implementing Dijkstra's Algorithm

IMPORT HEAPQ

def dijkstra(graph, start):

Initialize distances and priority queue

distances = {vertex: float('infinity') for vertex in graph}

distances[start] = 0

priority_queue = [(0, start)]

while priority_queue:

current_distance, current_vertex = heapq.heappop(priority_queue)

if current_distance > distances[current_vertex]:

continue

for neighbor, weight in graph[current_vertex]:

distance = current_distance + weight

Only consider this new path if it's shorter

```
if distance < distances[neighbor]:
distances[neighbor] = distance
heapq.heappush(priority_queue, (distance, neighbor))
return distances
# Example weighted graph
graph = {
'A': [('B', 1), ('C', 4)],
'B': [('A', 1), ('C', 2), ('D', 5)],
'C': [('A', 4), ('B', 2), ('D', 1)],
'D': [('B', 5), ('C', 1)]
}
# Finding shortest path from node 'A'
print(dijkstra(graph, 'A')) # Output: {'A': 0, 'B': 1, 'C': 3, 'D': 4}
```

In this example, Dijkstra's algorithm calculates the shortest path from a start node to all other nodes in a weighted graph. We use a priority queue (min-heap) to efficiently track the node with the smallest distance.

Real-World Use Case

DIJKSTRA'S ALGORITHM is used in GPS navigation systems to find the shortest route between two locations. It is also used in network routing protocols to optimize data transmission and ensure that packets follow the least-cost path through a network.

This algorithm is foundational in logistics, transportation, and network optimization problems.

Conclusion

THESE EXAMPLES DEMONSTRATE how complex data structures like tries, graphs, and heaps can be used to solve practical problems in areas such as search systems, social networks, job scheduling, and shortest path finding. Understanding how to implement and apply these structures enables the development of efficient and scalable solutions for real-world challenges. The ability to combine these data structures with algorithms unlocks the potential for optimizing performance and achieving significant improvements in various domains of software development.

Chapter 10: Introduction to Web Scraping with Python

What Is Web Scraping?

WEB SCRAPING IS THE process of automatically extracting data from websites. It allows developers and data enthusiasts to gather large amounts of information from the web in a structured format. Instead of manually copying and pasting data from a website, web scraping automates this process, making it more efficient and scalable.

At its core, web scraping involves sending a request to a web server, receiving the HTML of a webpage, and then extracting useful information from it. This process can be broken down into a few key steps:

1. **Requesting a webpage**: This involves sending an HTTP request to the server that hosts the website and receiving the HTML (or other content) of the webpage.
2. **Parsing the HTML**: After receiving the HTML, the next step is to parse it and extract the relevant information. This is typically done using a library that can navigate through the HTML structure, such as BeautifulSoup.
3. **Handling dynamic content**: Some websites load their content dynamically using JavaScript. In these cases, libraries like Selenium can be used to simulate a browser and scrape the dynamically loaded content.
4. **Storing the extracted data**: Finally, the extracted data needs to be saved in a structured format, such as CSV, JSON, or a database.

Why Web Scraping?

THERE ARE MANY REASONS to use web scraping, from gathering data for research to monitoring competitors in business. Here are a few common use cases:

- **Price Monitoring**: Companies often scrape e-commerce websites to track the prices of their products and competitors' products.
- **Content Aggregation**: News websites or blogs may scrape other websites to aggregate content or track breaking news.
- **SEO Analysis**: Marketers use web scraping to collect data on how competitors rank for keywords, backlinks, or meta descriptions.
- **Data Collection for Research**: Researchers often scrape websites to collect large datasets that are not publicly available in a structured format.

Despite its many applications, web scraping must be done responsibly and ethically. It's important to respect the website's terms of service and avoid overloading the server with requests.

The Basics of Web Scraping

TO START SCRAPING DATA from the web, you'll need to have some basic understanding of HTML, the structure of web pages, and Python libraries such as requests and BeautifulSoup. Let's dive into these concepts and then go step-by-step to scrape our first website.

HTML: The Structure of Web Pages

HTML (HYPERTEXT MARKUP Language) is the standard language used to create web pages. It consists of tags that define the structure of the page. A basic HTML document might look like this:

```
<!DOCTYPE html>

<html>

<head>

<title>Example Page</title>

</head>

<body>

<h1>Welcome to the Example Page</h1>

<p>This is a simple web page.</p>

<div class="content">

<p>Here is some additional content.</p>

</div>

</body>

</html>
```

In this document, there are several key components:

- <html>: The root element of the page.

• <head>: Contains metadata about the page, such as the title.

• <body>: The main content of the page, which includes headings (<h1>), paragraphs (<p>), and other elements like divs (<div>).

When scraping a website, you'll use this structure to identify and extract the data you need.

Libraries for Web Scraping

THERE ARE SEVERAL PYTHON libraries that are commonly used for web scraping. Two of the most important ones are:

1. **Requests**: A simple and elegant HTTP library that allows you to send HTTP requests to a web server and get the HTML content of a page.
2. **BeautifulSoup**: A library that makes it easy to parse HTML and extract specific elements from a webpage.

Let's look at how to install and use these libraries.

Installing Required Libraries

BEFORE YOU CAN START scraping, you'll need to install the necessary Python libraries. You can do this using pip, the Python package manager.

pip install requests

pip install beautifulsoup4

These commands will install the requests library for making HTTP requests and the beautifulsoup4 library for parsing HTML.

Making HTTP Requests with requests

THE FIRST STEP IN WEB scraping is to fetch the HTML of the webpage you want to scrape. You can do this easily with the requests library. Here's an example of how to fetch a webpage:

```
import requests

url = 'https://example.com'

response = requests.get(url)

# Print the HTML of the webpage

print(response.text)
```

In this example, we're sending an HTTP GET request to the URL https://example.com. The response.text property contains the HTML of the page, which we can then parse and extract data from.

Parsing HTML with BeautifulSoup

ONCE YOU HAVE THE HTML of a webpage, the next step is to parse it and extract the relevant information. BeautifulSoup is a powerful tool for navigating through the HTML structure and selecting the elements you want.

Here's an example of how to use BeautifulSoup to parse the HTML and extract specific elements:

```
from bs4 import BeautifulSoup

# Assuming you have already fetched the HTML using requests
```

```
html = response.text

# Create a BeautifulSoup object and specify the parser

soup = BeautifulSoup(html, 'html.parser')

# Extract the title of the page

title = soup.title.text

print(f"Title of the page: {title}")

# Extract all paragraphs

paragraphs = soup.find_all('p')

for p in paragraphs:

print(p.text)
```

In this example, we create a BeautifulSoup object by passing in the HTML and specifying the parser (html.parser). Then, we use the soup.title.text property to extract the title of the page. Similarly, we use soup.find_all('p') to find all the paragraph elements and print their content.

Navigating the HTML Structure

BEAUTIFULSOUP PROVIDES several methods for navigating through the HTML structure and selecting elements:

- **find()**: Returns the first element that matches a specified tag or condition.
- **find_all()**: Returns a list of all elements that match a specified tag or condition.

- **select()**: Allows you to use CSS selectors to find elements.

- **get_text()**: Extracts the text content from an HTML element.

Here's an example of how to use some of these methods:

```
# Find the first div element with the class 'content'

content_div = soup.find('div', class_='content')

# Extract the text content of the div

print(content_div.get_text())

# Use CSS selectors to find elements

h1_tag = soup.select('h1')

print(h1_tag[0].get_text())
```

In this example, we use find() to locate the first <div> element with the class content, and then extract its text using get_text(). We also use the select() method to find the <h1> element using a CSS selector.

Scraping Real-World Websites

NOW THAT YOU UNDERSTAND the basics of web scraping, let's look at a more practical example. Imagine you want to scrape the latest articles from a news website. You could use the following approach:

```
import requests

from bs4 import BeautifulSoup
```

```
url = 'https://news.ycombinator.com/'

response = requests.get(url)

soup = BeautifulSoup(response.text, 'html.parser')

# Find all article titles

titles = soup.find_all('a', class_='storylink')

for i, title in enumerate(titles, 1):

print(f"{i}. {title.text}")
```

In this example, we're scraping the Hacker News homepage to get a list of article titles. We use the find_all() method to locate all <a> tags with the class storylink, and then print the text of each title.

This is a simple example, but the same principles can be applied to more complex websites.

Handling Dynamic Content with Selenium

SOME WEBSITES USE JAVASCRIPT to load content dynamically, which means that the content may not be present in the initial HTML that you retrieve with requests. To scrape such websites, you can use Selenium, a tool that simulates a real browser and allows you to interact with JavaScript-driven pages.

Selenium requires a browser driver, such as ChromeDriver, to control the browser. Here's an example of how to use Selenium to scrape a page with dynamic content:

```
from selenium import webdriver

from selenium.webdriver.common.by import By
```

```
# Set up the browser driver (make sure to download the appropriate driver)

driver = webdriver.Chrome(executable_path='/path/to/chromedriver')

# Navigate to the website

driver.get('https://example.com')

# Wait for the content to load (if necessary)

driver.implicitly_wait(10)

# Find an element by its tag or class

element = driver.find_element(By.CLASS_NAME, 'dynamic-content')

print(element.text)

# Close the browser

driver.quit()
```

Selenium is a powerful tool for scraping dynamic websites, but it's also slower and more resource-intensive than using requests and BeautifulSoup. It should be used only when necessary, such as when scraping pages that rely heavily on JavaScript.

Ethical Considerations in Web Scraping

WHILE WEB SCRAPING can be a powerful tool for gathering data, it's important to use it ethically. Here are a few guidelines to follow:

1. **Check the website's terms of service**: Some websites

explicitly forbid web scraping in their terms of service. Make sure you are aware of and comply with these rules.

2. **Respect the robots.txt file**: The robots.txt file specifies which parts of a website are off-limits to web crawlers. Always check this file before scraping.
3. **Avoid overloading the server**: Sending too many requests to a server in a short period of time can overload it and cause performance issues. Be considerate and implement rate limiting if necessary.
4. **Always give credit**: If you are using scraped data in a public or commercial project, be sure to give proper attribution to the source.

By following these guidelines, you can ensure that your web scraping activities are legal, ethical, and respectful of the website owners.

Conclusion

WEB SCRAPING IS A POWERFUL tool for automating the extraction of data from websites. By using Python libraries such as requests, BeautifulSoup, and Selenium, you can scrape static and dynamic content efficiently. Remember to always be ethical and respectful when scraping websites, and ensure that you are following the website's terms of service and legal guidelines.

With these tools and techniques, you can start building your own web scrapers to gather the data you need for your projects.

Using Requests to Fetch Web Pages

IN WEB SCRAPING, THE first step is to obtain the HTML of a web page so that we can later parse and extract the desired data. Python's requests library is an excellent tool for this task. It is simple, easy to use, and can handle HTTP requests such as GET and POST. Before diving into fetching web pages with requests, it is important to understand the HTTP protocol, the types of requests it supports, and how requests helps abstract this complexity.

Understanding HTTP Requests

THE WEB OPERATES ON the HyperText Transfer Protocol (HTTP), which defines how data is exchanged between a client (usually a web browser or a Python script) and a web server. Each interaction between the client and the server begins with a request. There are several types of HTTP requests, but the two most important for web scraping are:

- **GET**: Requests data from a specified resource. In web scraping, this is typically the main type of request used to retrieve the HTML of a webpage.

- **POST**: Sends data to a server to create or update a resource. POST requests are used when a form is submitted, or data is sent to the server, such as login credentials.

Web scraping primarily relies on GET requests, as we are typically interested in retrieving information rather than sending it. The response to a GET request contains the HTML of the web page, which can then be parsed and processed.

Making a GET Request with requests

LET'S START BY MAKING a basic GET request using the requests library. First, ensure that you have the library installed:

```
pip install requests
```

Here's a simple example of making a GET request to retrieve a webpage:

```
import requests

# The URL of the webpage we want to scrape

url = 'https://example.com'

# Send a GET request to the server

response = requests.get(url)

# Print the response text (HTML of the page)

print(response.text)
```

In this code, we use the requests.get() function to send a GET request to the server hosting the page at https://example.com. The response object contains all the data sent back by the server, including the HTML of the page, which we can access through response.text.

Checking the Response Status

BEFORE WE DIVE INTO parsing the HTML, it's always a good idea to check whether the request was successful. The server sends back a status code in its response, indicating the result of the request. Common status codes include:

- **200 OK**: The request was successful, and the server returned the requested resource.

- **404 Not Found**: The requested resource could not be found on the server.
- **500 Internal Server Error**: The server encountered an error while processing the request.

You can check the status code of a request using the response.status_code attribute. Here's an example:

```
import requests

url = 'https://example.com'

response = requests.get(url)

# Check if the request was successful

if response.status_code == 200:

print("Request was successful!")

else:

print(f"Failed to retrieve the page. Status code: {response.status_code}")
```

This code checks if the request returned a 200 status code, indicating success. If the request was not successful, it prints the actual status code returned by the server, which can help you diagnose issues.

Understanding HTTP Headers

WHEN MAKING A REQUEST, you can also send additional information to the server in the form of HTTP headers. These headers provide context about the request, such as the type of content that the client can accept, or information about the client (e.g., the browser or application making the request). Some common headers include:

- **User-Agent**: Identifies the client making the request (such as a specific browser or bot). Some websites block scraping attempts by checking the User-Agent, so it's sometimes necessary to set this header.

- **Referer**: Indicates the URL from which the request was made.

- **Cookies**: Contains session data used for authentication or tracking purposes.

Here's an example of how to send a custom User-Agent header with a request:

```
import requests

url = 'https://example.com'

# Define custom headers

headers = {

'User-Agent': 'Mozilla/5.0 (Windows NT 10.0; Win64; x64) AppleWebKit/537.36 (KHTML, like Gecko) Chrome/91.0.4472.124 Safari/537.36'

}

# Send a GET request with custom headers

response = requests.get(url, headers=headers)

# Print the response status code
```

```
print(f"Response status code: {response.status_code}")
```

In this example, we define a custom User-Agent header that mimics a typical web browser. By doing so, we can sometimes avoid being blocked by websites that restrict bots or scrapers.

Handling Query Parameters in GET Requests

SOME WEB PAGES ACCEPT query parameters in their URL, which can be used to customize the response. For example, a news website might accept a page parameter to load different pages of articles. These parameters are passed as part of the URL, following a ?. For example:

https://example.com/search?query=python&page=2

In this case, the query parameter is set to python, and the page parameter is set to 2. You can send query parameters with a GET request using the params argument in requests.get().

Here's an example:

```
import requests

url = 'https://example.com/search'

# Define query parameters

params = {

'query': 'python',

'page': 2

}

# Send a GET request with query parameters
```

```
response = requests.get(url, params=params)

# Print the final URL after the parameters have been added

print(response.url)

# Print the response text

print(response.text)
```

In this code, we pass the query parameters as a dictionary to the params argument. The requests library automatically formats these parameters and appends them to the URL. The final URL is printed using response.url.

Handling POST Requests

WHILE GET REQUESTS are the most common for web scraping, there are cases where you need to send data to the server using a POST request. This is often the case when interacting with forms, such as logging in to a website or submitting a search query that is processed server-side.

To send a POST request with requests, use the requests.post() function, and pass the data you want to send in the data argument.

Here's an example of sending a POST request:

```
import requests

url = 'https://example.com/login'

# Define form data

data = {

'username': 'myusername',
```

```
'password': 'mypassword'

}

# Send a POST request with form data

response = requests.post(url, data=data)

# Print the response status code

print(f"Response status code: {response.status_code}")

# Print the response text

print(response.text)
```

In this example, we send a POST request to a login form at https://example.com/login. The form data is passed as a dictionary in the data argument, and the server responds with the appropriate page or an error message, which we can access through response.text.

Handling Sessions and Cookies

MANY WEBSITES USE COOKIES to track user sessions. For example, after logging in, the website might store a session cookie that allows you to stay logged in as you navigate between pages. If you're scraping a website that requires login, you'll need to maintain the session across multiple requests.

The requests library provides a Session object that allows you to persist cookies and other session-related data across requests. Here's how to use it:

```
import requests

# Create a session object
```

```
session = requests.Session()

# Send a POST request to log in

login_url = 'https://example.com/login'

login_data = {'username': 'myusername', 'password': 'mypassword'}

session.post(login_url, data=login_data)

# Now send a GET request using the same session

dashboard_url = 'https://example.com/dashboard'

response = session.get(dashboard_url)

# Print the dashboard page HTML

print(response.text)
```

In this code, we first create a session using requests.Session(). After logging in with a POST request, we send a GET request to another page (/dashboard). The session object automatically handles cookies, so we don't need to worry about passing them manually.

Handling Timeouts and Exceptions

WHEN MAKING REQUESTS to external servers, it's important to handle potential issues such as timeouts or server errors gracefully. The requests library provides mechanisms to handle these situations.

Timeouts

BY DEFAULT, REQUESTS will wait indefinitely for a response from the server. If the server is slow or unresponsive, this can cause your script to hang. To avoid this, you can set a timeout using the timeout argument.

Here's an example:

```
import requests

url = 'https://example.com'

# Set a timeout of 5 seconds

try:

response = requests.get(url, timeout=5)

print(response.text)

except requests.Timeout:

print("The request timed out")
```

In this code, we set a timeout of 5 seconds. If the server does not respond within that time, a requests.Timeout exception is raised, and we handle it by printing an error message.

Handling HTTP Errors

IF THE SERVER RETURNS an error (such as a 404 or 500 status code), requests will not raise an exception by default. However, you can check for errors manually or use the raise_for_status() method to raise an exception for HTTP errors.

Here's an example:

```
import requests

url = 'https://example.com/nonexistentpage'
```

```
response = requests.get(url)

# Raise an exception for 4xx or 5xx status codes

try:

response.raise_for_status()

except requests.HTTPError as e:

print(f"HTTP error occurred: {e}")
```

In this code, response.raise_for_status() checks if the server returned an error status code, and if so, raises an HTTPError exception. You can handle this exception as needed, such as by retrying the request or logging the error.

Conclusion

THE REQUESTS LIBRARY is a powerful and user-friendly tool for fetching web pages and handling HTTP requests in Python. By understanding how to send GET and POST requests, manage sessions and cookies, handle query parameters, and deal with potential errors, you can build robust web scrapers that interact with websites in a reliable and efficient way.

With these basics in mind, you're ready to move on to the next step of web scraping: parsing and extracting data from the HTML content of the pages you retrieve.

Parsing HTML with BeautifulSoup

PARSING HTML IS A CRUCIAL step in web scraping. After retrieving the raw HTML from a webpage using tools like requests, you need a way to navigate through and extract the data you want. The BeautifulSoup library provides a simple yet powerful way to parse and interact with HTML and XML documents. It allows you to search for and extract specific elements from a page, and to handle even malformed HTML gracefully.

What is BeautifulSoup?

BEAUTIFULSOUP IS A Python library that makes it easy to scrape information from web pages. It creates a parse tree from the page's source code, which can then be used to extract data based on tags, attributes, or even CSS selectors. BeautifulSoup can handle a variety of parsers, such as the default Python html.parser, or third-party parsers like lxml and html5lib.

The basic process of using BeautifulSoup involves:

1. Fetching the HTML content of a webpage.
2. Creating a BeautifulSoup object by parsing the HTML.
3. Searching and navigating through the parsed tree to find specific elements.
4. Extracting the relevant data.

Here's how to install BeautifulSoup using pip:

```
pip install beautifulsoup4
```

Additionally, if you want to use a faster parser like lxml, you can install it using:

```
pip install lxml
```

Once you have BeautifulSoup installed, you are ready to begin parsing HTML.

Creating a BeautifulSoup Object

AFTER FETCHING THE HTML of a page using requests, the next step is to create a BeautifulSoup object. The BeautifulSoup constructor takes two main arguments: the raw HTML content and the parser you want to use. You can choose between several parsers, but the built-in html.parser is generally sufficient for most cases.

Here's an example of creating a BeautifulSoup object:

```
import requests

from bs4 import BeautifulSoup

# Fetch the HTML content of a webpage

url = 'https://example.com'

response = requests.get(url)

html = response.text

# Create a BeautifulSoup object

soup = BeautifulSoup(html, 'html.parser')

# Print the prettified version of the HTML

print(soup.prettify())
```

In this example, we use the built-in html.parser to parse the HTML, but you can replace it with lxml or another parser if desired. The prettify() method is a helpful way to view a well-formatted version of the HTML, making it easier to inspect and navigate.

Navigating the HTML Tree

ONCE YOU HAVE A BEAUTIFULSOUP object, you can navigate the HTML tree using various methods. The most basic way to access elements is by using their tag names. BeautifulSoup allows you to access tags like properties of the object. For instance, to get the title of the page, you can simply do:

```
# Extract the title of the page

title = soup.title

print(title.text)
```

In this example, soup.title returns the <title> tag, and .text extracts the inner text. BeautifulSoup automatically finds the first occurrence of the specified tag, which is often sufficient for single instances like <title>.

Accessing Nested Elements

HTML DOCUMENTS ARE hierarchical, and BeautifulSoup makes it easy to navigate through nested elements. Each tag in the BeautifulSoup object contains information about its children and parent elements. For example:

```
# Access the body of the page

body = soup.body

# Find the first div inside the body

div = body.div

# Print the text inside the div
```

```
print(div.text)
```

In this code, we access the <body> tag and then the first <div> inside the body. BeautifulSoup allows you to traverse through nested elements by chaining tag names.

Finding Elements by Tag Name

WHILE ACCESSING ELEMENTS directly by tag name is useful, it's often more efficient to search for specific elements using methods like find() and find_all(). These methods allow you to search for tags that match specific criteria, such as tag name, attributes, or text content.

find(): Finding the First Matching Element

THE FIND() METHOD RETURNS the first tag that matches the specified criteria. You can search by tag name, class name, ID, or even CSS selectors.

```
# Find the first paragraph

first_paragraph = soup.find('p')

print(first_paragraph.text)
```

In this example, find('p') returns the first <p> tag in the document.

You can also search using attributes. For instance, if you want to find the first <div> with a specific class:

```
# Find the first div with class 'content'

content_div = soup.find('div', class_='content')

print(content_div.text)
```

Here, class_='content' specifies that we are looking for a <div> tag with the class attribute set to content.

find_all(): Finding All Matching Elements

WHILE FIND() RETURNS only the first match, find_all() returns a list of all matching elements. This is useful when you want to extract data from multiple elements with the same tag or attribute.

```
# Find all paragraphs on the page

paragraphs = soup.find_all('p')

# Loop through the paragraphs and print the text

for p in paragraphs:

print(p.text)
```

In this case, find_all('p') returns a list of all <p> tags on the page. We can then iterate through the list and extract the text from each paragraph.

Using CSS Selectors with select()

BEAUTIFULSOUP ALSO supports CSS selectors through the select() method. CSS selectors are a powerful way to target elements based on their tag names, classes, IDs, and hierarchical relationships.

```
# Use a CSS selector to find all elements with class 'content'

content_items = soup.select('.content')

# Print the text of each element with class 'content'
```

```
for item in content_items:

print(item.text)
```

In this example, .content is a CSS selector that targets all elements with the class content. The select() method is especially useful when you need to select elements based on complex relationships, such as nested elements or specific attribute combinations.

Extracting Attributes

IN ADDITION TO EXTRACTING the text inside an element, you can also extract its attributes, such as href for links or src for images. To do this, you can use the .get() method or treat the tag as a dictionary.

Here's an example of extracting the href attribute from a link:

```
# Find the first link on the page

link = soup.find('a')

# Extract the href attribute

href = link.get('href')

print(f"The first link points to: {href}")
```

Alternatively, you can use dictionary-like syntax to get attributes:

```
href = link['href']

print(f"The first link points to: {href}")
```

Both methods are equivalent, but the .get() method is more robust, as it returns None if the attribute doesn't exist, whereas accessing it like a dictionary raises a KeyError.

Searching for Elements with Specific Text

SOMETIMES, YOU MAY want to find an element based on the text it contains. BeautifulSoup allows you to search for elements whose text matches a specific string using the string argument in find() or find_all().

```
# Find the first paragraph that contains the text 'Python'

python_paragraph = soup.find('p', string='Python')

print(python_paragraph.text)
```

In this example, find('p', string='Python') returns the first <p> tag that contains the exact text "Python". You can also use regular expressions to search for more complex patterns.

```
import re

# Find all paragraphs that contain the word 'data'

data_paragraphs = soup.find_all('p', string=re.compile('data'))

for paragraph in data_paragraphs:

print(paragraph.text)
```

In this case, we use a regular expression to find all paragraphs that contain the word "data".

Modifying the HTML Document

BEAUTIFULSOUP NOT ONLY allows you to search for elements but also modify the document. You can change the text, attributes, or even structure of the document.

Changing the Text of an Element

TO MODIFY THE TEXT inside an element, you can simply assign a new value to its .string attribute.

```
# Find the first paragraph

first_paragraph = soup.find('p')

# Change its text

first_paragraph.string = "This is the new text."

# Print the modified HTML

print(soup.prettify())
```

This code modifies the text inside the first <p> tag and prints the updated HTML.

Adding or Removing Tags

YOU CAN ALSO ADD OR remove tags from the document. To add a new tag, you can use the new_tag() method, and to remove an existing tag, you can use the .decompose() method.

```
# Create a new <div> tag

new_div = soup.new_tag('div', class_='new-div')

new_div.string = "This is a new div."

# Insert the new div into the body

soup.body.append(new_div)

# Print the modified HTML
```

```
print(soup.prettify())
```

In this example, we create a new <div> tag, set its text content, and insert it into the body of the document.

Handling Malformed HTML

ONE OF THE STRENGTHS of BeautifulSoup is its ability to handle malformed HTML gracefully. Web pages often contain errors, missing closing tags, or other issues that can confuse parsers. BeautifulSoup automatically fixes these problems by converting the HTML into a valid tree structure.

For example, if a page contains unclosed tags like this:

```
<p>Unclosed paragraph

<div>Unclosed div
```

BeautifulSoup will automatically close them when parsing the document:

```
html = '<p>Unclosed paragraph<div>Unclosed div'

soup = BeautifulSoup(html, 'html.parser')

# Print the corrected HTML

print(soup.prettify())
```

Conclusion

BEAUTIFULSOUP IS A powerful and flexible library for parsing and manipulating HTML. Whether you are extracting data, modifying web pages, or handling malformed documents, BeautifulSoup makes it easy to work with HTML in Python. By combining find(), find_all(), select(), and other methods, you can navigate through and extract the information you need from any webpage.

Handling Dynamic Content with Selenium

WEB SCRAPING BECOMES more complex when you encounter websites that generate content dynamically using JavaScript. In such cases, the data you want to scrape may not be present in the raw HTML returned by a typical requests call. Instead, it may be loaded asynchronously after the page has rendered, making it difficult to access through basic scraping methods. This is where Selenium comes in.

Selenium is a powerful tool that allows you to interact with a web page just like a real user would. It simulates browser actions such as clicking buttons, filling out forms, scrolling, and waiting for JavaScript to execute. This makes it ideal for scraping dynamic content that requires the page to load fully before the data becomes available.

What is Selenium?

SELENIUM IS A PYTHON library that automates web browsers. It can drive different browsers (e.g., Chrome, Firefox, Safari) and perform various user actions like clicking, typing, scrolling, and interacting with JavaScript elements. Selenium is often used for testing web applications, but it is also highly effective for scraping content from websites that rely heavily on JavaScript.

The key components of Selenium include:

- **WebDriver**: A tool for automating web browsers. It provides methods for navigating, clicking, typing, and interacting with page elements.

- **Browser Drivers**: Each browser has its own driver (e.g., chromedriver for Chrome) that Selenium uses to control the browser.

- **Waits**: Selenium allows you to wait for elements to load or for certain conditions to be met before proceeding, which is crucial when dealing with dynamic content.

Before you can start using Selenium, you need to install it and download the appropriate browser driver.

Installing Selenium and Browser Drivers

YOU CAN INSTALL SELENIUM using pip:

```
pip install selenium
```

Next, you need to download a browser driver. For example, if you're using Chrome, you can download chromedriver from the official site: https://sites.google.com/a/chromium.org/chromedriver/. Make sure the driver version matches your installed version of Chrome.

Once you've downloaded the driver, ensure it's in your system's PATH, or specify its location when initializing the WebDriver in your code.

Setting Up Selenium with Chrome

NOW THAT YOU HAVE SELENIUM installed and a browser driver ready, let's look at how to set up a Selenium WebDriver for Chrome and navigate to a webpage.

```
from selenium import webdriver
```

```
# Specify the path to the chromedriver
driver_path = '/path/to/chromedriver'
# Initialize the Chrome WebDriver
driver = webdriver.Chrome(executable_path=driver_path)
# Navigate to a webpage
url = 'https://example.com'
driver.get(url)
# Print the page title
print(driver.title)
# Close the browser
driver.quit()
```

In this example, we initialize the Chrome WebDriver and use it to open a webpage. The driver.get() method navigates to the specified URL, and driver.title returns the page's title. Finally, we close the browser using driver.quit().

Handling Dynamic Content

ONE OF THE MAIN ADVANTAGES of Selenium is its ability to interact with dynamic content. JavaScript often loads data after the initial page load, so we need to wait for certain elements to appear before attempting to scrape the data.

Implicit Waits

SELENIUM PROVIDES IMPLICIT waits that allow the WebDriver to wait for a certain amount of time before throwing an exception if an element is not found. This is helpful when elements are loaded dynamically.

```
from selenium import webdriver

driver_path = '/path/to/chromedriver'

driver = webdriver.Chrome(executable_path=driver_path)

# Set an implicit wait time of 10 seconds

driver.implicitly_wait(10)

url = 'https://example.com'

driver.get(url)

# Try to find an element

element = driver.find_element_by_id('dynamic-element')

print(element.text)

driver.quit()
```

In this example, implicitly_wait(10) instructs Selenium to wait up to 10 seconds for elements to appear before throwing an exception. This is useful for handling elements that take a few seconds to load due to JavaScript.

Explicit Waits

IMPLICIT WAITS ARE convenient, but they wait for every element on the page, which can slow down the process. A more efficient approach is to use explicit waits, where you wait for a specific condition to be met before proceeding.

Selenium's WebDriverWait class allows you to set explicit waits. For example, you can wait until a particular element is present on the page, or until a specific condition (like text being visible) is met.

```
from selenium import webdriver

from selenium.webdriver.common.by import By

from selenium.webdriver.support.ui import WebDriverWait

from selenium.webdriver.support import expected_conditions as EC

driver_path = '/path/to/chromedriver'

driver = webdriver.Chrome(executable_path=driver_path)

url = 'https://example.com'

driver.get(url)

# Wait for the element to be present

try:

element = WebDriverWait(driver, 10).until(

EC.presence_of_element_located((By.ID, 'dynamic-element'))

)
```

```
print(element.text)

finally:

driver.quit()
```

In this example, we use WebDriverWait to wait up to 10 seconds for an element with the ID dynamic-element to appear. The expected_conditions module provides a variety of conditions you can wait for, such as the presence of an element, visibility of an element, or whether a certain text appears on the page.

Clicking and Interacting with Elements

DYNAMIC CONTENT OFTEN requires user interaction to load, such as clicking a button to reveal more data or filling out a form. Selenium allows you to simulate these actions.

Here's an example of clicking a button to load more content:

```
from selenium import webdriver

from selenium.webdriver.common.by import By

driver_path = '/path/to/chromedriver'

driver = webdriver.Chrome(executable_path=driver_path)

url = 'https://example.com'

driver.get(url)

# Click a button to load more content

load_more_button = driver.find_element(By.ID, 'load-more')

load_more_button.click()
```

```
# Wait for the new content to load and scrape it

new_content = driver.find_element(By.ID, 'new-content')

print(new_content.text)

driver.quit()
```

In this example, we find a button with the ID load-more and click it using the .click() method. After clicking the button, we wait for the new content to load and then scrape the data from it.

Selenium supports many other interactions as well, such as typing into input fields, submitting forms, or selecting items from dropdown menus.

Scrolling to Load More Content

SOME WEBSITES LOAD additional content when the user scrolls down the page, especially on infinite scrolling pages like social media feeds or search results. Selenium can simulate scrolling by using the execute_script() method to run JavaScript code that scrolls the page.

Here's how to scroll down the page and load more content:

```
from selenium import webdriver

import time

driver_path = '/path/to/chromedriver'

driver = webdriver.Chrome(executable_path=driver_path)

url = 'https://example.com'

driver.get(url)
```

```
# Scroll down the page multiple times to load more content

for i in range(5):

# Scroll down to the bottom of the page

driver.execute_script("window.scrollTo(0,
document.body.scrollHeight);")

# Wait for new content to load

time.sleep(2)

# Scrape the newly loaded content

new_content = driver.find_element_by_id('new-content')

print(new_content.text)

driver.quit()
```

In this code, we use window.scrollTo(0, document.body.scrollHeight) to scroll to the bottom of the page. We repeat this process five times, waiting 2 seconds between each scroll to give the new content time to load. After scrolling, we scrape the dynamically loaded content.

Taking Screenshots

SELENIUM ALSO ALLOWS you to take screenshots of the page, which can be useful for debugging or for visual verification of the page state during scraping.

Here's how to take a screenshot of the current page:

```
driver_path = '/path/to/chromedriver'

driver = webdriver.Chrome(executable_path=driver_path)
```

```
url = 'https://example.com'

driver.get(url)

# Take a screenshot and save it as 'screenshot.png'

driver.save_screenshot('screenshot.png')

driver.quit()
```

This saves a PNG image of the page as it appears in the browser window. This is particularly helpful when trying to verify that the page loaded correctly or when debugging issues with dynamic content not appearing as expected.

Headless Browsing

RUNNING A FULL BROWSER with a graphical user interface (GUI) can be resource-intensive and slow. For web scraping purposes, you often don't need to see the browser window at all. Selenium supports **headless browsing**, which allows you to run the browser in the background without rendering the GUI. This makes scraping faster and more efficient.

Here's how to run Chrome in headless mode:

```
from selenium import webdriver

from selenium.webdriver.chrome.options import Options

chrome_options = Options()

chrome_options.add_argument("—headless")

driver_path = '/path/to/chromedriver'
```

```
driver = webdriver.Chrome(executable_path=driver_path, options=chrome_options)

url = 'https://example.com'

driver.get(url)

# Scrape the content

content = driver.find_element_by_id('content')

print(content.text)

driver.quit()
```

In this example, we add the—headless argument to the Chrome options, which runs the browser in headless mode. The rest of the code works as usual, but without the browser window opening on your screen.

Dealing with Captchas and Anti-Scraping Mechanisms

MANY WEBSITES IMPLEMENT measures to prevent automated scraping, such as CAPTCHAs or bot detection systems. Selenium, in most cases, can bypass basic anti-scraping mechanisms, but CAPTCHAs present a significant challenge. CAPTCHAs are designed to differentiate between human users and bots, and solving them programmatically is difficult and often impractical.

If you encounter a CAPTCHA while scraping with Selenium, you have a few options:

1. **Manual Intervention**: You can set up Selenium to pause and wait for you to solve the CAPTCHA manually.

Once the CAPTCHA is solved, the script can continue.

2. **Use CAPTCHA Solving Services**: There are services like 2Captcha that provide APIs for solving CAPTCHAs. You can integrate such services into your script, but this approach may introduce latency and cost.
3. **Avoid CAPTCHAs**: Sometimes CAPTCHAs are triggered based on suspicious activity, such as making too many requests in a short period. Slowing down your scraping, using proxies, and mimicking human behavior (e.g., waiting between actions) can help avoid CAPTCHAs.

Conclusion

SELENIUM IS A POWERFUL tool for scraping dynamic content from websites that rely heavily on JavaScript. Its ability to simulate user actions, wait for elements to load, and interact with various page elements makes it ideal for handling complex scraping tasks that cannot be accomplished with basic tools like requests and BeautifulSoup. However, it's important to use Selenium responsibly and ethically, respecting the terms of service of the websites you are scraping.

By mastering Selenium, you can scrape even the most challenging websites, handling dynamic content, user interactions, and JavaScript-driven pages with ease.

Ethical Considerations in Web Scraping

WEB SCRAPING CAN BE an incredibly powerful tool for gathering data, automating tasks, and building real-world applications. However, it's essential to recognize that web scraping must be conducted ethically and legally. Just because it's technically possible to scrape a website doesn't mean it's always permissible or responsible to do so. When engaging in web scraping, there are several key ethical and legal considerations to keep in mind. This section will explore these considerations in depth, including website terms of service, compliance with legal frameworks, avoiding harm to web servers, respecting intellectual property, and strategies for ethical scraping.

Understanding Website Terms of Service

ONE OF THE FIRST STEPS before scraping a website is to thoroughly review its **Terms of Service (ToS)**. Many websites have specific guidelines regarding the use of automated tools to access their content. These terms can vary significantly between websites. Some websites explicitly forbid any form of automated access, including scraping, while others may allow scraping under certain conditions or for specific purposes.

For example, a ToS might include language such as:

> "You agree not to use any automated means, including robots, spiders, or scrapers, to access the website for any purpose without our express written permission."

In such cases, scraping the website would be a violation of the terms, and continuing to scrape could lead to legal consequences or being blocked from the website. It's essential to respect these rules and seek permission if necessary.

Reading and Interpreting Terms of Service

TERMS OF SERVICE AGREEMENTS are often long and complex. However, as a web scraper, you should focus on sections that refer to automated tools, data collection, intellectual property, and user conduct. Here's how you can approach interpreting a ToS:

1. **Search for Keywords**: Use your browser's search function to look for terms like "scraping," "automated," "robot," "spider," and "data." These sections will usually provide specific guidance on whether web scraping is allowed.
2. **Understand the Website's Intent**: Even if the ToS doesn't explicitly forbid scraping, consider the intent of the website owner. If the site is heavily monetized through advertisements, scraping could potentially hurt its revenue model. Respecting the purpose and business model of the website is key to ethical scraping.
3. **Get Explicit Permission**: If you are unsure about the site's stance on scraping or if scraping is essential for a project, consider reaching out to the website's administrators to ask for permission. A polite request can go a long way in fostering a positive relationship and ensuring you're on the right side of ethical and legal boundaries.

Compliance with Legal Frameworks

IN ADDITION TO ADHERING to the website's ToS, it's essential to ensure that your scraping activities comply with broader legal frameworks. Two of the most important legal areas to consider when scraping data are **copyright law** and **data protection regulations**.

Copyright Law

MANY WEBSITES CONTAIN original content that is protected under copyright law. Scraping this content without permission may infringe on the website's intellectual property rights. For example, scraping articles, images, or other creative works and using them without proper attribution or permission could lead to legal disputes.

When scraping content, ask yourself:

- **Who owns the data?**: Determine whether the data you're scraping is original content created by the website owner or whether it is public domain information.

- **How will you use the data?**: If you plan to redistribute, publish, or monetize the scraped data, you should be especially cautious about copyright infringement. Make sure to attribute content properly and avoid using copyrighted material in ways that violate fair use policies.

Data Protection Laws

IN RECENT YEARS, DATA privacy and protection laws have become increasingly strict, especially in regions such as the European Union with the **General Data Protection Regulation (GDPR)**. These laws are designed to protect individuals' personal information, such as names, email addresses, phone numbers, and other identifiable data.

If your scraping involves collecting personal data, you must ensure that you comply with data protection regulations. Here are some key principles to follow:

1. **Minimize Data Collection**: Only scrape the data that is absolutely necessary for your project. Collecting excessive or irrelevant personal data can increase the risk of violating privacy laws.
2. **Anonymize Data**: If possible, anonymize any personal data you collect so that individuals cannot be identified. For example, you might aggregate data or strip out identifiers.
3. **Provide Transparency**: If you are collecting personal data for a legitimate purpose, consider informing the individuals involved or making your intentions clear on the platform where the data is collected.
4. **Respect "Do Not Track" Requests**: If a user opts out of data collection or requests their data to be deleted, comply with their request. Many websites offer privacy settings that users can configure to limit tracking or data collection.

Violating data protection laws like GDPR can lead to significant fines and legal penalties, so it's crucial to stay informed about the regulations that apply to your scraping activities.

Avoiding Harm to Web Servers

WEB SCRAPING, IF DONE irresponsibly, can place a significant burden on a website's server infrastructure. This can lead to degraded performance, server downtime, or even being banned from the website. Ethical scraping involves using techniques that minimize the impact on the server and avoid overwhelming its resources.

Rate Limiting and Throttling

A KEY PRINCIPLE OF ethical web scraping is rate limiting, which means limiting the number of requests your scraper sends to the server over a period of time. Here's how you can implement rate limiting in your scraping scripts:

```
import time

import requests

from bs4 import BeautifulSoup

# URL to scrape

url = 'https://example.com'

# Set a delay between requests (in seconds)

delay = 2

# Perform multiple requests with a delay

for i in range(10):

response = requests.get(url)

soup = BeautifulSoup(response.text, 'html.parser')

# Process the response...

print(soup.title.text)

# Sleep for the specified delay before making the next request
```

```
time.sleep(delay)
```

In this example, we add a delay of 2 seconds between each request using time.sleep(). This reduces the risk of overloading the server and ensures that you are scraping responsibly.

Avoiding Infinite Loops

INFINITE LOOPS IN YOUR scraper can cause excessive load on the server if they continuously request data without any rate-limiting or stopping condition. Always ensure that your scraper has built-in stopping mechanisms and does not unintentionally scrape the same data repeatedly.

For example:

```
max_requests = 100

for i in range(max_requests):

# Scraping logic here

# Stop after max_requests iterations
```

This ensures that your scraper runs only for a limited number of requests and then stops, avoiding potential issues of server overload.

Scraping During Off-Peak Hours

ANOTHER WAY TO REDUCE the burden on a server is to scrape the website during off-peak hours when web traffic is likely to be lower. Many websites experience higher traffic during business hours, so running your scraper at night or on weekends can minimize its impact on server performance.

Respecting Robots.txt and Crawl Delay

THE **robots.txt** file is a publicly accessible file that tells web crawlers which parts of a website they are allowed to visit and which parts are off-limits. Ethical scrapers should always check the robots.txt file before scraping and respect the website owner's directives.

You can access a website's robots.txt file by visiting:

https://example.com/robots.txt

Here's an example of what a robots.txt file might look like:

```
User-agent: *

Disallow: /admin/

Disallow: /private/

User-agent: Googlebot

Crawl-delay: 10
```

In this example, all crawlers are disallowed from accessing the /admin/ and /private/ directories. Additionally, Googlebot is instructed to wait 10 seconds between requests (Crawl-delay: 10). Ethical scrapers should respect these directives and adjust their scraping behavior accordingly.

You can implement robots.txt compliance in your scraper by programmatically checking the file before scraping:

```
import requests

def is_scraping_allowed(url):

robots_url = url + '/robots.txt'
```

```
response = requests.get(robots_url)
if 'Disallow' in response.text:
return False
return True
url = 'https://example.com'
if is_scraping_allowed(url):
# Proceed with scraping
pass
else:
print("Scraping not allowed by robots.txt")
```

This code checks the website's robots.txt file for "Disallow" directives and halts scraping if the site disallows certain areas from being crawled.

Attribution and Fair Use of Data

WHEN SCRAPING DATA from websites, it's essential to attribute the source of the data, especially if you are using it in a public or commercial project. Failure to give proper credit can not only lead to legal issues but also damage your reputation as an ethical scraper.

Here are some best practices for attribution:

- **Cite the Source**: Always mention the website or organization from which you scraped the data. This is particularly important in academic or research contexts, where transparency is a key component of ethical data usage.

- **Link Back to the Source**: If you're publishing the scraped data online, provide a link back to the original website. This gives credit to the website owner and allows others to verify the data for themselves.

- **Don't Misuse Data**: Avoid using scraped data in misleading or deceptive ways. For example, don't misrepresent scraped reviews or testimonials, and don't use scraped product listings to create fraudulent e-commerce sites.

Conclusion

ETHICAL WEB SCRAPING is about balancing the power of automated data collection with respect for website owners, users, and legal frameworks. By adhering to website terms of service, complying with data protection regulations, minimizing your impact on web servers, and respecting intellectual property rights, you can ensure that your scraping activities are responsible and sustainable.

The key to ethical scraping is transparency and respect: be clear about what you're scraping, why you're scraping it, and how you plan to use the data. Ethical scrapers contribute positively to the data ecosystem by helping build trust and maintaining the integrity of the web as a shared resource for all.

Chapter 11: Introduction to Data Analysis with Python

Working with Pandas for Data Manipulation

PANDAS IS AN OPEN-SOURCE library that provides powerful data structures and tools for data manipulation and analysis in Python. It is particularly useful for dealing with structured data such as tables, CSV files, Excel sheets, or databases. The primary data structures in Pandas are the **Series** and **DataFrame**, which allow for efficient manipulation, filtering, and aggregation of data.

Installing Pandas

BEFORE STARTING WITH Pandas, you need to install the library. If you haven't installed it yet, you can use pip:

```
pip install pandas
```

Once installed, you can import it in your Python script:

```
import pandas as pd
```

What is a Pandas Series?

A **Series** is a one-dimensional labeled array capable of holding any data type such as integers, strings, floats, or even Python objects. The labels in a Series are called its index. Let's look at how we can create a Series:

```
import pandas as pd

# Creating a Series from a list

data = [1, 3, 5, 7, 9]
```

```
series = pd.Series(data)

print(series)
```

Output:

```
0 1

1 3

2 5

3 7

4 9

dtype: int64
```

In this case, the index is automatically generated as 0, 1, 2, etc. You can also provide custom indices:

```
series = pd.Series(data, index=['a', 'b', 'c', 'd', 'e'])

print(series)
```

Output:

```
a 1

b 3

c 5

d 7

e 9

dtype: int64
```

The **Series** object supports many useful operations. For example, you can perform arithmetic operations across the values in a Series:

print(series * 2)

Output:

a 2

b 6

c 10

d 14

e 18

dtype: int64

Introduction to DataFrame

THE **DataFrame** is the core structure of Pandas and represents a two-dimensional labeled data structure, much like a table with rows and columns. A **DataFrame** can be created in various ways, such as from a dictionary of lists, a NumPy array, or an external file like a CSV.

Here's an example of how to create a DataFrame from a dictionary of lists:

data = {

'Name': ['Alice', 'Bob', 'Charlie', 'David', 'Edward'],

'Age': [24, 27, 22, 32, 29],

'City': ['New York', 'Los Angeles', 'Chicago', 'Houston', 'Phoenix']

```
}
df = pd.DataFrame(data)
print(df)
```

Output:

```
Name Age City
0 Alice 24 New York
1 Bob 27 Los Angeles
2 Charlie 22 Chicago
3 David 32 Houston
4 Edward 29 Phoenix
```

Loading Data from External Files

PANDAS MAKES IT EASY to load data from external files such as CSV, Excel, or JSON. Here's how you can load a CSV file:

```
df = pd.read_csv('data.csv')
```

If you have data in an Excel file, you can use the following:

```
df = pd.read_excel('data.xlsx')
```

Once loaded, the data is represented as a DataFrame, which you can manipulate using various Pandas functions.

Exploring and Analyzing the Data

ONCE THE DATA IS LOADED into a DataFrame, you can start exploring it. A good first step is to inspect the first few rows of the data:

```
print(df.head())
```

You can also view the last few rows using the tail() method:

```
print(df.tail())
```

To get an overview of the DataFrame, including the number of rows and columns, as well as the data types, use the info() method:

```
print(df.info())
```

To get a statistical summary of the numeric columns, you can use the describe() method:

```
print(df.describe())
```

This will display useful metrics like the mean, standard deviation, minimum, maximum, and quartiles.

Selecting and Filtering Data

PANDAS MAKES IT VERY easy to select specific rows and columns from a DataFrame. You can select a column by passing the column name inside square brackets:

```
age_column = df['Age']

print(age_column)
```

To select multiple columns, pass a list of column names:

```
selected_columns = df[['Name', 'City']]
```

```
print(selected_columns)
```

You can also filter the data based on certain conditions. For example, to select rows where the age is greater than 25:

```
filtered_df = df[df['Age'] > 25]

print(filtered_df)
```

You can combine multiple conditions using logical operators:

```
filtered_df = df[(df['Age'] > 25) & (df['City'] == 'New York')]

print(filtered_df)
```

Data Manipulation: Adding, Deleting, and Modifying Columns

YOU CAN EASILY ADD a new column to the DataFrame. For instance, to add a new column called "Salary" based on some calculation:

```
df['Salary'] = [50000, 60000, 55000, 62000, 59000]

print(df)
```

To delete a column, you can use the drop() method:

```
df = df.drop('Salary', axis=1)

print(df)
```

You can also modify an existing column by applying operations to it. For example, you can increase the age of everyone by 1:

```
df['Age'] = df['Age'] + 1

print(df)
```

Handling Missing Data

REAL-WORLD DATA OFTEN contains missing values. Pandas provides several functions to handle missing data. You can check for missing values using the isna() function:

```
print(df.isna())
```

To fill missing values, use the fillna() method:

```
df['Age'] = df['Age'].fillna(df['Age'].mean())
```

To drop rows with missing values, use the dropna() method:

```
df = df.dropna()
```

Grouping and Aggregating Data

PANDAS PROVIDES POWERFUL grouping and aggregation functionality with the groupby() method. For example, if you want to group the data by the "City" column and calculate the average age for each city:

```
grouped_df = df.groupby('City')['Age'].mean()

print(grouped_df)
```

You can perform other aggregate functions such as sum(), count(), max(), etc., depending on your requirements.

Merging and Joining DataFrames

PANDAS ALLOWS YOU TO merge and join DataFrames, similar to SQL operations. For example, to merge two DataFrames on a common column:

```
df1 = pd.DataFrame({
```

```
'ID': [1, 2, 3],
'Name': ['Alice', 'Bob', 'Charlie']
})
df2 = pd.DataFrame({
'ID': [1, 2, 4],
'Age': [24, 27, 22]
})
merged_df = pd.merge(df1, df2, on='ID', how='inner')
print(merged_df)
```

```
ID NAME AGE
0 1 Alice 24
1 2 Bob 27
```

You can choose different types of joins (e.g., inner, outer, left, right) depending on your needs.

Conclusion

PANDAS IS AN INCREDIBLY powerful library for working with structured data in Python. From simple data manipulation tasks to complex data analysis workflows, Pandas provides a wide array of tools to help you handle data effectively.

Data Cleaning and Preprocessing

DATA CLEANING AND PREPROCESSING is a crucial step in the data analysis process, as raw data is often messy, incomplete, and inconsistent. Pandas, with its flexible and powerful data structures, provides an excellent set of tools for cleaning and transforming data. In this section, we'll cover various techniques for handling missing values, detecting outliers, removing duplicates, and transforming data for further analysis.

Understanding the Importance of Data Cleaning

DATA CLEANING IS ESSENTIAL because poor-quality data can lead to inaccurate analysis and misleading insights. Typical issues include:

- Missing values
- Incorrect data types
- Duplicates
- Outliers and anomalies
- Inconsistent data formatting

Addressing these issues early on ensures that the data is in a consistent, usable form and improves the reliability of the results.

Handling Missing Values

ONE OF THE MOST COMMON issues in data analysis is missing values. In Pandas, missing data is typically represented as NaN (Not a Number). The first step in handling missing values is to detect them. You can use the isna() or isnull() method to identify missing data in a DataFrame:

```
import pandas as pd

data = {

'Name': ['Alice', 'Bob', 'Charlie', None],

'Age': [24, 27, None, 32],

'City': ['New York', 'Los Angeles', None, 'Houston']

}

df = pd.DataFrame(data)

# Detect missing values

print(df.isna())
```

Output:

```
Name Age City

0 False False False

1 False False False

2 False True True

3 True False False
```

You can also get a summary of missing values for each column using the isna().sum() method:

```
print(df.isna().sum())
```

Output:

```
Name 1

Age 1
```

City 1

dtype: int64

Filling Missing Values

TO HANDLE MISSING DATA, you can fill the missing values with a specific value using the fillna() method. For example, you might want to replace missing values in the "Age" column with the average age:

```
df['Age'] = df['Age'].fillna(df['Age'].mean())

print(df)
```

Alternatively, you can forward-fill or backward-fill missing values based on adjacent data:

```
# Forward fill

df['City'] = df['City'].fillna(method='ffill')

# Backward fill

df['Name'] = df['Name'].fillna(method='bfill')

print(df)
```

Dropping Missing Values

IN CASES WHERE MISSING values are too frequent or it is not meaningful to fill them, you may want to drop rows or columns with missing data. Use the dropna() method to remove these rows or columns:

```
# Drop rows with missing values
```

```
df_cleaned = df.dropna()

print(df_cleaned)

# Drop columns with missing values

df_cleaned = df.dropna(axis=1)

print(df_cleaned)
```

Detecting and Removing Duplicates

DUPLICATE DATA CAN skew your analysis, so it's essential to identify and remove any duplicate entries in your dataset. You can use the duplicated() method to check for duplicate rows:

```
df = pd.DataFrame({

'Name': ['Alice', 'Bob', 'Charlie', 'Bob'],

'Age': [24, 27, 22, 27],

'City': ['New York', 'Los Angeles', 'Chicago', 'Los Angeles']

})

print(df.duplicated())
```

Output:

```
0 False

1 False

2 False

3 True

dtype: bool
```

You can then remove these duplicate rows using the drop_duplicates() method:

```
df_cleaned = df.drop_duplicates()

print(df_cleaned)
```

Handling Incorrect Data Types

SOMETIMES, DATA IS stored in the wrong format, such as numerical values being stored as strings. You can check the data types of your columns using the dtypes attribute:

```
print(df.dtypes)
```

If a column is in the wrong data type, you can convert it using the astype() method. For example, to convert a string representation of numbers into actual integers:

```
df['Age'] = df['Age'].astype(int)

print(df)
```

For date columns, you can convert them to a datetime format using the pd.to_datetime() function:

```
df['Date'] = pd.to_datetime(df['Date'])

print(df)
```

Standardizing Data Formatting

INCONSISTENT DATA FORMATTING is another common issue in datasets. For example, you may encounter inconsistencies in how dates are formatted or how categorical values (e.g., gender, location) are represented. You can standardize data formatting by applying string operations in Pandas.

To standardize text columns (e.g., converting everything to lowercase):

```
df['City'] = df['City'].str.lower()

print(df)
```

You can also use string replacement functions to fix specific formatting issues:

```
df['Name'] = df['Name'].str.replace('Bob', 'Robert')

print(df)
```

Outlier Detection and Removal

OUTLIERS ARE DATA POINTS that deviate significantly from the rest of the data. While not always incorrect, outliers can distort statistical analysis. Pandas and NumPy provide tools to detect and handle outliers.

A simple method to detect outliers is using the Interquartile Range (IQR):

```
import numpy as np

Q1 = df['Age'].quantile(0.25)

Q3 = df['Age'].quantile(0.75)

IQR = Q3 - Q1

# Define outlier range

lower_bound = Q1 - 1.5 * IQR

upper_bound = Q3 + 1.5 * IQR
```

```
# Filter out outliers

df_filtered = df[(df['Age'] >= lower_bound) & (df['Age'] <= upper_bound)]

print(df_filtered)
```

Another method is Z-score, which measures how many standard deviations a data point is from the mean:

```
from scipy import stats

z_scores = np.abs(stats.zscore(df['Age']))

df_filtered = df[(z_scores < 3)]

print(df_filtered)
```

Encoding Categorical Data

WHEN DEALING WITH CATEGORICAL data, it is often necessary to convert it into numerical form for analysis. Pandas provides several techniques for encoding categorical variables.

Label Encoding

LABEL ENCODING IS THE process of converting categorical text labels into numerical values. You can do this manually or use the factorize() method:

```
df['City_encoded'] = pd.factorize(df['City'])[0]

print(df)
```

One-Hot Encoding

ONE-HOT ENCODING CREATES binary columns for each category, which is useful for machine learning models that require numerical input. You can perform one-hot encoding using the get_dummies() function:

```
df = pd.get_dummies(df, columns=['City'])

print(df)
```

Feature Scaling and Normalization

FEATURE SCALING IS the process of normalizing or standardizing your numerical data so that it falls within a certain range, typically between 0 and 1 or around the mean with a standard deviation of 1. This is particularly important when using algorithms that rely on distance measurements (e.g., K-Nearest Neighbors, SVM).

You can use the Min-Max scaling method to scale your data to a range between 0 and 1:

```
from sklearn.preprocessing import MinMaxScaler

scaler = MinMaxScaler()

df[['Age']] = scaler.fit_transform(df[['Age']])

print(df)
```

Alternatively, you can standardize your data to have a mean of 0 and a standard deviation of 1 using the StandardScaler:

```
from sklearn.preprocessing import StandardScaler

scaler = StandardScaler()
```

```
df[['Age']] = scaler.fit_transform(df[['Age']])

print(df)
```

Data Transformation

DATA TRANSFORMATION involves changing the structure of your data for better analysis. Common transformations include:

- **Log Transformation**: Useful when dealing with highly skewed data.

```
df['Log_Age'] = np.log(df['Age'] + 1)
```

- **Binning**: Grouping continuous variables into bins or categories.

```
df['Age_group'] = pd.cut(df['Age'], bins=[0, 18, 35, 60], labels=['Youth', 'Adult', 'Senior'])

print(df)
```

Conclusion

DATA CLEANING AND PREPROCESSING are essential tasks in the data analysis workflow, as they directly affect the quality of insights derived from the data. By handling missing values, detecting duplicates, standardizing formats, dealing with outliers, encoding categorical variables, and scaling features, you can prepare your data for robust and accurate analysis. The techniques outlined in this section provide a foundation for cleaning and transforming data effectively using Pandas.

Visualizing Data with Matplotlib

DATA VISUALIZATION is a key part of the data analysis process, as it allows us to see trends, patterns, and relationships in the data that might not be immediately obvious. **Matplotlib** is one of the most widely used libraries for creating visualizations in Python. It provides an extensive range of plotting capabilities, from simple line plots to complex multi-dimensional visualizations. In this section, we'll explore how to create various types of plots and customize them for effective data communication.

Installing and Importing Matplotlib

BEFORE WE DIVE INTO visualizations, we need to install Matplotlib. If you haven't installed it yet, you can use pip to install it:

```
pip install matplotlib
```

Once installed, you can import the library and start plotting:

```
import matplotlib.pyplot as plt
```

By convention, matplotlib.pyplot is imported as plt. This is the standard alias used throughout the Python community.

Basic Plotting

THE SIMPLEST TYPE OF plot is the **line plot**, which shows how one variable changes as another variable changes. Let's start with a basic example of a line plot:

```
import matplotlib.pyplot as plt

# Example data
```

```
x = [1, 2, 3, 4, 5]

y = [10, 20, 25, 30, 35]

# Create a line plot

plt.plot(x, y)

plt.title('Basic Line Plot')

plt.xlabel('X-axis')

plt.ylabel('Y-axis')

plt.show()
```

This generates a simple line plot, where x is plotted on the horizontal axis and y is plotted on the vertical axis.

Customizing Plots

MATPLOTLIB PROVIDES a wide variety of ways to customize your plots, making it easy to create professional-quality visualizations.

Adding Titles and Labels

YOU CAN ADD TITLES and axis labels to make your plot more informative. Use the title(), xlabel(), and ylabel() functions to add these elements:

```
plt.plot(x, y)

plt.title('My Customized Plot')

plt.xlabel('Independent Variable')
```

```
plt.ylabel('Dependent Variable')

plt.show()
```

Changing Line Styles and Colors

YOU CAN CUSTOMIZE THE appearance of your lines using various line styles ('-', '—', '-.', ':') and colors ('r', 'g', 'b', etc.). Here's an example:

```
# Change line style to dashed and color to red

plt.plot(x, y, linestyle='—', color='r')

plt.title('Dashed Red Line')

plt.show()
```

You can also specify line width (linewidth) and marker style (marker):

```
plt.plot(x, y, color='b', linewidth=2.0, marker='o', markersize=8)

plt.title('Customized Line with Markers')

plt.show()
```

Creating Multiple Plots in One Figure

YOU CAN CREATE MULTIPLE plots in one figure using the subplot() function, which allows you to arrange multiple subplots in a grid layout. Here's an example of creating two subplots in a 1x2 grid:

```
# Create a figure with two subplots (1 row, 2 columns)

plt.subplot(1, 2, 1)
```

```
plt.plot(x, y)

plt.title('Plot 1')

plt.subplot(1, 2, 2)

plt.plot(y, x)

plt.title('Plot 2')

plt.tight_layout() # Adjusts spacing to prevent overlap

plt.show()
```

The subplot() function takes three arguments: the number of rows, the number of columns, and the index of the current subplot.

Plotting Different Types of Charts

IN ADDITION TO LINE plots, Matplotlib supports a wide range of chart types, including bar charts, scatter plots, histograms, and pie charts. Let's go over each of these.

Bar Charts

A **bar chart** is used to compare quantities across categories. Here's an example of how to create a bar chart:

```
categories = ['A', 'B', 'C', 'D']

values = [4, 7, 1, 8]

plt.bar(categories, values)

plt.title('Basic Bar Chart')

plt.xlabel('Category')
```

```
plt.ylabel('Values')

plt.show()
```

You can also create horizontal bar charts using the barh() function:

```
plt.barh(categories, values)

plt.title('Horizontal Bar Chart')

plt.show()
```

Scatter Plots

A **scatter plot** shows the relationship between two variables. It's particularly useful for identifying correlations or clusters in the data:

```
x = [1, 2, 3, 4, 5, 6, 7, 8, 9]

y = [5, 6, 7, 8, 7, 6, 5, 4, 3]

plt.scatter(x, y)

plt.title('Basic Scatter Plot')

plt.xlabel('X-axis')

plt.ylabel('Y-axis')

plt.show()
```

You can add color and size to the points in the scatter plot to convey more information:

```
sizes = [20, 50, 80, 100, 200, 300, 400, 500, 600]
```

```
colors = ['red', 'blue', 'green', 'purple', 'orange', 'brown', 'pink', 'gray', 'yellow']

plt.scatter(x, y, s=sizes, c=colors)

plt.title('Scatter Plot with Custom Sizes and Colors')

plt.show()
```

Histograms

A **histogram** is a type of plot that shows the frequency distribution of a dataset. It's useful for understanding the underlying distribution of a variable:

```
data = [1, 2, 2, 3, 3, 3, 4, 4, 4, 4, 5, 5, 5, 5, 5]

plt.hist(data, bins=5, edgecolor='black')

plt.title('Basic Histogram')

plt.xlabel('Value')

plt.ylabel('Frequency')

plt.show()
```

You can adjust the number of bins (intervals) using the bins parameter to control the granularity of the distribution.

Pie Charts

A **pie chart** is a circular chart divided into segments, where each segment represents a proportion of the whole. Here's how to create a simple pie chart:

```
labels = ['Category A', 'Category B', 'Category C', 'Category D']

sizes = [15, 30, 45, 10]

plt.pie(sizes, labels=labels, autopct='%1.1f%%', startangle=90)

plt.title('Basic Pie Chart')

plt.show()
```

The autopct='%1.1f%%' parameter displays the percentage values, and startangle=90 rotates the start of the pie chart to improve readability.

Adding Legends

FOR MULTI-LINE OR MULTI-category plots, it's important to include a legend to explain what each element represents. You can add a legend using the legend() function:

```
plt.plot(x, y, label='Line 1')

plt.plot(y, x, label='Line 2')

plt.legend() # Adds a legend

plt.title('Plot with Legend')

plt.show()
```

You can customize the location of the legend using the loc parameter:

```
plt.legend(loc='upper left')
```

Annotating Plots

ANNOTATIONS ARE USEFUL for adding specific information to a plot, such as highlighting a particular data point. You can use the annotate() function to add text at a specific location in the plot:

```
plt.plot(x, y)

plt.title('Annotated Plot')

# Add annotation at x=3, y=25

plt.annotate('Important Point', xy=(3, 25), xytext=(4, 30),

arrowprops=dict(facecolor='black', arrowstyle='->'))

plt.show()
```

Saving Plots to Files

YOU CAN SAVE YOUR PLOTS as image files (e.g., PNG, JPG, PDF) using the savefig() function. This is useful when you need to include plots in reports or presentations:

```
plt.plot(x, y)

plt.title('Plot to Save')

# Save the plot as a PNG file

plt.savefig('my_plot.png')

# Save the plot as a PDF file

plt.savefig('my_plot.pdf')

plt.show()
```

Advanced Customizations

MATPLOTLIB ALLOWS FOR extensive customizations, including control over the appearance of ticks, grids, and axes. Let's look at some advanced customizations.

Customizing Ticks

YOU CAN CUSTOMIZE THE ticks on both the x-axis and y-axis to make your plot more readable:

```
plt.plot(x, y)

# Customize ticks

plt.xticks([1, 2, 3, 4, 5], ['One', 'Two', 'Three', 'Four', 'Five'])

plt.yticks([10, 20, 30, 40], ['Low', 'Medium', 'High', 'Very High'])

plt.title('Plot with Custom Ticks')

plt.show()
```

Adding Gridlines

GRIDLINES CAN HELP guide the eye across the plot. You can add gridlines using the grid() function:

```
plt.plot(x, y)

plt.grid(True) # Add gridlines

plt.title('Plot with Gridlines')

plt.show()
```

You can also customize the gridlines' style and appearance:

```
plt.grid(color='gray', linestyle='—', linewidth=0.5)
```

Customizing Axes

YOU CAN CONTROL THE appearance and range of the axes using the xlim() and ylim() functions:

```
plt.plot(x, y)

plt.xlim(0, 10) # Set x-axis limits

plt.ylim(0, 40) # Set y-axis limits

plt.title('Plot with Custom Axes')

plt.show()
```

Conclusion

MATPLOTLIB IS A VERSATILE and powerful library for creating visualizations in Python. Whether you're creating simple line plots, complex multi-plot figures, or customizing every aspect of a chart's appearance, Matplotlib provides the tools to produce high-quality visualizations. Through careful use of customizations, legends, annotations, and various chart types, you can effectively communicate the insights from your data analysis.

Analyzing Data with NumPy

NUMPY IS ONE OF THE most powerful libraries in Python for numerical computing. It provides support for multi-dimensional arrays and matrices, along with a wide variety of mathematical functions to operate on these arrays. NumPy is the foundation for many other scientific computing libraries, including Pandas, Matplotlib, and SciPy. In this section, we will explore the basic and advanced capabilities of NumPy, covering topics such as array creation, mathematical operations, array indexing, and more.

Why Use NumPy?

NUMPY IS HIGHLY EFFICIENT for numerical computations, especially when working with large datasets. Unlike Python lists, NumPy arrays are stored in contiguous blocks of memory, allowing faster access and manipulation. Moreover, NumPy functions are written in C, which provides much better performance than standard Python loops or list comprehensions when performing mathematical operations on large datasets.

Here are some key advantages of using NumPy:

- **Vectorized operations**: Mathematical operations are applied to entire arrays rather than individual elements.
- **Multidimensional arrays**: NumPy arrays (also called ndarrays) can have multiple dimensions, allowing you to work with matrices and tensors.
- **Broadcasting**: NumPy automatically handles element-wise operations between arrays of different shapes.
- **Memory efficiency**: NumPy uses less memory than traditional Python lists.

Let's dive into how you can use NumPy to analyze data effectively.

Installing and Importing NumPy

IF YOU DON'T HAVE NUMPY installed, you can install it using pip:

```
pip install numpy
```

Once installed, you can import it into your Python script as follows:

```
import numpy as np
```

By convention, numpy is imported as np. This short alias is used throughout the Python community and allows for easier code readability.

Creating NumPy Arrays

A NUMPY ARRAY, ALSO known as an **ndarray** (n-dimensional array), is the fundamental building block of NumPy. You can create an array in several ways, such as converting a Python list or tuple into an array, or using specialized functions to create arrays of zeros, ones, or random numbers.

Creating Arrays from Lists

YOU CAN CREATE A NUMPY array from a Python list or tuple using the np.array() function:

```
import numpy as np

# Creating a 1D array from a list

arr = np.array([1, 2, 3, 4, 5])

print(arr)

# Creating a 2D array (matrix) from a list of lists

matrix = np.array([[1, 2, 3], [4, 5, 6], [7, 8, 9]])

print(matrix)
```

Output:

[1 2 3 4 5]

[[1 2 3]

[4 5 6]

[7 8 9]]

Using NumPy Functions to Create Arrays

NUMPY PROVIDES A VARIETY of functions to generate arrays without explicitly defining their elements:

- **np.zeros()**: Creates an array filled with zeros.

```
zeros_array = np.zeros((3, 4))

print(zeros_array)
```

- **np.ones()**: Creates an array filled with ones.

```
ones_array = np.ones((2, 3))

print(ones_array)
```

- **np.arange()**: Creates an array with evenly spaced values between a start and stop value.

```
range_array = np.arange(0, 10, 2) # Start at 0, stop before 10, step by 2

print(range_array)
```

- **np.linspace()**: Creates an array with a specified number of evenly spaced values between two endpoints.

```
linspace_array = np.linspace(0, 1, 5) # 5 evenly spaced numbers between 0 and 1

print(linspace_array)
```

- **np.random.rand()**: Creates an array of random values between 0 and 1.

```
random_array = np.random.rand(4, 4)

print(random_array)
```

Array Data Types

BY DEFAULT, NUMPY AUTOMATICALLY infers the data type of an array from the input data, but you can explicitly specify the data type using the dtype parameter. NumPy supports various data types, including int, float, bool, and more.

```
float_array = np.array([1, 2, 3], dtype=float)

print(float_array)
```

You can check the data type of an array using the dtype attribute:

```
print(float_array.dtype)
```

Array Indexing and Slicing

NUMPY ARRAYS CAN BE indexed and sliced in ways similar to Python lists. This allows you to access individual elements or subsets of an array.

Indexing One-Dimensional Arrays

YOU CAN ACCESS INDIVIDUAL elements of a 1D array using square brackets:

```
arr = np.array([10, 20, 30, 40, 50])

print(arr[0]) # Access the first element (index 0)

print(arr[3]) # Access the fourth element (index 3)
```

Indexing Multi-Dimensional Arrays

FOR MULTI-DIMENSIONAL arrays, you can access elements by specifying the row and column indices:

```
matrix = np.array([[1, 2, 3], [4, 5, 6], [7, 8, 9]])

print(matrix[1, 2]) # Access the element at row 2, column 3 (value 6)
```

You can also use slicing to extract a subset of an array. For example:

```
# Slicing a 2D array to extract the first two rows and the first two columns

sub_matrix = matrix[0:2, 0:2]

print(sub_matrix)
```

Basic Array Operations

NUMPY MAKES IT EASY to perform mathematical operations on arrays. These operations are vectorized, meaning that they are applied element-wise, which is much faster than using loops.

Element-Wise Operations

YOU CAN PERFORM OPERATIONS such as addition, subtraction, multiplication, and division directly on arrays:

```
arr1 = np.array([1, 2, 3])

arr2 = np.array([4, 5, 6])

# Element-wise addition

result = arr1 + arr2

print(result)

# Element-wise multiplication

result = arr1 * arr2

print(result)
```

Matrix Multiplication

FOR MULTI-DIMENSIONAL arrays (matrices), you can perform matrix multiplication using the np.dot() function or the @ operator:

```
matrix1 = np.array([[1, 2], [3, 4]])

matrix2 = np.array([[5, 6], [7, 8]])

# Matrix multiplication using np.dot()

result = np.dot(matrix1, matrix2)

print(result)

# Matrix multiplication using @ operator
```

```
result = matrix1 @ matrix2

print(result)
```

Broadcasting

NUMPY SUPPORTS BROADCASTING, which allows operations between arrays of different shapes. Broadcasting automatically expands smaller arrays to match the dimensions of the larger array.

```
arr = np.array([1, 2, 3])

matrix = np.array([[1, 2, 3], [4, 5, 6]])

# Broadcasting allows element-wise addition of a 1D array to a 2D array

result = matrix + arr

print(result)
```

Mathematical Functions

NUMPY PROVIDES A WIDE variety of mathematical functions for performing operations such as trigonometry, logarithms, exponentiation, and more. These functions operate element-wise on arrays.

```
arr = np.array([1, 2, 3, 4])

# Exponentiation

result = np.exp(arr)

print(result)
```

```
# Logarithm

result = np.log(arr)

print(result)

# Square root

result = np.sqrt(arr)

print(result)
```

You can also perform aggregation functions such as sum(), mean(), min(), and max():

```
arr = np.array([1, 2, 3, 4, 5])

print(np.sum(arr)) # Sum of all elements

print(np.mean(arr)) # Mean (average)

print(np.min(arr)) # Minimum value

print(np.max(arr)) # Maximum value
```

Working with Multi-Dimensional Arrays

NUMPY ARRAYS CAN HAVE more than two dimensions, allowing you to work with data structures like 3D matrices (tensors). For example, you might use a 3D array to represent a collection of 2D images.

Creating Multi-Dimensional Arrays

YOU CAN CREATE A MULTI-dimensional array by specifying a tuple of dimensions:

tensor = np.zeros((3, 3, 3)) # A 3x3x3 array filled with zeros

print(tensor)

Indexing Multi-Dimensional Arrays

YOU CAN ACCESS ELEMENTS in multi-dimensional arrays using a combination of row, column, and depth indices:

tensor = np.array([[[1, 2, 3], [4, 5, 6], [7, 8, 9]],

[[10, 11, 12], [13, 14, 15], [16, 17, 18]],

[[19, 20, 21], [22, 23, 24], [25, 26, 27]]])

Accessing an element at depth=1, row=2, column=3

print(tensor[1, 2, 2]) # Output: 18

Reshaping Arrays

NUMPY ALLOWS YOU TO reshape arrays without changing their data. You can use the reshape() function to change the shape of an array:

arr = np.array([1, 2, 3, 4, 5, 6])

reshaped_arr = arr.reshape(2, 3) # Reshape the array into a 2x3 matrix

print(reshaped_arr)

You can also flatten a multi-dimensional array into a 1D array using the flatten() method:

flattened_arr = reshaped_arr.flatten()

```
print(flattened_arr)
```

Advanced Indexing and Masking

NUMPY SUPPORTS ADVANCED indexing techniques, including boolean masking, which allows you to filter arrays based on conditions:

```
arr = np.array([1, 2, 3, 4, 5, 6])

# Create a boolean mask for elements greater than 3

mask = arr > 3

print(mask)

# Apply the mask to filter the array

filtered_arr = arr[mask]

print(filtered_arr)
```

You can combine multiple conditions using logical operators:

```
arr = np.array([1, 2, 3, 4, 5, 6])

# Filter for elements greater than 2 and less than 5

filtered_arr = arr[(arr > 2) & (arr < 5)]

print(filtered_arr)
```

Conclusion

NUMPY PROVIDES A COMPREHENSIVE set of tools for numerical computing in Python. From basic array creation and manipulation to advanced operations like matrix multiplication and broadcasting, NumPy makes it easy to perform complex mathematical operations efficiently. Its capabilities extend beyond basic numerical analysis, supporting multi-dimensional arrays, broadcasting, and advanced indexing, making it a foundational library for data analysis, machine learning, and scientific computing.

Real-World Case Studies

IN THIS SECTION, WE will explore real-world case studies that demonstrate how Python can be used for data analysis across various domains. These case studies will help solidify the concepts of working with data, visualizing patterns, and extracting insights using libraries like Pandas, NumPy, and Matplotlib. We'll walk through each case study, examining data preparation, analysis techniques, and visualizations that help convey meaningful information.

Case Study 1: Analyzing Sales Data

Background

A RETAIL COMPANY WANTS to analyze its sales data to understand customer behavior, identify trends in product sales, and optimize inventory management. The dataset contains information on products sold, quantities, prices, customer demographics, and time of purchase.

Step 1: Loading and Exploring the Data

THE FIRST STEP IS TO load the sales data, which is stored in a CSV file. We will use Pandas to read the data into a DataFrame and explore its structure.

```
import pandas as pd

# Load the dataset

sales_data = pd.read_csv('sales_data.csv')

# Display the first few rows of the dataset

print(sales_data.head())

# Get a summary of the dataset

print(sales_data.info())
```

The dataset might include columns like:

- Order ID: Unique identifier for each order
- Product: Name of the product sold
- Quantity: Number of units sold
- Price: Price per unit
- Total: Total revenue for the sale (Price * Quantity)
- Customer ID: Unique identifier for each customer
- Region: Geographical region of the sale
- Date: Date and time of the sale

Step 2: Cleaning the Data

BEFORE CONDUCTING THE analysis, we need to clean the dataset. Common tasks include handling missing values, converting data types, and removing duplicates.

```
# Check for missing values

print(sales_data.isnull().sum())

# Drop rows with missing values

sales_data_cleaned = sales_data.dropna()

# Ensure that 'Date' is in datetime format

sales_data_cleaned['Date'] =
pd.to_datetime(sales_data_cleaned['Date'])

# Remove duplicate rows, if any

sales_data_cleaned = sales_data_cleaned.drop_duplicates()

# Check the cleaned dataset

print(sales_data_cleaned.info())
```

Step 3: Analyzing Sales by Product

WE WANT TO UNDERSTAND which products are the top performers in terms of sales volume and revenue. Using the groupby() function in Pandas, we can aggregate sales data by product.

```
# Group by product and calculate total quantity sold and total revenue

product_sales = sales_data_cleaned.groupby('Product').agg({

'Quantity': 'sum',

'Total': 'sum'

}).sort_values(by='Total', ascending=False)
```

```
# Display the top 10 products by total revenue

print(product_sales.head(10))
```

This analysis reveals which products generate the most revenue and which products sell the most units. For example, high-revenue products may not necessarily have the highest unit sales but may have higher prices.

Step 4: Visualizing Sales Trends Over Time

NEXT, WE WANT TO ANALYZE sales trends over time to identify any seasonal patterns or monthly trends. We can group the data by month and visualize the total revenue over time.

```
import matplotlib.pyplot as plt

# Create a new column for the month

sales_data_cleaned['Month'] =
sales_data_cleaned['Date'].dt.to_period('M')

# Group by month and calculate total revenue

monthly_sales =
sales_data_cleaned.groupby('Month')['Total'].sum()

# Plot the sales trend over time

plt.plot(monthly_sales.index.astype(str), monthly_sales.values)

plt.title('Monthly Sales Trend')

plt.xlabel('Month')

plt.ylabel('Total Revenue')
```

```
plt.xticks(rotation=45)

plt.grid(True)

plt.show()
```

This plot can help the company identify peak sales months, which may correspond to holidays, promotional periods, or seasonal buying trends.

Step 5: Customer Segmentation

WE CAN ALSO ANALYZE customer behavior by segmenting customers based on their total purchase amounts. This segmentation can help the company tailor marketing efforts to different customer groups.

```
# Group by customer and calculate total purchase amounts

customer_sales = sales_data_cleaned.groupby('Customer ID')['Total'].sum()

# Define customer segments based on purchase amounts

def segment_customer(total_purchase):

if total_purchase > 1000:

return 'High Value'

elif total_purchase > 500:

return 'Medium Value'

else:

return 'Low Value'
```

```
# Apply the segmentation function to the customer data

customer_segments = customer_sales.apply(segment_customer)

# Display the count of customers in each segment

print(customer_segments.value_counts())
```

This segmentation provides insights into how many customers fall into each value category, enabling targeted marketing and loyalty programs.

Case Study 2: Analyzing Financial Market Data

Background

A FINANCIAL ANALYST wants to analyze stock market data to identify trends, calculate moving averages, and evaluate the performance of different stocks over time. The dataset contains daily stock prices for several companies, including open, close, high, and low prices.

Step 1: Loading and Exploring the Data

WE START BY LOADING the stock price data into a Pandas DataFrame and exploring its structure.

```
# Load stock price data

stock_data = pd.read_csv('stock_prices.csv')

# Display the first few rows of the dataset

print(stock_data.head())

# Get a summary of the dataset
```

```
print(stock_data.info())
```

The dataset might include columns like:

- Date: The date of the trading day
- Company: The name of the company
- Open: The opening price of the stock
- Close: The closing price of the stock
- High: The highest price during the trading day
- Low: The lowest price during the trading day
- Volume: The number of shares traded

Step 2: Calculating Moving Averages

MOVING AVERAGES HELP smooth out short-term fluctuations in stock prices and reveal longer-term trends. We will calculate the 20-day and 50-day moving averages for each stock.

```
# Ensure 'Date' is in datetime format

stock_data['Date'] = pd.to_datetime(stock_data['Date'])

# Sort the dataset by company and date

stock_data = stock_data.sort_values(by=['Company', 'Date'])

# Calculate 20-day and 50-day moving averages

stock_data['20_MA'] = stock_data.groupby('Company')['Close'].transform(lambda x: x.rolling(window=20).mean())
```

```
stock_data['50_MA'] = stock_data.groupby('Company')['Close'].transform(lambda x: x.rolling(window=50).mean())

# Display the stock data with moving averages

print(stock_data[['Date', 'Company', 'Close', '20_MA', '50_MA']].head())
```

Step 3: Visualizing Stock Price Trends

WE CAN PLOT THE STOCK prices and their moving averages to visualize how the stock has performed over time.

```
# Filter data for a specific company

company_data = stock_data[stock_data['Company'] == 'Company A']

# Plot the stock price and moving averages

plt.plot(company_data['Date'], company_data['Close'], label='Close Price')

plt.plot(company_data['Date'], company_data['20_MA'], label='20-Day MA', linestyle='—')

plt.plot(company_data['Date'], company_data['50_MA'], label='50-Day MA', linestyle='—')

plt.title('Stock Price and Moving Averages for Company A')

plt.xlabel('Date')

plt.ylabel('Price')

plt.legend()
```

```
plt.grid(True)

plt.show()
```

This plot provides a clear visual representation of the stock's short-term and long-term trends, helping investors make informed decisions.

Step 4: Analyzing Stock Volatility

STOCK VOLATILITY IS a measure of how much a stock's price fluctuates over time. We can calculate volatility by determining the standard deviation of daily returns.

```
# Calculate daily returns

stock_data['Daily_Return'] = stock_data.groupby('Company')['Close'].pct_change()

# Calculate rolling volatility (standard deviation) over a 20-day window

stock_data['20_Volatility'] = stock_data.groupby('Company')['Daily_Return'].transform(lambda x: x.rolling(window=20).std())

# Display stock data with volatility

print(stock_data[['Date', 'Company', 'Daily_Return', '20_Volatility']].head())
```

Step 5: Identifying Trends and Patterns

WE CAN USE THE CALCULATED moving averages and volatility to identify trends in stock prices. For example, a common signal in technical analysis is the crossover between short-term and long-term moving averages. If the short-term moving average crosses above the long-term moving average, it may signal a potential buying opportunity.

```
# Identify crossover points where the 20-day MA crosses above the 50-day MA

stock_data['Signal'] = 0

stock_data.loc[stock_data['20_MA'] > stock_data['50_MA'], 'Signal'] = 1

# Display stock data with crossover signals

print(stock_data[['Date', 'Company', 'Close', '20_MA', '50_MA', 'Signal']].head())
```

Case Study 3: Customer Churn Analysis in a Telecom Company

Background

A TELECOM COMPANY WANTS to analyze its customer churn data to identify factors that contribute to customer attrition. The dataset includes customer demographics, service usage patterns, contract details, and whether the customer has churned (i.e., canceled the service).

Step 1: Loading and Exploring the Data

WE BEGIN BY LOADING the churn dataset and exploring its structure.

```
# Load the churn dataset
```

```
churn_data = pd.read_csv('churn_data.csv')

# Display the first few rows of the dataset

print(churn_data.head())

# Get a summary of the dataset

print(churn_data.info())
```

The dataset might include columns like:

- CustomerID: Unique identifier for each customer
- Gender: Gender of the customer
- SeniorCitizen: Whether the customer is a senior citizen
- Tenure: Number of months the customer has been with the company
- MonthlyCharges: The amount the customer pays each month
- Churn: Whether the customer has churned (Yes/No)

Step 2: Analyzing Churn by Tenure

WE WANT TO ANALYZE churn rates by customer tenure to see if customers are more likely to churn after a certain period.

```
# Group by tenure and calculate churn rate

tenure_churn =
churn_data.groupby('Tenure')['Churn'].value_counts(normalize=True).uns
```

```
# Plot churn rate by tenure

plt.plot(tenure_churn.index, tenure_churn['Yes'], label='Churn Rate')

plt.title('Churn Rate by Customer Tenure')

plt.xlabel('Tenure (Months)')

plt.ylabel('Churn Rate')

plt.grid(True)

plt.show()
```

Step 3: Analyzing Churn by Monthly Charges

WE ALSO WANT TO ANALYZE whether customers who pay higher monthly charges are more likely to churn.

```
# Group by monthly charges and calculate churn rate

monthly_churn = churn_data.groupby('MonthlyCharges')['Churn'].value_counts(normaliz

# Plot churn rate by monthly charges

plt.plot(monthly_churn.index, monthly_churn['Yes'], label='Churn Rate')

plt.title('Churn Rate by Monthly Charges')

plt.xlabel('Monthly Charges')

plt.ylabel('Churn Rate')

plt.grid(True)
```

```
plt.show()
```

Step 4: Segmenting Customers by Churn Probability

FINALLY, WE CAN SEGMENT customers based on their probability of churn, using machine learning models or simple decision rules based on the factors analyzed.

```
# Define a function to segment customers based on churn risk

def segment_churn_risk(monthly_charges, tenure):

if monthly_charges > 80 and tenure < 12:

return 'High Risk'

elif monthly_charges > 50:

return 'Medium Risk'

else:

return 'Low Risk'

# Apply the segmentation function to the dataset

churn_data['Churn_Risk'] = churn_data.apply(lambda row: segment_churn_risk(row['MonthlyCharges'], row['Tenure']), axis=1)

# Display customer churn risk segments

print(churn_data[['CustomerID', 'MonthlyCharges', 'Tenure', 'Churn_Risk']].head())
```

Conclusion

THESE CASE STUDIES demonstrate how Python can be applied to analyze real-world data in various domains, from sales and stock markets to customer churn analysis. By leveraging libraries like Pandas, NumPy, and Matplotlib, you can efficiently clean data, explore patterns, and extract actionable insights that drive informed decision-making.

Chapter 12: Next Steps in Python Programming

Exploring Advanced Topics: Machine Learning, AI, and Automation

AS YOU ADVANCE IN YOUR Python programming journey, you'll eventually reach a point where the basic concepts are second nature. From data structures to control flow, you'll have developed a firm grasp on Python's core functionalities. Now, the real fun begins: diving into advanced topics like Machine Learning, Artificial Intelligence, and Automation. These fields are at the cutting edge of technology, and Python is one of the most popular languages to explore them. In this section, we'll discuss how you can start learning about these advanced topics, tools you'll need, and best practices for applying these concepts in real-world scenarios.

Machine Learning: An Overview

MACHINE LEARNING (ML) is a subfield of Artificial Intelligence (AI) that enables computers to learn from data. Instead of being explicitly programmed to perform a task, a machine learning model can generalize from examples and make decisions based on new, unseen data. It's widely used in various industries, including finance, healthcare, e-commerce, and entertainment.

In Python, several libraries make machine learning accessible, even to those who are not data scientists by training. Key libraries you will use include:

1. **Scikit-learn**: This is the go-to library for most basic machine learning tasks. It provides simple and efficient tools for data mining, data analysis, and machine learning.
2. **TensorFlow**: Created by Google, TensorFlow is used for deep learning and artificial neural networks.
3. **PyTorch**: Developed by Facebook, PyTorch is popular for research and experimentation in deep learning.

Let's dive into the basic steps for building a machine learning model:

Steps to Build a Machine Learning Model in Python

Step 1: Data Collection and Preparation

THE FIRST STEP IS GATHERING data. Your model will learn from data, so the quality and quantity of your data are crucial. Datasets can come in different forms—CSV files, databases, or APIs.

```
import pandas as pd

# Load data into a pandas DataFrame

data = pd.read_csv('your_dataset.csv')

# Inspect the first few rows of the dataset

print(data.head())
```

Once the data is loaded, you need to clean it. This process involves handling missing values, correcting data types, and removing duplicates.

```
# Handle missing data

data.fillna(method='ffill', inplace=True)

# Remove duplicate rows

data.drop_duplicates(inplace=True)
```

Step 2: Feature Engineering

FEATURE ENGINEERING is the process of transforming raw data into meaningful inputs for a machine learning model. It might involve selecting important features, creating new ones, or normalizing the data to bring all values to the same scale.

```
from sklearn.preprocessing import StandardScaler

# Normalize data

scaler = StandardScaler()

scaled_data = scaler.fit_transform(data[['feature1', 'feature2']])
```

Step 3: Splitting the Data

BEFORE TRAINING A MACHINE learning model, it's essential to split the data into training and testing sets. The training set is used to train the model, while the testing set is used to evaluate its performance on unseen data.

```
from sklearn.model_selection import train_test_split

# Split data into training and testing sets

X_train, X_test, y_train, y_test = train_test_split(scaled_data, data['target'], test_size=0.2)
```

Step 4: Choosing a Model

THE CHOICE OF MODEL depends on the problem you are solving. Scikit-learn provides several models such as linear regression, decision trees, and support vector machines.

```
from sklearn.linear_model import LogisticRegression

# Create a logistic regression model

model = LogisticRegression()

# Train the model

model.fit(X_train, y_train)
```

Step 5: Evaluating the Model

AFTER TRAINING THE model, you'll want to evaluate its performance on the test set.

```
# Evaluate the model's accuracy

accuracy = model.score(X_test, y_test)

print(f'Accuracy: {accuracy * 100:.2f}%')
```

If the accuracy is not satisfactory, you may need to tweak your model, adjust the features, or even switch to a different algorithm.

Artificial Intelligence and Neural Networks

ARTIFICIAL INTELLIGENCE (AI) encompasses a broader range of techniques than machine learning. While machine learning focuses on algorithms that can learn from data, AI attempts to create systems that mimic human intelligence, such as problem-solving, understanding language, and recognizing patterns.

One of the most important techniques in AI is **deep learning,** which involves training neural networks to perform tasks like image recognition or natural language processing.

Neural Networks in Python with TensorFlow

A NEURAL NETWORK IS a model inspired by the human brain. It consists of layers of nodes (neurons), where each layer transforms the input data in some way. The output layer produces the final prediction.

Here's a simple example of building a neural network with TensorFlow:

```
import tensorflow as tf

from tensorflow.keras.models import Sequential

from tensorflow.keras.layers import Dense

# Initialize the neural network

model = Sequential()

# Add layers to the neural network

model.add(Dense(units=32, activation='relu', input_shape=(X_train.shape[1],)))

model.add(Dense(units=16, activation='relu'))

model.add(Dense(units=1, activation='sigmoid'))

# Compile the model
```

```
model.compile(optimizer='adam', loss='binary_crossentropy', metrics=['accuracy'])

# Train the model

model.fit(X_train, y_train, epochs=10, batch_size=32)
```

Neural networks are particularly powerful when working with unstructured data like images, text, and sound.

Automation with Python

AUTOMATION IS ANOTHER area where Python excels. Whether you're automating a simple task like file handling or more complex workflows like scraping websites and interacting with APIs, Python offers a range of tools to help you get the job done.

Automating Tasks with Python

LET'S LOOK AT A FEW common automation tasks that Python can simplify.

1. **Automating File Operations**: You can use Python's built-in libraries to automate file handling tasks, such as moving files, renaming them, or even zipping them.

```
import os

import shutil

# Move a file

shutil.move('source/file.txt', 'destination/file.txt')

# Rename a file
```

```
os.rename('file.txt', 'new_file.txt')
```

1. **Web Scraping**: Python's BeautifulSoup and Selenium libraries allow you to automate the extraction of data from websites.

```
from bs4 import BeautifulSoup

import requests

# Fetch web page content

response = requests.get('http://example.com')

soup = BeautifulSoup(response.content, 'html.parser')

# Extract data

print(soup.title.text)
```

1. **API Automation**: Python can automate tasks involving APIs, such as interacting with third-party services like Slack, Google Sheets, or Twitter.

```
import requests

# Send a request to an API

response = requests.get('https://api.github.com/users/username')

data = response.json()

print(data['name'])
```

Best Practices for Advanced Python Projects

AS YOU DELVE INTO MORE complex Python projects, it becomes increasingly important to follow best practices. Here are some tips to ensure your projects remain scalable and maintainable:

- **Use Version Control**: Git is an excellent tool for tracking changes and collaborating on projects.

- **Write Tests**: Unit testing ensures that your code behaves as expected. Python's unittest library makes it easy to create tests.

```
import unittest

class TestExample(unittest.TestCase):

def test_sum(self):

self.assertEqual(sum([1, 2, 3]), 6)

if __name__ == '__main__':

unittest.main()
```

- **Documentation**: Commenting your code and writing documentation is critical for large projects, especially if you work in a team.

```
def add_numbers(a, b):

"""

Adds two numbers together.

Args:
```

```
a (int): The first number.

b (int): The second number.

Returns:

int: The sum of a and b.

"""

return a + b
```

- **Follow Pythonic Practices**: The term "Pythonic" refers to writing code that adheres to the idiomatic conventions of Python. These include writing clean, readable code and leveraging Python's features, such as list comprehensions and generator expressions.

```
# Example of Pythonic code

squares = [x**2 for x in range(10)]
```

Conclusion

EXPLORING ADVANCED topics like machine learning, artificial intelligence, and automation with Python opens up new possibilities for building impactful applications. The libraries and tools mentioned in this section are just the beginning—once you get comfortable with these, you'll find even more opportunities to innovate and solve complex problems using Python.

Contributing to Open Source Python Projects

CONTRIBUTING TO OPEN-source Python projects is an excellent way to deepen your understanding of the language, build your skills, and connect with a global community of developers. It's also an opportunity to give back to a community that provides numerous libraries and tools for free. Many Python projects are maintained by volunteers, and contributing even small improvements can significantly help these projects grow and remain useful.

In this section, we'll explore how to contribute to open-source Python projects. We'll discuss the benefits of contributing, how to find suitable projects, the process of contributing code, and best practices for making impactful contributions. We'll also look at some common challenges and how to overcome them.

Benefits of Contributing to Open Source

CONTRIBUTING TO OPEN-source projects has several advantages, both personally and professionally. Here are a few key benefits:

1. **Learning**: By contributing to open source, you learn how large-scale projects are structured, how code reviews work, and how developers collaborate.
2. **Networking**: You get to interact with other developers, project maintainers, and possibly even companies, all of which can expand your professional network.
3. **Reputation**: Having a portfolio of contributions on platforms like GitHub demonstrates your coding skills to potential employers and collaborators.
4. **Real-World Experience**: Open-source contributions give you hands-on experience with real-world applications and problems. It's a chance to apply what you've learned in a practical environment.
5. **Giving Back**: Contributing helps the Python community

grow and flourish. Many open-source projects are free, and your contributions help keep them viable for others.

Finding the Right Project to Contribute To

FINDING THE RIGHT OPEN-source project can be challenging if you're new to contributing. Here are a few strategies to help you find a suitable project:

1. Start with Projects You Use

A GOOD STARTING POINT is contributing to projects you already use. Whether it's a library, a framework, or a tool, you are already familiar with its purpose, and you may have encountered bugs or thought of improvements. For example, if you use Django, Flask, or Pandas, these are great projects to explore for contributions.

To get started:

- Visit the project's GitHub repository.
- Look at the open issues to see if any are marked as "good first issue" or "beginner-friendly."
- Familiarize yourself with the contributing guidelines, often located in a file called CONTRIBUTING.md.

2. Explore Popular Python Projects

IF YOU'RE UNSURE WHERE to start, you can explore popular Python projects on GitHub by filtering repositories by language (Python) and sorting them by stars or forks. Some commonly contributed-to Python projects include:

- **Requests**: A popular library for making HTTP requests.
- **Scikit-learn**: A library for machine learning algorithms.
- **Flask**: A lightweight web framework.
- **Pandas**: A powerful data manipulation and analysis library.

```
# Example: Using the Requests library

import requests

response = requests.get('https://api.github.com')

print(response.status_code)
```

These projects often have well-documented contribution guidelines and a welcoming community, making them a good place for beginners to get started.

3. Use GitHub's Search Features

GITHUB PROVIDES POWERFUL search filters to help you find repositories that need contributors. For instance, you can search for repositories labeled "good first issue" by using the following query in the GitHub search bar:

```
label:"good first issue" language:Python
```

This query will return Python repositories with issues that maintainers have specifically marked as beginner-friendly.

4. Contribute to Documentation

NOT ALL CONTRIBUTIONS need to be code. Many projects need help with documentation, tutorials, and translations. If you're not yet confident in your coding skills or simply enjoy writing, contributing to documentation is a valuable way to support a project.

```
# Example of a docstring in Python

def add(a, b):

"""

Adds two numbers together.

Args:

a (int): The first number.

b (int): The second number.

Returns:

int: The sum of a and b.

"""

return a + b
```

The Contribution Process

ONCE YOU'VE FOUND A project and identified an issue or area where you want to contribute, the next step is understanding the contribution process. Open-source projects typically follow a standard workflow, which can be broken down into the following steps:

1. Fork the Repository

FORKING A REPOSITORY creates a copy of the project under your own GitHub account. You will be working on your fork before submitting changes to the original repository.

```
# Fork the repository on GitHub, then clone it to your local machine

git clone https://github.com/your-username/repository-name.git

cd repository-name
```

2. Create a New Branch

IT'S A GOOD PRACTICE to create a new branch for your contributions. This keeps your work separate from the main branch and allows you to work on multiple features or bug fixes simultaneously.

```
# Create a new branch

git checkout -b my-new-feature
```

3. Make Your Changes

NOW THAT YOU HAVE A new branch, you can make your changes to the codebase. Be sure to follow the project's coding standards and guidelines. Many projects include linters and style guides (e.g., PEP 8 for Python), so it's important to adhere to these.

```
# Example of following PEP 8 style guide

def greet(name):
```

```
"""Returns a greeting for the provided name."""

return f"Hello, {name}!"
```

4. Test Your Changes

BEFORE SUBMITTING YOUR changes, you should test them thoroughly to ensure they work as expected. Many projects include automated tests, and you can run these to check if your code breaks any existing functionality.

```
# Run the test suite

python -m unittest discover
```

If the project doesn't have automated tests, you may need to write your own tests or manually verify that your changes work.

5. Commit Your Changes

ONCE YOU'RE HAPPY WITH your changes and have tested them, it's time to commit your work. Use descriptive commit messages that explain what changes you've made.

```
# Add and commit your changes

git add .

git commit -m "Added feature to greet user by name"
```

6. Push Your Changes

AFTER COMMITTING YOUR changes, you need to push them to your forked repository on GitHub.

```
# Push your changes to GitHub

git push origin my-new-feature
```

7. Create a Pull Request

ONCE YOUR CHANGES ARE pushed, you can create a pull request (PR). A pull request is a way to notify the maintainers of the project that you've made changes and would like them to be reviewed and merged into the main project.

In your pull request:

- Provide a clear description of what your changes do.
- Reference any issues your changes address by using keywords like "Closes #123" to automatically close the issue once the PR is merged.
- Be open to feedback from the maintainers, and be prepared to make revisions based on their comments.

```
# Example of linking an issue in a pull request description

"""

This PR implements a new feature that allows the program to greet users by name.

Closes #123

"""
```

Best Practices for Open-Source Contributions

CONTRIBUTING TO OPEN source involves more than just writing code. To be a successful contributor, you should follow some best practices to ensure your contributions are valuable and align with the project's goals.

1. Understand the Project's Goals

BEFORE DIVING INTO a codebase, take the time to understand the project's mission, goals, and future roadmap. This will help you focus on contributions that align with the project's vision.

2. Start Small

IF YOU'RE NEW TO A project, it's best to start with small contributions. Fixing typos in documentation, improving error messages, or adding test cases are all good ways to familiarize yourself with the codebase and build a rapport with the maintainers.

3. Follow Coding Standards

MOST PROJECTS HAVE coding standards or style guides that contributors must follow. In Python, PEP 8 is a widely accepted style guide, but individual projects may have additional rules. Ensure your contributions adhere to these guidelines.

4. Be Responsive and Open to Feedback

WHEN YOU SUBMIT A PULL request, it's common for maintainers to provide feedback. Be open to suggestions and willing to make changes. Responsiveness is key to getting your contributions merged quickly.

5. Collaborate and Communicate

OPEN-SOURCE PROJECTS thrive on collaboration. If you're unsure about something, ask questions. Use GitHub issues, project forums, or chat platforms like Discord or Slack to communicate with other contributors and maintainers.

Overcoming Common Challenges

CONTRIBUTING TO OPEN-source projects isn't always smooth sailing. You may encounter a few common challenges, especially when starting out.

1. Imposter Syndrome

MANY NEW CONTRIBUTORS feel like they're not "good enough" to contribute to open source. Remember that everyone starts somewhere, and even small contributions are valuable. The open-source community is generally welcoming and supportive of beginners.

2. Complex Codebases

LARGE PROJECTS CAN have complex and unfamiliar codebases. Take your time to understand the project's structure, and don't hesitate to ask for help. Many projects have documentation specifically for new contributors.

3. Time Commitment

CONTRIBUTING TO OPEN source can be time-consuming, especially when you're balancing it with work or personal commitments. Start with small, manageable tasks, and contribute at your own pace.

Conclusion

CONTRIBUTING TO OPEN-source Python projects is one of the best ways to improve your skills, gain experience, and become part of a global community. By following the steps and best practices outlined in this section, you'll be well-equipped to make meaningful contributions to the Python ecosystem. Whether you're fixing bugs, writing documentation, or building new features, every contribution counts, and the experience you gain is invaluable.

Python Community and Learning Resources

THE PYTHON PROGRAMMING language has one of the most active and welcoming communities in the world. From forums, meetups, and conferences to online tutorials and books, the Python ecosystem offers a wide range of resources for both beginners and experienced developers. In this section, we will explore the various ways you can engage with the Python community, the resources available to deepen your learning, and how to make the most of this supportive environment. Engaging with the community not only accelerates your learning but also helps you stay updated on the latest trends and developments in the Python world.

Python Community Engagement

ONE OF THE BEST WAYS to improve your skills and grow as a Python developer is to actively engage with the community. The Python community is vast, and there are numerous platforms where you can participate, contribute, and learn.

1. Python Forums and Mailing Lists

ONLINE FORUMS AND MAILING lists are excellent places to ask questions, discuss programming challenges, and get advice from other Python developers. The official Python mailing list, Python-Dev, is a primary channel for discussing developments related to Python's core features. However, there are many other forums where Python enthusiasts gather to share knowledge.

- **Python.org**: The official Python website hosts various mailing lists and forums where developers can participate in discussions.

- **Stack Overflow**: This is one of the most popular platforms for asking and answering programming-related questions. Thousands of Python-related questions are asked daily, and it's an excellent resource for troubleshooting and getting quick help.

- **Reddit**: Subreddits like r/Python and r/learnpython are vibrant communities where people share tutorials, ask questions, and discuss news related to Python.

Being active on these forums not only helps you solve problems but also allows you to help others, which reinforces your own learning. Don't hesitate to ask questions, but always make sure to provide enough context when doing so. Similarly, answering other people's questions is a great way to solidify your understanding of a topic.

```
# Example of a common Stack Overflow question: How to reverse a string in Python?

def reverse_string(s):

return s[::-1]

# Test the function

reverse_string("Python") # Output: 'nohtyP'
```

2. Meetups and Local User Groups

IN-PERSON MEETUPS AND user groups are another fantastic way to engage with the Python community. Python user groups (PUGs) exist in cities around the world, providing opportunities for Python enthusiasts to meet, network, and collaborate on projects. These groups often organize talks, hackathons, and study sessions. Participating in such events allows you to gain insights from experienced developers, share your knowledge, and form lasting professional relationships.

You can find local meetups through platforms like:

- **Meetup.com**: Search for Python-related events in your area.
- **PyLadies**: A global community focused on helping women become active participants and leaders in the

Python community. PyLadies chapters exist in many cities and host regular events.

- **Django Girls**: A non-profit organization that aims to bring more women into the tech industry by offering free, beginner-friendly programming workshops.

3. Python Conferences

ATTENDING PYTHON CONFERENCES is one of the best ways to stay connected to the latest developments in the Python world. These conferences feature talks by prominent developers, workshops, and opportunities to network with peers. Some well-known Python conferences include:

- **PyCon**: The largest annual Python conference, organized by the Python Software Foundation (PSF). PyCon events are held in different regions around the world, and they feature talks, tutorials, and sprints (collaborative coding sessions).

- **EuroPython**: One of the biggest Python conferences in Europe, attracting developers from across the continent.

- **DjangoCon**: A conference specifically focused on Django, one of the most popular web frameworks built with Python.

Attending a Python conference can be an eye-opening experience, offering you exposure to cutting-edge technologies, best practices, and new libraries. If attending in person is not feasible, many conferences provide livestreams or post recorded sessions online, making it easy to participate remotely.

Learning Resources

PYTHON'S POPULARITY means there are a wealth of resources available to help you learn and grow as a developer. Whether you're just starting out or looking to advance your skills, you can find books, online courses, blogs, and videos that cater to your learning needs.

1. Books on Python Programming

BOOKS ARE AN EXCELLENT way to gain a deep understanding of Python. Whether you prefer a beginner-friendly introduction or an advanced dive into specific topics like data science or web development, there are many high-quality Python books available.

Here are some popular Python books:

- **"Automate the Boring Stuff with Python" by Al Sweigart**: A beginner-friendly book that teaches practical Python programming by automating tasks.
- **"Python Crash Course" by Eric Matthes**: A fast-paced introduction to Python, focusing on hands-on projects.
- **"Fluent Python" by Luciano Ramalho**: A comprehensive guide to writing Pythonic code, with a focus on advanced Python features and idiomatic programming techniques.

- **"Effective Python" by Brett Slatkin**: This book offers 59 specific ways to improve your Python programs, covering best practices and performance optimizations.

Reading books not only improves your coding skills but also provides context and deeper insights into Python's philosophy and best practices.

```
# Example inspired by "Automate the Boring Stuff with Python"

import pyautogui

# Automate a simple task of opening an application (for example, a calculator)

pyautogui.hotkey('command', 'space') # Open Spotlight (on macOS)

pyautogui.typewrite('calculator')

pyautogui.press('enter')
```

2. Online Courses and Tutorials

FOR LEARNERS WHO PREFER a more structured and interactive approach, online courses are an excellent resource. Many platforms offer comprehensive Python courses that cover a wide range of topics, from basic syntax to advanced data science and machine learning.

Some popular platforms for Python courses include:

- **Coursera**: Coursera offers courses from top universities and companies. Courses like the Python for

Everybody specialization by the University of Michigan are highly rated.

- **edX**: edX provides courses from renowned institutions like MIT and Harvard, with Python programming often featured in their computer science and data science curricula.

- **Udemy**: Udemy offers a wide variety of Python courses at affordable prices. Popular courses include "The Complete Python Bootcamp" by Jose Portilla.

- **Real Python**: A dedicated Python learning platform offering tutorials, videos, and quizzes. Real Python is great for continuous learning as they frequently update their content.

Many of these courses include hands-on projects and assignments that help reinforce your learning. You can apply what you've learned immediately, gaining confidence with each new concept.

3. Blogs and Tutorials

MANY EXPERIENCED PYTHON developers share their knowledge through blogs and tutorials. Regularly reading these can help you stay updated with new features, best practices, and emerging libraries. Some notable Python blogs include:

- **Real Python**: In addition to offering structured courses, Real Python publishes high-quality articles on Python programming, with topics ranging from beginner to advanced.

- **The Mouse Vs. The Python**: A blog run by Mike Driscoll, offering Python tips, tutorials, and book reviews.

- **Full Stack Python**: This blog is focused on full-stack development with Python, covering everything from backend frameworks like Flask and Django to deployment strategies.

- **Planet Python**: A collection of blog posts from Python developers across the globe. It's a great resource for finding diverse perspectives and learning from different parts of the community.

Blogs are an excellent way to dive deep into niche topics or new Python libraries that may not yet have comprehensive documentation.

```
# Example inspired by a blog tutorial: Using Python's itertools for combinations

import itertools

# Create a list of items

items = ['A', 'B', 'C']

# Get all possible combinations of two items

combinations = list(itertools.combinations(items, 2))

print(combinations) # Output: [('A', 'B'), ('A', 'C'), ('B', 'C')]
```

4. Video Tutorials

IF YOU PREFER LEARNING by watching and listening, video tutorials are an excellent option. Many YouTube channels and video platforms offer high-quality content for Python learners.

Popular YouTube channels for Python tutorials include:

- **Corey Schafer**: Corey Schafer's channel offers comprehensive Python tutorials on various topics, including web development, automation, and data science.

- **Programming with Mosh**: Mosh Hamedani's tutorials are known for their clarity and are perfect for beginners.

- **Tech With Tim**: Tim Ruscica provides Python tutorials with a focus on game development, AI, and algorithms.

Video tutorials allow you to see code in action, often with real-world examples that are easier to follow compared to written guides.

5. Python Documentation and Official Resources

THE OFFICIAL PYTHON documentation is one of the most valuable resources for any Python developer. It contains everything from tutorials and guides for beginners to in-depth references for experienced developers.

- **The Python Documentation**: Available at python.org/doc, this resource covers the entire Python language, including tutorials for beginners, a detailed explanation of built-in functions, and advanced topics like C extensions and Python internals.

- **PEP 8 – Python Style Guide**: PEP 8 is the official style guide for Python code. Adhering to it ensures your code is readable and consistent with the wider Python community's standards.

6. Python Cheat Sheets

FOR QUICK REFERENCE, Python cheat sheets can be incredibly helpful. These one- or two-page documents summarize essential Python syntax, functions, and libraries. You can find cheat sheets for topics like regular expressions, list comprehensions, and object-oriented programming. Some websites, like Python Cheat Sheet (pythoncheatsheet.org), offer comprehensive downloadable resources.

Best Practices for Continuous Learning

LEARNING PYTHON IS a journey that doesn't stop after mastering the basics. Here are some best practices to ensure you keep progressing as a Python developer:

- **Practice Regularly**: The best way to learn Python is to practice regularly. Building small projects, solving coding challenges on platforms like LeetCode or HackerRank, and contributing to open-source projects can reinforce your learning.

- **Keep Up with New Python Features**: Python is a continuously evolving language. New features are added in every release, and staying up to date ensures you're using the latest and most efficient tools. You can follow Python release notes and PEPs (Python Enhancement Proposals) to learn about upcoming changes.

- **Collaborate with Others**: Coding with others, whether in a pair programming session or on a team project, exposes you to different ways of thinking and solving problems. It also helps improve your collaboration and communication skills.

- **Work on Real-World Projects**: Apply what you've learned by working on real-world projects. Whether you're automating tasks at work or building a personal project, the experience of applying Python in a real-world context is invaluable.

Conclusion

THE PYTHON COMMUNITY offers a wealth of resources to support developers at all levels, from beginner to advanced. By engaging with the community, attending events, reading blogs, and utilizing the wide array of learning resources available, you can continue to grow your Python skills and stay up-to-date with the latest advancements in the language. Whether you prefer reading books, taking courses, or contributing to open source, the Python ecosystem provides everything you need to become a proficient and successful Python developer.

Building Real-World Python Projects

BUILDING REAL-WORLD projects is one of the most effective ways to solidify your Python skills and gain practical experience. It takes your theoretical knowledge and applies it to solving tangible problems, often using multiple libraries, frameworks, and concepts at once. This section will guide you through the process of planning, developing, and refining Python projects that mirror real-world applications, giving you the tools to tackle larger and more complex challenges in your Python journey.

1. Planning Your Python Project

THE FIRST STEP IN BUILDING any project, whether it's a small script or a full-fledged application, is to plan effectively. A well-thought-out plan not only saves time but also ensures you have a clear roadmap for development. Here are some key points to consider when planning your project:

a. Defining the Scope and Purpose

ASK YOURSELF: WHAT problem is the project trying to solve? Who will use it, and how will it benefit them? Defining the scope of your project early on will help you stay focused on the most important aspects and avoid unnecessary complications.

For instance, if you're building a web scraping tool, the purpose could be to gather specific data from multiple websites. The scope could involve scraping data from websites, handling dynamic content, and exporting the data in a user-friendly format such as CSV or JSON.

Example purpose: Web scraper for gathering product prices from an e-commerce website

b. Breaking Down the Project into Modules

AFTER DEFINING THE scope, break down your project into smaller, manageable tasks. Think about the components or modules needed to make the project functional. For example, if you are building a web application, your project might include:

- A user authentication system.
- A database to store user data.
- An interface for users to interact with the system.

For a smaller project, such as a file automation tool, you could break the project into input handling, file manipulation, and output generation modules.

```
# Example structure for a web application project

# - User authentication module

# - Database management module

# - Frontend and backend communication

# - Error handling and logging
```

c. Selecting Libraries and Tools

PYTHON'S ECOSYSTEM is vast, offering a variety of libraries and frameworks to make development faster and more efficient. Choosing the right tools can drastically simplify the development process. Here are some libraries commonly used for specific project types:

- **Web Development**: Flask, Django

- **Data Analysis**: Pandas, NumPy, Matplotlib
- **Machine Learning**: Scikit-learn, TensorFlow, Keras
- **Automation**: Selenium, PyAutoGUI, Requests
- **Database Management**: SQLAlchemy, SQLite, PostgreSQL

Make sure to choose libraries that fit your project's needs. For instance, if you're working on a small web application, Flask might be a better choice than Django due to its lightweight nature.

```
# Example: Using Flask for a web application

from flask import Flask

app = Flask(__name__)

@app.route('/')

def home():

return "Welcome to My Web Application!"

if __name__ == "__main__":

app.run(debug=True)
```

2. Building the Foundation

ONCE YOUR PROJECT IS planned, you can begin laying the foundation. Start by setting up your environment, organizing your code, and implementing the core features. During this stage, focus on writing clean, modular code that can be easily extended and maintained.

a. Setting Up a Virtual Environment

A VIRTUAL ENVIRONMENT helps manage dependencies, ensuring that your project's libraries are isolated from the system's global packages. This is especially useful for larger projects that may require specific versions of libraries.

```
# Setting up a virtual environment

python -m venv myprojectenv

# Activating the virtual environment

# On Windows:

myprojectenv\Scripts\activate

# On macOS/Linux:

source myprojectenv/bin/activate
```

Once the environment is activated, you can install the necessary libraries using pip. This ensures that the dependencies are specific to your project.

```
# Installing Flask in the virtual environment

pip install Flask
```

b. Structuring Your Code

HOW YOU STRUCTURE YOUR code can greatly affect the maintainability of your project. For most Python projects, it's a good idea to follow a standard folder structure that separates different components. Here's a common structure for a Python project:

```
my_project/
│
├── app/ # Application code
│ ├── __init__.py # Initialize the module
│ ├── views.py # Code handling user interaction
│ ├── models.py # Database models
│ ├── static/ # Static files (CSS, images, etc.)
│ └── templates/ # HTML templates
│
├── tests/ # Test files
│ └── test_app.py
│
├── venv/ # Virtual environment
│
├── requirements.txt # List of dependencies
└── README.md # Project documentation
```

This structure keeps your project organized, allowing for scalability and collaboration. If your project grows, this modularity ensures that new components can be added without causing confusion.

3. Core Features Development

NOW THAT YOUR ENVIRONMENT is set up and the project structure is in place, you can begin coding the core features. Here are some tips for developing different types of real-world projects.

a. Building a Web Application

WEB DEVELOPMENT IS one of the most common use cases for Python. Whether you're building a personal blog, a portfolio site, or a more complex web application, Python's web frameworks provide a great foundation.

Example: A Simple Flask Web Application

```
from flask import Flask, render_template, request

app = Flask(__name__)

# Route to display homepage

@app.route('/')

def index():

return render_template('index.html')

# Route to process form data

@app.route('/submit', methods=['POST'])

def submit():

name = request.form['name']

return f"Hello, {name}!"
```

```
if __name__ == "__main__":

app.run(debug=True)
```

This simple web application displays a homepage and processes form submissions. You can expand on it by adding a database, user authentication, or API integrations.

b. Data Analysis Project

IF YOUR PROJECT INVOLVES data, Python's data analysis libraries like Pandas and NumPy are invaluable. You can use these libraries to clean, process, and visualize data. A common real-world example might involve analyzing sales data or processing survey results.

Example: Analyzing Sales Data with Pandas

```
import pandas as pd

# Load sales data

data = pd.read_csv('sales_data.csv')

# Perform basic analysis

total_sales = data['Sales'].sum()

average_sales = data['Sales'].mean()

print(f"Total Sales: {total_sales}")

print(f"Average Sales: {average_sales}")

# Visualize data with Matplotlib

import matplotlib.pyplot as plt
```

```
data['Sales'].plot(kind='bar')

plt.show()
```

In this example, we load sales data from a CSV file, perform basic aggregation, and visualize the data. Depending on the scope of your project, you could further analyze trends, correlations, and seasonal patterns in the data.

c. Automating Repetitive Tasks

AUTOMATION PROJECTS are popular in the Python community because they help reduce time spent on repetitive tasks. These projects can range from simple file manipulation to complex workflows that integrate with APIs and other services.

Example: Automating File Renaming

```
import os

# Directory containing files

directory = "C:/path/to/files"

# Rename all .txt files in the directory

for filename in os.listdir(directory):

if filename.endswith(".txt"):

new_name = filename.replace(" ", "_")

os.rename(os.path.join(directory, filename), os.path.join(directory, new_name))
```

This simple script renames all text files in a directory, replacing spaces with underscores. You could expand on this by integrating it into a larger automation pipeline that processes, categorizes, and moves files to different folders.

4. Testing and Debugging

ONCE YOU'VE IMPLEMENTED the core features, it's important to test and debug your code to ensure that everything works as expected. Python offers several tools for writing tests and identifying bugs.

a. Unit Testing

UNIT TESTS VERIFY THAT individual components of your project work correctly. Python's unittest module makes it easy to write tests for your project.

Example: Writing Unit Tests for a Calculator

```
import unittest

# Simple calculator class

class Calculator:

def add(self, x, y):

return x + y

# Unit tests for the calculator

class TestCalculator(unittest.TestCase):

def test_add(self):

calc = Calculator()

self.assertEqual(calc.add(2, 3), 5)
```

```
if __name__ == '__main__':
unittest.main()
```

In this example, we define a simple Calculator class and a corresponding test case to verify that the add method works as expected. When writing real-world projects, ensure that your core functionalities are covered by unit tests to catch any regressions or bugs early.

b. Debugging Tools

BUGS ARE INEVITABLE, especially in larger projects. Fortunately, Python provides robust debugging tools. The built-in pdb (Python Debugger) allows you to step through your code, inspect variables, and identify where things are going wrong.

```
# Example of using pdb for debugging
import pdb
def divide(a, b):
pdb.set_trace() # This will open an interactive debugging session
return a / b
divide(10, 0)
```

In this example, the debugger will pause execution at pdb.set_trace() and allow you to inspect the state of the program. This is particularly useful for identifying tricky bugs that are hard to catch with simple print statements.

5. Documenting and Sharing Your Project

GOOD DOCUMENTATION is essential for any real-world project. Whether you're sharing your code with collaborators or releasing it as an open-source project, clear documentation ensures that others can understand and use your work.

a. Writing a README File

EVERY PROJECT SHOULD have a README.md file that explains the project's purpose, installation instructions, and usage. A well-written README helps others get started with your project quickly.

Here's an example of what a README.md might include:

My Web Scraping Tool

Description

This tool scrapes product prices from e-commerce websites and exports the data to a CSV file.

Installation

1. Clone the repository:

git clonehttps://github.com/username/my-web-scraper.git

2. Install dependencies:

pip install -r requirements.txt

USAGE

Run the tool with the following command:

---

b. Commenting Your Code

CLEAR, CONCISE COMMENTS within your code help others (and yourself) understand the logic and purpose of different sections. Be sure to comment on any non-obvious code, particularly if you're using complex algorithms or workarounds.

```
# Calculate the total sales for each region

region_totals = data.groupby('Region')['Sales'].sum()
```

c. Sharing Your Project on GitHub

IF YOU WANT TO SHARE your project with the world, GitHub is an excellent platform for hosting open-source projects. After creating a repository, you can upload your project, document it, and even invite collaborators.

```
# Steps to upload a project to GitHub

git init

git add .

git commit -m "Initial commit"

git remote add origin https://github.com/username/my-project.git

git push -u origin master
```

6. Deploying Your Project

THE FINAL STEP IN BUILDING a real-world project is deploying it so that others can use it. Depending on your project, deployment might involve:

- **Hosting a Web Application**: Use platforms like Heroku, AWS, or DigitalOcean to host your web app.
- **Distributing a Python Package**: Publish your code to PyPI (Python Package Index) if you want others to install it using pip.
- **Automating with Cron Jobs**: For automation scripts, you might set up cron jobs (on Linux) or Task Scheduler (on Windows) to run your Python script at regular intervals.

Conclusion

BUILDING REAL-WORLD Python projects is both challenging and rewarding. It allows you to apply your knowledge in practical ways, collaborate with others, and tackle increasingly complex problems. By following the steps outlined in this section—planning your project, writing clean code, testing thoroughly, and documenting and sharing your work—you'll develop the skills necessary to succeed in real-world development scenarios. Whether you're building a small automation script or a large web application, Python's versatility makes it an ideal language for solving real-world problems.

Final Thoughts: Mastering Python Beyond the Basics

AS YOU PROGRESS THROUGH your Python journey, moving beyond the basics involves not only mastering advanced technical skills but also adopting a mindset that promotes continuous learning, improvement, and creativity. Python, as a language, opens doors to numerous fields, such as web development, data science, artificial intelligence, and automation. However, mastering Python goes far beyond syntax and libraries; it involves a deep understanding of problem-solving, algorithmic thinking, and real-world application.

In this section, we will explore key strategies, concepts, and mindsets that will help you move from being an intermediate Python user to mastering the language. We will discuss how to approach complex challenges, how to integrate Python into larger systems, and the importance of coding best practices. These final thoughts aim to equip you with a holistic approach to Python, preparing you for projects that demand more than just a working knowledge of the language.

1. Developing a Problem-Solving Mindset

AT THE CORE OF EVERY successful developer lies an effective problem-solving mindset. The ability to break down complex problems into manageable components and then solve them efficiently is what distinguishes experienced developers from beginners. Python is an excellent language for fostering this mindset because of its simplicity and readability, allowing you to focus on the logic rather than the intricacies of syntax.

a. Breaking Down Complex Problems

WHEN CONFRONTED WITH a complex problem, the first step is to break it down into smaller, more manageable pieces. This technique is called decomposition. By solving each smaller piece independently, you can assemble the solutions to solve the overarching problem.

For instance, if you're tasked with building an application that processes and analyzes customer data, you could break the project down into the following tasks:

- Parsing and validating input data
- Storing data in a database
- Performing statistical analysis on the data
- Visualizing the results using charts and graphs

Each of these tasks can be handled separately, allowing you to focus on solving one problem at a time.

```
# Example: Breaking down a problem into smaller tasks

def parse_data(file_path):

# Read and validate data from a file

pass

def store_data(database, data):

# Store data in a database

pass
```

```
def analyze_data(data):

# Perform data analysis

pass

def visualize_results(results):

# Visualize analysis results using charts

pass
```

b. Leveraging Python's Built-In Libraries

ONE OF THE ADVANTAGES of Python is its extensive standard library, which includes modules and packages designed to solve common problems. Instead of reinventing the wheel, a true Python master knows how to leverage these libraries effectively.

For example, you can handle file operations using the os and shutil libraries, perform mathematical computations using math, or manage time-based tasks using datetime. Knowing when and how to use these libraries can significantly improve your productivity.

```
import os

import shutil

from datetime import datetime

# Example: Using built-in libraries for common tasks

def backup_files(source_dir, backup_dir):

if not os.path.exists(backup_dir):

os.makedirs(backup_dir)
```

```
for filename in os.listdir(source_dir):

shutil.copy(os.path.join(source_dir, filename), backup_dir)

# Example of using datetime to timestamp backups

backup_name = f"backup_{datetime.now().strftime('%Y%m%d_%H%M%S')}"

backup_files('/path/to/source', f'/path/to/backup/{backup_name}')
```

c. Thinking Algorithmically

AS YOU DIVE DEEPER into Python, understanding algorithmic thinking becomes essential. Mastery of algorithms and data structures allows you to write efficient, scalable programs. Learning algorithms like sorting, searching, recursion, and dynamic programming will help you tackle problems that require optimized solutions.

One common algorithm is **binary search**, which is more efficient than linear search when working with sorted data. Here's a simple implementation in Python:

```
# Example: Implementing binary search in Python

def binary_search(arr, target):

low = 0

high = len(arr) - 1

while low <= high:

mid = (low + high) // 2
```

```
if arr[mid] == target:
return mid
elif arr[mid] < target:
low = mid + 1
else:
high = mid - 1
return -1
# Usage
arr = [1, 3, 5, 7, 9, 11]
result = binary_search(arr, 7) # Output: 3
```

Algorithmic thinking doesn't always mean inventing algorithms from scratch. In most cases, it's about recognizing which existing algorithm fits a problem and implementing it effectively.

2. Integrating Python with Other Technologies

AS YOU GROW IN YOUR Python expertise, you'll likely work on projects that require integrating Python with other technologies. Python's flexibility allows it to interact with various databases, web frameworks, APIs, and even other programming languages. Being comfortable with these integrations is essential for tackling larger, more complex projects.

a. Database Integration

MANY REAL-WORLD APPLICATIONS require storing and retrieving data from a database. Python provides several libraries for interacting with databases, such as SQLite, PostgreSQL, and MySQL. For instance, the sqlite3 module in Python allows you to easily work with SQLite databases.

```
import sqlite3

# Example: Working with SQLite in Python

def create_database(db_name):

conn = sqlite3.connect(db_name)

cursor = conn.cursor()

cursor.execute('''CREATE TABLE IF NOT EXISTS users (

id INTEGER PRIMARY KEY,

name TEXT NOT NULL,

age INTEGER NOT NULL)''')

conn.commit()

conn.close()

def add_user(db_name, name, age):

conn = sqlite3.connect(db_name)

cursor = conn.cursor()

cursor.execute("INSERT INTO users (name, age) VALUES (?, ?)",
(name, age))

conn.commit()

conn.close()
```

```
# Create a new database and add a user

create_database('users.db')

add_user('users.db', 'Alice', 25)
```

When your applications need to scale, understanding how to interact with larger database systems (e.g., PostgreSQL or MySQL) will be crucial. You can use libraries like SQLAlchemy to abstract and simplify database interactions.

b. Web Development and APIs

PYTHON IS COMMONLY used for web development, and frameworks like Flask and Django make building web applications relatively straightforward. Moreover, Python can integrate with external APIs to either provide or consume data.

For example, consuming a third-party API might involve using the requests library:

```
import requests

# Example: Fetching data from an external API

def fetch_weather(city):

api_key = "your_api_key"

url = f"http://api.openweathermap.org/data/2.5/weather?q={city}&appid={api_key}"

response = requests.get(url)

if response.status_code == 200:

data = response.json()
```

```
return data
else:
return None
weather_data = fetch_weather("London")
print(weather_data)
```

Similarly, Python is frequently used to build APIs using frameworks like Flask and Django REST framework.

```
from flask import Flask, jsonify
app = Flask(__name__)
# Example: Creating a simple API in Flask
@app.route('/api/greet/<name>', methods=['GET'])
def greet(name):
return jsonify({"message": f"Hello, {name}!"})
if __name__ == '__main__':
app.run(debug=True)
```

Understanding how to integrate Python with APIs and web technologies allows you to create more interactive, user-facing applications, further expanding your project possibilities.

3. Writing Efficient, Scalable Code

EFFICIENCY AND SCALABILITY are critical when moving beyond basic Python applications. As you tackle more substantial projects, you'll need to consider how well your code performs, especially when dealing with large datasets, high traffic, or complex computations.

a. Code Efficiency

WRITING EFFICIENT CODE ensures that your programs run faster and consume fewer resources. One way to improve efficiency is by selecting the appropriate data structures. For instance, using a set rather than a list can significantly speed up membership tests:

```
# Example: Efficiency comparison between list and set membership tests

my_list = [1, 2, 3, 4, 5]

my_set = {1, 2, 3, 4, 5}

# Checking membership

print(3 in my_list) # O(n) time complexity

print(3 in my_set) # O(1) time complexity
```

You can also profile your code using Python's built-in timeit module or external tools like cProfile to identify bottlenecks and optimize performance.

b. Scalability Considerations

WHEN BUILDING SCALABLE applications, you need to think about how your code will behave as the application grows in complexity, traffic, or data volume. For example, a web application that handles thousands of users per minute requires different design considerations than one that serves only a few.

One way to improve scalability is through the use of **caching**, which can reduce the load on your system by storing the results of expensive operations. Tools like **Redis** and **Memcached** can help you implement caching solutions in Python applications.

Another strategy is **load balancing**, which distributes incoming requests across multiple servers to prevent any single server from becoming overloaded. Python frameworks like Flask or Django can easily be scaled using cloud platforms like AWS, Google Cloud, or Heroku.

4. Adopting Best Practices for Python Code

BECOMING A MASTER OF Python also means adhering to best practices. This involves writing clean, readable code that follows Pythonic principles, adhering to style guidelines, and maintaining your codebase in a way that facilitates collaboration and scalability.

a. Follow PEP 8 Guidelines

PEP 8 IS THE OFFICIAL style guide for Python code, and following it ensures that your code is readable and consistent with the broader Python community. Some key points include:

- Use 4 spaces per indentation level (avoid tabs).
- Limit lines to 79 characters.
- Use descriptive variable names and avoid single-letter variables except for counters or iterators.

Example: Following PEP 8 style guide

```
def calculate_area(radius):

"""Calculate the area of a circle given its radius."""

pi = 3.14159

return pi * radius ** 2
```

b. Write Tests

TESTING IS AN INTEGRAL part of writing maintainable code. Unit tests help ensure that your code works as expected and prevent regressions when making changes. Python's unittest module provides an easy way to write and run tests.

```
import unittest

# Example: Writing a simple unit test

def multiply(a, b):

return a * b

class TestMultiply(unittest.TestCase):

def test_multiply(self):

self.assertEqual(multiply(3, 4), 12)

if __name__ == '__main__':

unittest.main()
```

Writing tests not only improves code quality but also makes it easier for others to contribute to your project confidently.

c. Document Your Code

GOOD DOCUMENTATION makes your codebase accessible to others and your future self. Whether you're writing a small utility script or a large application, documenting your code helps others (and you) understand its purpose, structure, and usage.

You can use docstrings to describe the functionality of your functions and classes:

```
# Example: Using docstrings for documentation

def greet(name):

"""

Greets a person by name.

Args:

name (str): The person's name.

Returns:

str: A greeting message.

"""

return f"Hello, {name}!"
```

For larger projects, consider maintaining a README.md file and using tools like **Sphinx** to generate professional documentation from your docstrings.

Conclusion

MASTERING PYTHON GOES far beyond learning syntax and libraries. It involves developing a problem-solving mindset, thinking algorithmically, and integrating Python into broader technological ecosystems. Writing efficient, scalable code and adhering to best practices are essential components of Python mastery. By continuously applying these concepts, engaging with real-world challenges, and staying curious, you will not only master Python but also become a highly effective and versatile developer, capable of tackling complex projects and contributing meaningfully to the tech industry.

Chapter 13: Appendices

Glossary of Python Terms

THIS SECTION SERVES as a detailed glossary of essential Python terms that you will frequently encounter as you continue your Python programming journey. Each term is defined in a way that not only explains what it means but also provides examples of how it fits into the broader context of Python programming. Whether you're a beginner or an experienced developer, understanding these terms will help you navigate the Python language with more confidence.

1. Argument

AN ARGUMENT IS A VALUE that is passed to a function when the function is called. Functions in Python can take one or more arguments, which are specified within the parentheses following the function name. Arguments allow functions to operate on data that is passed to them.

Example:

```
def greet(name):

return f"Hello, {name}!"

print(greet("Alice"))
```

In the example above, "Alice" is the argument passed to the greet function.

2. Assignment

ASSIGNMENT IN PYTHON refers to the act of assigning a value to a variable. The assignment operator in Python is the equals sign =. This operator assigns the value on its right to the variable on its left.

Example:

x = 10

name = "John"

In this case, the value 10 is assigned to the variable x, and the string "John" is assigned to the variable name.

3. Boolean

A BOOLEAN IS A DATA type that represents one of two values: True or False. Booleans are often used in conditions to control the flow of a program, such as in if statements or loops.

Example:

is_student = True

if is_student:

print("The user is a student.")

else:

print("The user is not a student.")

In the example above, the Boolean is_student is used to determine which block of code to execute.

4. Class

A CLASS IS A BLUEPRINT for creating objects (instances of that class). Classes define properties and behaviors (via methods) that the objects created from the class will have. Python supports object-oriented programming, where classes play a central role.

Example:

```
class Dog:

def __init__(self, name, breed):

self.name = name

self.breed = breed

def bark(self):

return f"{self.name} says woof!"

my_dog = Dog("Buddy", "Golden Retriever")

print(my_dog.bark())
```

Here, Dog is a class, and my_dog is an object (or instance) of the class.

5. Data Types

DATA TYPES DEFINE THE type of value that can be stored in a variable. Common Python data types include:

- int: for integers (whole numbers)
- float: for floating-point numbers (decimals)
- str: for strings (text)

- bool: for Boolean values (True or False)
- list: for ordered collections of items
- dict: for key-value pairs

Example:

age = 25 # int

height = 5.9 # float

name = "John" # str

is_student = True # bool

6. Dictionary

A DICTIONARY IS A COLLECTION of key-value pairs. In Python, dictionaries are defined using curly braces {} and each key is mapped to a value. Dictionaries are useful when you need to associate values with unique keys.

Example:

student = {

"name": "Alice",

"age": 22,

"major": "Computer Science"

}

print(student["name"])

In this case, the key "name" is associated with the value "Alice".

7. Exception

AN EXCEPTION IS AN error that occurs during the execution of a program. When an exception is raised, Python generates an error message and halts the program unless the exception is handled using try and except blocks.

Example:

```
try:

result = 10 / 0

except ZeroDivisionError:

print("You cannot divide by zero.")
```

Here, a ZeroDivisionError exception is raised because division by zero is not allowed in Python. The exception is caught, and the program prints a message instead of crashing.

8. Function

A FUNCTION IS A BLOCK of code that performs a specific task. Functions allow you to reuse code by defining a task once and calling the function whenever you need to perform that task. In Python, functions are defined using the def keyword.

Example:

```
def add_numbers(a, b):

return a + b

print(add_numbers(3, 5))
```

In this case, the add_numbers function takes two arguments (a and b) and returns their sum.

9. Immutable

AN OBJECT IS CONSIDERED immutable if its value cannot be changed after it is created. In Python, types such as int, float, bool, str, and tuple are immutable. If you try to modify an immutable object, Python will create a new object instead of modifying the original one.

Example:

name = "Alice"

name[0] = "B" # This will raise an error because strings are immutable

Since strings are immutable, attempting to modify one of its characters will result in an error.

10. List

A LIST IS A COLLECTION of items that can be of different data types. Lists are mutable, meaning you can change their content (e.g., adding, removing, or modifying items) after they are created. Lists are defined using square brackets [].

Example:

fruits = ["apple", "banana", "cherry"]

print(fruits[1]) # Output: banana

fruits.append("orange")

print(fruits) # Output: ['apple', 'banana', 'cherry', 'orange']

11. Loop

A LOOP IS A PROGRAMMING construct that repeats a block of code multiple times. Python supports two types of loops: for and while. Loops allow you to iterate over data structures like lists, strings, and ranges.

Example of a for loop:

```
for i in range(5):

print(i)
```

This for loop will print the numbers from 0 to 4.

Example of a while loop:

```
count = 0

while count < 5:

print(count)

count += 1
```

12. Method

A METHOD IS A FUNCTION that is associated with an object. Methods in Python are defined within classes and operate on the data within the object. Methods are called using the object name followed by a dot and the method name.

Example:

```
class Car:

def __init__(self, model, year):
```

```
self.model = model
self.year = year
def start(self):
return f"The {self.model} is starting."
my_car = Car("Toyota Corolla", 2020)
print(my_car.start())
```

Here, start is a method of the Car class.

13. Mutable

AN OBJECT IS MUTABLE if it can be changed after it is created. Lists, dictionaries, and sets are examples of mutable objects in Python. Unlike immutable objects, mutable objects can have their contents altered in place.

Example:

```
numbers = [1, 2, 3]
numbers[0] = 10
print(numbers) # Output: [10, 2, 3]
```

14. Object-Oriented Programming (OOP)

OBJECT-ORIENTED PROGRAMMING (OOP) is a programming paradigm that revolves around the concept of objects. Objects are instances of classes, and they contain both data (attributes) and functions (methods) that operate on that data. OOP encourages code reuse and modularity by allowing programmers to define custom data types using classes.

Key concepts of OOP include:

- **Class**: A blueprint for creating objects.
- **Object**: An instance of a class.
- **Encapsulation**: Bundling of data and methods within a class.
- **Inheritance**: The ability to create new classes based on existing ones.
- **Polymorphism**: The ability to define methods that behave differently based on the object that invokes them.

Example:

```
class Animal:

def speak(self):

return "Animal sound"

class Dog(Animal):

def speak(self):

return "Bark!"

my_dog = Dog()

print(my_dog.speak()) # Output: Bark!
```

In this example, Dog inherits from Animal, but it overrides the speak method to return a different output.

15. Parameter

A PARAMETER IS A VARIABLE listed in a function's definition. Parameters act as placeholders for the values (arguments) that are passed to the function when it is called.

Example:

```
def greet(name):

return f"Hello, {name}!"

print(greet("Alice"))
```

In the function greet, name is a parameter that is used to customize the greeting.

16. Slice

A SLICE IS A SUBSET of a sequence (like a list or string) and is defined by specifying a start and end index. Slicing allows you to extract parts of sequences.

Example:

```
numbers = [0, 1, 2, 3, 4, 5]

print(numbers[1:4]) # Output: [1, 2, 3]
```

In this case, the slice [1:4] extracts the elements from index 1 to index 3.

17. Tuple

A TUPLE IS A COLLECTION of items that are ordered and immutable. Once a tuple is created, its contents cannot be changed.

Tuples are useful when you need to store multiple items that should not be modified.

Example:

coordinates = (10, 20)

print(coordinates[0]) # Output: 10

Tuples cannot be modified

coordinates[0] = 15 # This will raise an error

18. Variable

A VARIABLE IS A NAME that is used to refer to a value stored in memory. Variables in Python are created when you assign a value to them, and they can store different types of data such as numbers, strings, and lists.

Example:

age = 30

name = "Alice"

19. Virtual Environment

A VIRTUAL ENVIRONMENT is an isolated Python environment where you can install packages and dependencies for a specific project without affecting the global Python environment on your system. Virtual environments help avoid conflicts between different projects that require different versions of the same package.

To create a virtual environment:

```
python -m venv myenv
```

To activate a virtual environment:

```
# On Windows
myenv\Scripts\activate
# On macOS/Linux
source myenv/bin/activate
```

20. Whitespace

WHITESPACE REFERS TO spaces, tabs, and newline characters. In Python, whitespace is significant and is used to define blocks of code. For example, functions and loops must be indented consistently to indicate that the code belongs to the same block.

Example:

```
if True:
print("This is indented correctly.")
```

Misusing whitespace can lead to IndentationError:

```
if True:
print("This will raise an error.")
```

Resources for Further Learning

IN THE WORLD OF PROGRAMMING, continuous learning is crucial, and Python is no exception. Whether you're a beginner or an experienced programmer, there is always more to explore in

Python's rich ecosystem. This section provides an extensive guide to the various resources available for further learning, including books, websites, online courses, and tools that will help you deepen your Python knowledge.

Books

BOOKS ARE A TIMELESS resource for learning programming concepts in-depth. Here is a list of highly recommended Python books that cater to different levels of expertise.

1. **"Python Crash Course" by Eric Matthes**

   This book is perfect for beginners. It covers the basics of Python programming and leads the reader through more complex projects such as games and data visualization. Each chapter contains exercises to solidify your understanding of key concepts.

   Topics covered:

   ○ Python fundamentals

   ○ Data structures

   ○ Object-oriented programming (OOP)

   ○ Web development and data visualization

"Automate the Boring Stuff with Python" by Al Sweigart

One of the most popular Python books for beginners and intermediate programmers, this book focuses on real-world tasks that you can automate using Python. It walks you through automating tasks such as file manipulation, web scraping, and handling Excel spreadsheets.

Example of a task from the book:

python

import os

for folder_name, sub_folders, file_names in os.walk('C:/Users/Example'):

for file_name in file_names:

if file_name.endswith('.txt'):

print(os.path.join(folder_name, file_name))

2.

3. **"Fluent Python" by Luciano Ramalho**

For experienced Python developers, "Fluent Python" dives deep into the language's more sophisticated aspects, including metaprogramming, decorators, and concurrency. It is a must-read if you want to write Pythonic code that is both efficient and elegant.

Key chapters:

- Data model and special methods
- First-class functions
- Object-oriented idioms
- Concurrency with asyncio

4. "Effective Python" by Brett Slatkin

This book presents 90 specific recommendations for writing better Python code. It is divided into sections that cover various Pythonic best practices, performance tips, and how to avoid common pitfalls.

Example recommendation:

Prefer comprehensions over for loops when generating lists or dictionaries:

python

```
squares = [x**2 for x in range(10)]
```

○

5. "Learning Python" by Mark Lutz

Often considered the Python bible, "Learning Python" provides an exhaustive overview of the Python language. It covers both Python 2 and Python 3, making it a versatile reference guide for programmers of all levels.

Topics covered:

- ○ Python installation and setup
- ○ Core language syntax and semantics
- ○ Data types and structures
- ○ Functions, modules, and libraries

○ Advanced topics like decorators, metaclasses, and generators

Online Documentation

READING PYTHON'S OFFICIAL documentation is one of the most reliable ways to learn the language in-depth. Below are some key documentation sources that can help you as you learn.

1. **Official Python Documentation**

The official documentation of Python (https://docs.python.org) is the primary source of truth for Python syntax, libraries, and features. It provides extensive examples and guides on how to use Python's built-in modules and functions.

Sections worth exploring:

○ Python Standard Library (https://docs.python.org/3/library/)

○ Python Language Reference (https://docs.python.org/3/reference/)

○ What's New in Python 3.x (https://docs.python.org/3/whatsnew/)

○ Tutorials and how-tos

2. **Pandas Documentation**

Pandas is one of the most powerful libraries for data manipulation and analysis in Python. The official documentation (https://pandas.pydata.org/docs/) is well-structured and includes detailed examples of how to work with DataFrame and Series objects.

3. **NumPy Documentation**

NumPy is fundamental for scientific computing in Python. It supports large, multi-dimensional arrays and matrices, along with a collection of mathematical functions to operate on them. Visit https://numpy.org/doc/ for comprehensive coverage of all NumPy features.

4. **Matplotlib Documentation**

For data visualization, Matplotlib is the go-to library in Python. Its official documentation (https://matplotlib.org/stable/contents.html) provides examples of how to create a wide range of plots, including line plots, bar charts, histograms, and 3D plots.

Online Learning Platforms

THERE ARE NUMEROUS online platforms that offer interactive Python courses. These platforms are especially useful if you prefer learning through videos, quizzes, and hands-on projects.

1. **Coursera**

Coursera offers a vast array of Python courses for all levels, many of which are taught by professors from prestigious universities such as Stanford and MIT. Some of the most popular Python-related courses on Coursera include:

○ "Python for Everybody" by Dr. Charles Severance

○ "Applied Data Science with Python" by the University of Michigan

○ "Introduction to Data Science in Python"

2. **edX**

Like Coursera, edX provides a variety of Python courses, often from universities and institutions. Their Python offerings range from beginner to advanced, covering areas such as data science, machine learning, and artificial intelligence.

3. **Udemy**

Udemy hosts a massive selection of Python courses. Many of these courses come with lifetime access, so you can learn at your own pace. Popular Python courses on Udemy include:

○ "Complete Python Bootcamp" by Jose Portilla

○ "Python for Data Science and Machine Learning Bootcamp"

○ "The Python Mega Course: Build 10 Real-World Applications"

4. **Codecademy**

Codecademy is known for its interactive approach to learning Python. Its courses are highly interactive, and you can practice coding directly in your browser as you learn. Codecademy offers:

- "Learn Python 3"
- "Build Chatbots with Python"
- "Data Science: Analyze Data with Python"

5. **DataCamp**

Focused primarily on data science, DataCamp offers Python courses that emphasize hands-on coding and real-world data analysis tasks. The platform includes specialized courses such as:

- "Introduction to Python for Data Science"
- "Data Manipulation with Pandas"
- "Machine Learning with Scikit-learn"

Python Conferences and Meetups

ATTENDING PYTHON CONFERENCES and meetups is an excellent way to connect with the Python community, learn about the latest advancements in the language, and stay inspired. Here are some prominent Python events worth attending or exploring online.

1. **PyCon**

PyCon is the largest annual conference for the Python community. It includes presentations from Python experts, coding sprints, and workshops. PyCon is also a great place to meet fellow Python developers and exchange ideas.

PyCon events around the world:

- PyCon US
- PyCon UK
- EuroPython

2. **DjangoCon**

DjangoCon is a community-driven conference for the Django web framework. It is particularly useful if you are interested in web development with Python and want to deepen your understanding of Django.

3. **PyData**

PyData is a series of international conferences focused on data science and machine learning using Python. It features presentations from data scientists, machine learning engineers, and researchers who use Python to solve complex problems.

4. **Local Meetups**

Websites like Meetup.com offer Python meetups in cities around the world. These meetups are a great way to connect with local Python programmers, attend workshops, and participate in coding challenges.

To find a local Python meetup, simply search for "Python" on Meetup.com and enter your location.

Open Source Contributions

ONE OF THE BEST WAYS to improve your Python skills and give back to the community is by contributing to open-source projects. There are countless Python projects that welcome contributions from developers of all skill levels.

1. **Contributing to Python Itself**

Python is an open-source language, and you can contribute to its development. Whether it's fixing bugs, improving documentation, or proposing new features, the Python development community welcomes contributions. You can start by visiting the official Python GitHub repository:https://github.com/python/cpython.

Python's contribution guide:https://devguide.python.org/

2. **Open Source Python Projects**

There are numerous popular Python libraries and frameworks that accept contributions. Some of these include:

○ **Django**: A high-level web framework GitHub:https://github.com/django/django

○ **Flask:** A lightweight web framework GitHub:https://github.com/pallets/flask

○ **Requests:** A simple HTTP library GitHub:https://github.com/psf/requests

○ **Pandas**: A library for data manipulation GitHub:https://github.com/pandas-dev/pandas

3. Contributing to these projects can significantly improve your understanding of how Python libraries are structured and how real-world applications are built.

Tools for Python Development

USING THE RIGHT TOOLS can make a big difference in your productivity as a Python developer. Below are some essential tools and environments you should consider using.

1. **Integrated Development Environments (IDEs)**

IDEs provide a comprehensive environment for coding, debugging, and testing your Python programs. Some of the most popular Python IDEs include:

○ **PyCharm**: A full-featured Python IDE by JetBrains, offering features such as code completion, debugging, and integration with frameworks like Django and Flask.

○ **VS Code**: A lightweight editor by Microsoft with excellent Python support, including a powerful debugger and integrated terminal.

○ **Jupyter Notebooks**: An interactive development environment primarily used for data science and machine learning. It allows you to write code and see results inline, which is ideal for data analysis tasks.

Version Control with Git

Git is a version control system that helps you track changes in your codebase and collaborate with others. GitHub and GitLab are popular platforms for hosting Git repositories. Learning Git is essential for any Python developer working in a team or contributing to open-source projects.

Example of using Git:

bash

```
# Initialize a new repository

git init

# Add files to the repository

git add .

# Commit the changes

git commit -m "Initial commit"
```

2.

Virtual Environments

Python's venv module allows you to create isolated environments for different projects. This prevents conflicts between packages and dependencies across projects.

Example:

bash

```
python -m venv myproject_env

source myproject_env/bin/activate # Activate the virtual environment
```

pip install -r requirements.txt # Install project dependencies

3.

4. **Linters and Formatters**

Code quality tools like linters and formatters help you maintain clean and readable code. Popular Python linters include:

○ **Flake8**: Checks for style guide violations (PEP8) and common errors.

○ **Pylint**: A more comprehensive tool that checks for errors, enforces coding standards, and looks for code smells.

5. For formatting, tools like **Black** automatically format your Python code to follow standard conventions.

Conclusion

LEARNING PYTHON IS an ongoing journey, and the resources available to you are vast. Whether you prefer books, online courses, meetups, or open-source contributions, there is always something new to learn. By continually engaging with the Python community and using these resources, you will be well-equipped to master the language and apply it to a wide variety of real-world projects.

Sample Projects and Code Snippets

ONE OF THE BEST WAYS to solidify your understanding of Python is by working on real-world projects. Whether you're automating repetitive tasks, building web applications, or analyzing data, hands-on projects can enhance your problem-solving skills and make you more confident in using Python. This section provides several sample projects and accompanying code snippets to guide you through practical applications of Python concepts. Each project covers different aspects of Python, such as data manipulation, web development, file handling, and automation. These projects are suitable for both beginners and intermediate programmers who want to challenge themselves.

Project 1: Command-Line To-Do List Application

A COMMAND-LINE TO-DO list application is a great beginner project that helps you practice handling user input, working with files, and managing data in a structured way. The application will allow users to add, view, and delete tasks from their to-do list.

Key Concepts

- User input handling
- File reading and writing
- Lists and dictionaries for task management
- Basic exception handling

Steps:

1. **Create a text file to store tasks**
   The tasks will be stored in a text file, where each line represents a task. The file will be read and updated as the user adds or deletes tasks.
2. **Implement task addition and deletion functions**

Write functions that allow users to add tasks to the file and delete tasks by their task number.

3. **Display the to-do list**
   Write a function to read the file and display the tasks along with their indices so that users can reference tasks by their number.
4. **Basic Exception Handling**
   Add error handling to manage cases where users enter invalid input, such as selecting a non-existent task number for deletion.

```
IMPORT OS

TODO_FILE = "todo.txt"

def add_task(task):

with open(TODO_FILE, "a") as file:

file.write(task + "\n")

def delete_task(task_number):

try:

with open(TODO_FILE, "r") as file:

tasks = file.readlines()

if 0 < task_number <= len(tasks):

tasks.pop(task_number - 1)

with open(TODO_FILE, "w") as file:

file.writelines(tasks)
```

```
else:
print("Invalid task number!")
except FileNotFoundError:
print("No tasks found!")
def view_tasks():
try:
with open(TODO_FILE, "r") as file:
tasks = file.readlines()
if tasks:
print("To-Do List:")
for idx, task in enumerate(tasks, 1):
print(f"{idx}. {task.strip()}")
else:
print("Your to-do list is empty!")
except FileNotFoundError:
print("No tasks found!")
# Main loop
while True:
print("\n1. View Tasks")
print("2. Add Task")
```

```
print("3. Delete Task")

print("4. Exit")

choice = input("Choose an option: ")

if choice == "1":

view_tasks()

elif choice == "2":

task = input("Enter the task: ")

add_task(task)

elif choice == "3":

task_number = int(input("Enter the task number to delete: "))

delete_task(task_number)

elif choice == "4":

break

else:

print("Invalid choice!")
```

This basic command-line to-do list application can be expanded further by adding features like editing tasks, setting priorities, or saving the list in JSON format.

Project 2: Web Scraper with BeautifulSoup

WEB SCRAPING IS A COMMON task in data analysis and automation. In this project, you'll use the BeautifulSoup library to scrape information from a website. We'll build a simple web scraper that extracts article titles and URLs from a news website.

Key Concepts

- Making HTTP requests using the requests library
- Parsing HTML content with BeautifulSoup
- Extracting data from web pages (titles, links, etc.)
- Writing data to a CSV file

Steps:

INSTALL THE NECESSARY libraries

You'll need the requests and beautifulsoup4 libraries to scrape data from websites.

pip install requests beautifulsoup4

1.
2. **Fetch the web page content**
   Use the requests library to send an HTTP request to the website and retrieve the HTML content.
3. **Parse the HTML with BeautifulSoup**
   Use BeautifulSoup to parse the HTML content and extract specific elements, such as article titles and URLs.
4. **Save the data to a CSV file**
   Once the data is extracted, save it to a CSV file for future use or analysis.

import requests

```
from bs4 import BeautifulSoup

import csv

URL = "https://news.ycombinator.com/"

response = requests.get(URL)

# Parse the page content

soup = BeautifulSoup(response.content, "html.parser")

# Find all article titles and URLs

articles = soup.find_all("a", class_="storylink")

# Save data to a CSV file

with open("articles.csv", mode="w", newline="") as file:

writer = csv.writer(file)

writer.writerow(["Title", "URL"])

for article in articles:

title = article.get_text()

url = article['href']

writer.writerow([title, url])

print("Scraping completed. Data saved to articles.csv.")
```

In this example, the scraper retrieves the article titles and URLs from a news website and saves them into a CSV file. You can customize the script to scrape other websites by modifying the CSS selectors or HTML tags you want to target.

Project 3: Simple Portfolio Tracker

IF YOU'RE INTERESTED in finance or investment, a portfolio tracker can help you manage and monitor the performance of your assets. In this project, you will build a simple portfolio tracker that retrieves the current prices of stocks using an API and calculates the portfolio's total value.

Key Concepts

- Fetching data from APIs
- Working with JSON data
- Simple arithmetic operations to calculate asset values
- Storing and retrieving portfolio information

Steps:

1. **Set up the API**
   Use a free financial API like Alpha Vantage (https://www.alphavantage.co/) or Yahoo Finance to fetch real-time stock data.
2. **Fetch and parse the API response**
   Retrieve stock prices from the API in JSON format and parse the data.
3. **Calculate portfolio value**
   Define a portfolio as a list of dictionaries, where each dictionary contains a stock symbol, the number of shares, and the purchase price. Calculate the total value of the portfolio based on the current stock prices.
4. **Display the portfolio performance**
   Display the current value of each stock along with the

overall portfolio value.

```
IMPORT REQUESTS
API_KEY = "your_alpha_vantage_api_key"
BASE_URL = "https://www.alphavantage.co/query?"
# Sample portfolio: symbol, shares, purchase price
portfolio = [
{"symbol": "AAPL", "shares": 10, "purchase_price": 150.00},
{"symbol": "MSFT", "shares": 5, "purchase_price": 200.00},
]
def get_stock_price(symbol):
params = {
"function": "TIME_SERIES_INTRADAY",
"symbol": symbol,
"interval": "1min",
"apikey": API_KEY
}
response = requests.get(BASE_URL, params=params)
data = response.json()
# Extract the latest close price
last_refreshed = list(data['Time Series (1min)'].keys())[0]
```

```
return float(data['Time Series (1min)'][last_refreshed]['4. close'])

def calculate_portfolio_value(portfolio):

total_value = 0.0

for stock in portfolio:

current_price = get_stock_price(stock["symbol"])

stock_value = current_price * stock["shares"]

total_value += stock_value

print(f"{stock['symbol']}: {stock['shares']} shares @ ${current_price:.2f} = ${stock_value:.2f}")

print(f"\nTotal Portfolio Value: ${total_value:.2f}")

calculate_portfolio_value(portfolio)
```

This simple portfolio tracker can be expanded to include features like tracking historical prices, calculating profit/loss, and sending notifications when stock prices reach certain levels.

Project 4: Automating Email Reports

IN THIS PROJECT, YOU'LL build a Python script that sends daily email reports with automated data summaries. This can be useful in business settings where you need to send recurring reports or alerts based on certain conditions.

Key Concepts

- Working with email using the smtplib library

- Automating repetitive tasks with a scheduler like cron (on Linux/macOS) or Task Scheduler (on Windows)

- Fetching and summarizing data (e.g., stock prices, website statistics)

Steps:

1. **Set up email credentials**
   Use an email provider's SMTP server (e.g., Gmail) to send emails. You will need your email address and an app-specific password (if using Gmail, you can generate this in your Google account settings).
2. **Create a report**
   Gather the data for your report, such as web statistics, sales data, or stock prices. Summarize the data in a format suitable for an email.
3. **Send the email**
   Use Python's smtplib to send the report via email to your recipients.

```
IMPORT SMTPLIB

from email.mime.text import MIMEText

from email.mime.multipart import MIMEMultipart

SMTP_SERVER = "smtp.gmail.com"

SMTP_PORT = 587

EMAIL = "your_email@gmail.com"

PASSWORD = "your_app_specific_password"
```

```
def send_email(subject, body, to_email):
msg = MIMEMultipart()
msg['From'] = EMAIL
msg['To'] = to_email
msg['Subject'] = subject
msg.attach(MIMEText(body, 'plain'))
server = smtplib.SMTP(SMTP_SERVER, SMTP_PORT)
server.starttls()
server.login(EMAIL, PASSWORD)
server.sendmail(EMAIL, to_email, msg.as_string())
server.quit()
# Example report
subject = "Daily Stock Report"
body = "Here is your daily stock report:\n\nAAPL: $150.00\nMSFT: $220.00"
send_email(subject, body, "recipient@example.com")
```

This basic email automation can be scheduled to run at specific intervals using cron or Task Scheduler, allowing you to send daily, weekly, or monthly reports without manual intervention.

Conclusion

THESE SAMPLE PROJECTS and code snippets offer a practical way to apply your Python skills to real-world scenarios. Each project builds on different aspects of Python programming, such as file handling, web scraping, API interactions, and automation. By completing these projects, you'll gain a deeper understanding of how Python can be used to solve various challenges and create useful tools in your day-to-day activities or professional work.

Python Reference Guide

THIS SECTION SERVES as a comprehensive reference guide to Python's core features, providing detailed explanations, examples, and best practices for using essential Python functions, data types, and constructs. It is structured to help you understand and quickly look up Python's basic and advanced functionalities, ensuring that you can efficiently use them in your own projects. Whether you are working on small scripts or large applications, this guide will give you a solid foundation for writing clean, efficient, and Pythonic code.

1. Python Built-in Functions

PYTHON COMES WITH A variety of built-in functions that allow you to perform common tasks without having to import any external libraries. Below are some of the most commonly used built-in functions and examples of how to use them.

1.1 print()

THE PRINT() FUNCTION outputs text to the console. It can accept multiple arguments and supports formatting using f-strings or the format() method.

Example:

```
# Basic print
```

```
print("Hello, World!")

# Printing multiple items

name = "Alice"

age = 25

print("Name:", name, "Age:", age)

# Using f-strings for formatting

print(f"Name: {name}, Age: {age}")

# Using format()

print("Name: {}, Age: {}".format(name, age))
```

1.2 len()

THE LEN() FUNCTION returns the number of items in an object. It works with sequences like strings, lists, and tuples, as well as collections like dictionaries.

Example:

```
# Length of a string

text = "Hello"

print(len(text)) # Output: 5

# Length of a list

numbers = [1, 2, 3, 4, 5]

print(len(numbers)) # Output: 5
```

```
# Length of a dictionary

data = {"name": "Alice", "age": 25}

print(len(data)) # Output: 2
```

1.3 range()

THE RANGE() FUNCTION generates a sequence of numbers. It is commonly used with loops to iterate over a specific range of values.

Example:

```
# Generating a sequence of numbers from 0 to 4

for i in range(5):

print(i)

# Generating a sequence with a step value

for i in range(0, 10, 2):

print(i) # Output: 0, 2, 4, 6, 8
```

1.4 sum()

THE SUM() FUNCTION adds all the items in an iterable (such as a list or tuple).

Example:

```
# Summing a list of numbers

numbers = [1, 2, 3, 4, 5]
```

```
print(sum(numbers)) # Output: 15

# Summing with a starting value

print(sum(numbers, 10)) # Output: 25
```

1.5 sorted()

THE SORTED() FUNCTION returns a new sorted list from the items in an iterable. It can sort numbers, strings, or any other comparable objects.

Example:

```
# Sorting a list of numbers

numbers = [5, 2, 9, 1, 5, 6]

sorted_numbers = sorted(numbers)

print(sorted_numbers) # Output: [1, 2, 5, 5, 6, 9]

# Sorting in reverse order

sorted_numbers = sorted(numbers, reverse=True)

print(sorted_numbers) # Output: [9, 6, 5, 5, 2, 1]
```

2. Data Types and Their Methods

PYTHON PROVIDES SEVERAL built-in data types, each with its own set of methods for performing operations. This section explores the key data types and the most commonly used methods for working with them.

2.1 Strings

A STRING IS A SEQUENCE of characters enclosed in single, double, or triple quotes. Strings are immutable, meaning that once they are created, their contents cannot be changed.

String Methods

- **upper()**: Converts all characters to uppercase.
- **lower()**: Converts all characters to lowercase.
- **replace(old, new)**: Replaces occurrences of a substring with another substring.
- **split(delimiter)**: Splits the string into a list based on a delimiter.
- **strip()**: Removes leading and trailing whitespace.

EXAMPLE:

```
text = " Hello, World! "

# Convert to uppercase

print(text.upper()) # Output: " HELLO, WORLD! "

# Remove leading and trailing spaces

print(text.strip()) # Output: "Hello, World!"

# Replace a substring

print(text.replace("World", "Python")) # Output: " Hello, Python!
"
```

Split the string into a list of words

words = text.split(", ")

print(words) # Output: [' Hello', 'World! ']

2.2 Lists

A LIST IS A COLLECTION of items that are ordered and changeable. Lists allow duplicate elements.

List Methods

- **append(item)**: Adds an item to the end of the list.
- **extend(iterable)**: Adds all items from an iterable to the list.
- **remove(item)**: Removes the first occurrence of an item.
- **pop(index)**: Removes and returns the item at the specified index.
- **sort()**: Sorts the list in ascending order.

EXAMPLE:

fruits = ["apple", "banana", "cherry"]

Append a new item

fruits.append("orange")

print(fruits) # Output: ["apple", "banana", "cherry", "orange"]

Remove an item

```
fruits.remove("banana")

print(fruits) # Output: ["apple", "cherry", "orange"]

# Pop the last item

last_fruit = fruits.pop()

print(last_fruit) # Output: "orange"
```

2.3 Dictionaries

A DICTIONARY IS A COLLECTION of key-value pairs. Dictionaries are unordered, changeable, and do not allow duplicate keys.

Dictionary Methods

- **get(key)**: Returns the value for the specified key. If the key is not found, it returns None.
- **keys()**: Returns a view of all the keys in the dictionary.
- **values()**: Returns a view of all the values in the dictionary.
- **items()**: Returns a view of all key-value pairs as tuples.
- **update(other_dict)**: Updates the dictionary with key-value pairs from another dictionary.

EXAMPLE:

```
person = {"name": "Alice", "age": 25, "city": "New York"}

# Get the value of a key
```

print(person.get("name")) # Output: Alice

Get all keys

print(person.keys()) # Output: dict_keys(["name", "age", "city"])

Update the dictionary

person.update({"age": 26, "job": "Developer"})

print(person) # Output: {"name": "Alice", "age": 26, "city": "New York", "job": "Developer"}

2.4 Tuples

A TUPLE IS A COLLECTION of items that are ordered and immutable. Tuples allow duplicate elements. Once created, the elements in a tuple cannot be changed.

Tuple Methods

- **count(item)**: Returns the number of times the specified item appears in the tuple.
- **index(item)**: Returns the index of the first occurrence of the specified item.

EXAMPLE:

colors = ("red", "green", "blue", "green")

Count occurrences of an item

print(colors.count("green")) # Output: 2

Find the index of an item

print(colors.index("blue")) # Output: 2

2.5 Sets

A SET IS A COLLECTION of unique items that are unordered and unindexed. Sets are useful when you want to store items without duplicates.

Set Methods

- **add(item)**: Adds an item to the set.
- **remove(item)**: Removes the specified item from the set. Raises a KeyError if the item is not found.
- **union(other_set)**: Returns a new set with all elements from both sets.
- **intersection(other_set)**: Returns a set containing only the items that exist in both sets.
- **difference(other_set)**: Returns a set containing items that are in the first set but not in the second.

EXAMPLE:

set1 = {1, 2, 3}

set2 = {3, 4, 5}

Add an item

set1.add(6)

print(set1) # Output: {1, 2, 3, 6}

```
# Union of two sets

union_set = set1.union(set2)

print(union_set) # Output: {1, 2, 3, 4, 5, 6}

# Intersection of two sets

intersection_set = set1.intersection(set2)

print(intersection_set) # Output: {3}
```

3. Control Flow Statements

CONTROL FLOW STATEMENTS allow you to control the execution of your program based on conditions and loops. Python provides several ways to manage control flow, including if statements, loops, and exception handling.

3.1 if, elif, else Statements

THE IF STATEMENT ALLOWS you to execute a block of code only if a certain condition is met. You can use elif to check multiple conditions and else to execute code when none of the conditions are met.

Example:

```
age = 20

if age < 18:

print("You are a minor.")

elif age < 65:

print("You are an adult.")
```

```
else:

print("You are a senior.")
```

3.2 for Loops

A FOR LOOP IS USED to iterate over a sequence (such as a list, tuple, or string). Python's for loops are versatile and work with any iterable.

Example:

```
# Looping over a list

fruits = ["apple", "banana", "cherry"]

for fruit in fruits:

print(fruit)

# Looping over a string

for letter in "Python":

print(letter)
```

3.3 while Loops

A WHILE LOOP REPEATS a block of code as long as a condition is True.

Example:

```
count = 0

while count < 5:
```

```
print(count)

count += 1
```

3.4 break and continue

THE BREAK STATEMENT exits the loop prematurely, while the continue statement skips the current iteration and moves to the next one.

Example:

```
for i in range(10):

if i == 5:

break # Exit the loop when i is 5

print(i)

for i in range(10):

if i % 2 == 0:

continue # Skip even numbers

print(i)
```

4. Exception Handling

PYTHON PROVIDES A ROBUST mechanism for handling runtime errors via exceptions. You can use try, except, finally, and else blocks to manage exceptions in a clean and controlled manner.

4.1 try and except

THE TRY BLOCK LETS you test a block of code for errors, while the except block allows you to handle the error.

Example:

```
try:
x = 1 / 0
except ZeroDivisionError:
print("Cannot divide by zero!")
```

4.2 finally

THE FINALLY BLOCK IS always executed, regardless of whether an error occurs. It is typically used for cleanup actions, such as closing files or releasing resources.

Example:

```
try:
file = open("example.txt", "r")
content = file.read()
finally:
file.close() # Ensure the file is always closed
```

4.3 Custom Exceptions

YOU CAN CREATE YOUR own exceptions by subclassing the Exception class.

Example:

```
class CustomError(Exception):

pass

try:

raise CustomError("This is a custom error!")

except CustomError as e:

print(e)
```

Conclusion

THIS REFERENCE GUIDE provides a solid foundation for understanding Python's most essential features. By mastering these basic and advanced constructs, you will be well-equipped to write efficient and clean code. Keep this guide handy as you work on Python projects, and don't hesitate to refer back to it whenever you need a quick refresher.

Frequently Asked Questions

IN THIS SECTION, WE will address some of the most common questions that Python developers frequently encounter. Whether you're a beginner struggling with syntax or an experienced programmer looking to refine your skills, these questions and answers will help clarify core concepts, provide useful tips, and resolve typical challenges in Python programming.

1. What is the difference between Python 2 and Python 3?

PYTHON 2 AND PYTHON 3 are two major versions of Python, with Python 3 being the latest. Although Python 2 is no longer officially supported (as of January 1, 2020), some projects still use it. However, most modern applications should be written in Python 3.

Key differences include:

- **Print Statement**: In Python 2, print is a statement (print "Hello"), while in Python 3, it is a function (print("Hello")).

- **Integer Division**: In Python 2, dividing two integers truncates the result (5 / 2 yields 2), while Python 3 returns a float (5 / 2 yields 2.5). To perform integer division in Python 3, you need to use the floor division operator //.

- **Unicode**: In Python 3, strings are stored as Unicode by default, while in Python 2, they are stored as ASCII unless explicitly defined as Unicode.

- **xrange vs range**: In Python 2, xrange() is used for generating numbers lazily, while range() creates a list. In Python 3, range() returns a generator-like object, similar to xrange() in Python 2.

Example:

PYTHON 2:

```
print "Hello, World!"

print 5 / 2 # Output: 2
```

Python 3:

```
print("Hello, World!")

print(5 / 2) # Output: 2.5
```

2. How do I install Python packages?

PYTHON USES A PACKAGE manager called pip to install and manage third-party libraries. You can install packages from the Python Package Index (PyPI) using pip. To install a package, run the following command in your terminal or command prompt:

```
pip install package_name
```

For example, to install the popular data manipulation library pandas:

```
pip install pandas
```

Creating and Using Virtual Environments:

WHEN WORKING ON PROJECTS, it's a best practice to use virtual environments. A virtual environment isolates the dependencies for a project, preventing conflicts between different projects that require different package versions.

1. Create a virtual environment:

```
python -m venv myenv
```

1. Activate the virtual environment:

- On Windows:

myenv\Scripts\activate

- On macOS/Linux:

source myenv/bin/activate

1. Install packages within the environment:

pip install package_name

1. Deactivate the environment when done:

deactivate

3. What is the difference between a list and a tuple?

BOTH LISTS AND TUPLES are data structures used to store collections of items in Python. However, there are significant differences between the two:

- **Mutability**: Lists are mutable, meaning you can change, add, or remove elements after the list is created. Tuples, on the other hand, are immutable, meaning their contents cannot be changed once they are created.

- **Syntax**: Lists are created using square brackets [], while tuples are created using parentheses ().

- **Performance**: Because tuples are immutable, they are generally faster than lists for lookups or iterations, and they can be used as keys in dictionaries.

Example:

```
# LIST (MUTABLE)

fruits = ["apple", "banana", "cherry"]

fruits.append("orange")

print(fruits) # Output: ['apple', 'banana', 'cherry', 'orange']

# Tuple (immutable)

colors = ("red", "green", "blue")

# colors.append("yellow") # This would raise an error
```

4. What is a lambda function?

A LAMBDA FUNCTION IS a small anonymous function that can have any number of arguments, but only one expression. It is often used when a small function is required for a short period of time, especially as an argument to higher-order functions like map(), filter(), or sorted().

Example:

```
# LAMBDA FUNCTION TO add two numbers

add = lambda x, y: x + y

print(add(3, 5)) # Output: 8

# Using lambda with sorted() to sort a list of tuples by the second item

pairs = [(1, 'one'), (2, 'two'), (3, 'three')]
```

```
sorted_pairs = sorted(pairs, key=lambda x: x[1])

print(sorted_pairs) # Output: [(1, 'one'), (3, 'three'), (2, 'two')]
```

5. How do I handle errors in Python?

IN PYTHON, ERRORS OR exceptions can be caught and handled using try and except blocks. The try block contains the code that might raise an exception, while the except block contains code to handle the exception.

Basic Error Handling Example:

```
TRY:

x = 1 / 0

except ZeroDivisionError:

print("Cannot divide by zero!")
```

Handling Multiple Exceptions:

YOU CAN CATCH MULTIPLE types of exceptions by specifying multiple except clauses:

```
try:

x = int(input("Enter a number: "))

result = 10 / x

except ZeroDivisionError:

print("Cannot divide by zero!")

except ValueError:
```

```
print("Invalid input! Please enter a valid number.")
```

Using finally:

THE FINALLY BLOCK IS executed regardless of whether an exception occurred. It is typically used for cleanup actions, such as closing a file or releasing resources.

```
try:

file = open("example.txt", "r")

# Perform file operations

finally:

file.close() # This will always execute
```

6. What are list comprehensions?

LIST COMPREHENSIONS provide a concise way to create lists in Python. They consist of brackets containing an expression followed by a for clause and optionally one or more if clauses. List comprehensions are often used to make code more readable and Pythonic.

Example:

```
# WITHOUT LIST COMPREHENSION

squares = []

for i in range(10):

squares.append(i ** 2)
```

```
# With list comprehension

squares = [i ** 2 for i in range(10)]
```

You can also add conditions to list comprehensions:

```
# List of even squares

even_squares = [i ** 2 for i in range(10) if i % 2 == 0]

print(even_squares) # Output: [0, 4, 16, 36, 64]
```

7. What is the __init__() method in classes?

THE __INIT__() METHOD is a special method in Python classes. It is the constructor method that gets called when you create an instance of a class. This method allows you to initialize the object's attributes.

Example:

```
CLASS DOG:

def __init__(self, name, breed):

self.name = name

self.breed = breed

def bark(self):

return f"{self.name} says woof!"

my_dog = Dog("Buddy", "Golden Retriever")

print(my_dog.bark()) # Output: Buddy says woof!
```

In this example, __init__() initializes the attributes name and breed when a new Dog object is created.

8. How do I read and write files in Python?

PYTHON PROVIDES BUILT-in functions to work with files. The open() function is used to open a file, which can then be read from or written to using methods like read(), write(), and close().

Reading a File:

OPENING A FILE AND reading its contents

with open("example.txt", "r") as file:

content = file.read()

print(content)

The with statement ensures that the file is properly closed after its block of code is executed, even if an error occurs.

Writing to a File:

WRITING TO A FILE

with open("example.txt", "w") as file:

file.write("Hello, World!")

Appending to a File:

APPENDING TEXT TO a file

with open("example.txt", "a") as file:

```
file.write("\nAppended text")
```

9. What is the self keyword in Python?

IN PYTHON, SELF REFERS to the instance of the class. It is used in instance methods to access variables and methods associated with the instance. It must be explicitly defined as the first parameter of any method inside the class.

Example:

```
CLASS CAR:

def __init__(self, model):

self.model = model

def start(self):

return f"{self.model} is starting."

my_car = Car("Tesla Model S")

print(my_car.start()) # Output: Tesla Model S is starting.
```

Here, self.model refers to the model attribute of the instance my_car.

10. What are decorators in Python?

DECORATORS ARE A WAY to modify or extend the behavior of functions or methods without permanently modifying them. In Python, decorators are defined using the @ symbol above the function definition.

Example:

```
DEF DECORATOR(FUNC):
def wrapper():
print("Before the function runs")
func()
print("After the function runs")
return wrapper
@decorator
def say_hello():
print("Hello!")
say_hello()
```

Output:

```
Before the function runs
Hello!
After the function runs
```

Decorators are commonly used for logging, enforcing access control, and measuring execution time.

Conclusion

THESE FREQUENTLY ASKED questions address some of the most common challenges and concepts that Python developers encounter. By understanding these topics, you will be better equipped to write efficient, clean, and Pythonic code. This FAQ is a living document, so feel free to revisit and expand your knowledge as you continue your Python journey.